STRATFORD-UPON-AVON STUDIES 13

General Editors

MALCOLM BRADBURY

& DAVID PALMER

Already published in this series

* *Under the general editorship of John Russell Brown and Bernard Harris*

STRATFORD-UPON-AVON STUDIES 13

THE AMERICAN NOVEL AND THE NINETEEN TWENTIES

EDWARD ARNOLD

© EDWARD ARNOLD (PUBLISHERS) LTD 1971

First published 1971 by
Edward Arnold (Publishers) Ltd
41 Maddox Street, London W1R 0AN

Cloth edition ISBN: 0 7131 5615 5
Paper edition ISBN: 0 7131 5616 3

Printed in Great Britain by
Butler & Tanner Ltd, Frome and London

Contents

Preface

THE aim of this collection of essays is to look afresh at the American novel in one of its most remarkable phases—that period of change and literary experimentalism that occurred after the First World War. In this period a new passion and consciousness, and a new experimentalism, comes into American writing—a famous 'coming-of-age', to use Van Wyck Brooks' phrase, in which the American novel both asserted itself positively as a national form and at the same time took on international power and influence. At the same time, appropriately, some of the great American writers of the past, notably Melville, were being rediscovered, so that the sense that the novel in America was a distinct, modern and potentially very naturally American species grew —and has kept on growing, in performance and in criticism, ever since. To see why this is so, we need to look directly at the remarkable body of novelists that emerged in the decade, or emerged shortly before it, and did their best work in it: the great names are of course Sherwood Anderson, Sinclair Lewis, Scott Fitzgerald, William Faulkner, Ernest Hemingway and John Dos Passos. But this book, while looking at these and other novelists in detail, contains another theme; for it is necessary, in considering these writers whose work still obsesses us and whose merits are still matters of intense discussion and disagreement, to look behind them at the decade of the twenties itself, and at the developments in the American culture of the time which helped to bring about a new stylistic era. The twenties in America remain fascinating as a cultural spectacle because the decade enshrines a paradox. It is thought of as a classic decade of materialism, of business-ethics and of prohibition, of what the writers who so regularly condemned it and expatriated themselves from it called 'puritanism'; but it is also the decade of 'the greatest, gaudiest spree in history', as Fitzgerald told us, when 'something subtle passed to America, the style of man', of cultural ebullience and experiment. In short, the relationship between the literature and culture is a good deal more complex than has often been represented; and that is one reason why a number of the essays which follow—notably those by Lawrence W. Levine, Henry Dan Piper and Eric Mottram—deal with the cultural complexity of the decade. For the American twenties pose fascinating problems about the relationship between social changes and transformations in a decade which has been thought of by many as the first modern decade in American life, changes so vast and so rapid as totally to reshape mores and patterns of human behaviour, and changes of style in another sense—the change in literary forms and structures, the growth of a more modernist mode of writing, the shift of writers towards bohemianism and towards a much more intense obsession both with their craft and with the distinctive and exposed moral conditions of their generation.

The writers we are concerned with in this volume are those who seem to form a community as a 'twenties generation', as the popularity of the famous phrase that Hemingway attributed to Gertrude Stein in the epigraph to his novel, *The Sun Also Rises*—'you are all a lost generation'—makes clear. This stylistic and aesthetic community exists even though most of those writers produced their work over several decades, and some did their most remarkable writing after the twenties were over. Part of this community seems to lie in a situation that has deep roots in the twenties, a deep cultural tension deriving from the marked shifts of social power, from the rural to the urban, from the *Gemeinschaft* to the *Gesellschaft*, from the pre-technological to the mass-technological, that run as essential themes in any account of the decade. And it also seems to lie in something that went with that process, the spectacle of a society seeking to find its model of historical progress through the expansion of personal identity. If the twenties is indeed an age of contradictions, an age shaped by two apocalyptic moments, the war that begins the decade and the slump which ends it, then its contradictions are notoriously not deeply felt as matters of politics. To many in the thirties, this was a moral absence; and that view has helped encourage the notion of the American twenties as an age of frenzied and even more ridiculous social fantasies, from the flappers and the Fords, the flagpole sitters and the sports spectaculars, to the climate of wild boom and speculation which reached its peak and then toppled into the economic disaster of the Wall Street Crash. But the twenties was a decade deeply immersed in its own modernity, a decade quite as radical in its way as any species of politically-orientated social revolution. Similarly, the writers of the decade, while themselves usually more aesthetic than political in orientation (though as Henry Dan Piper and Eric Mottram show, they sensed a malaise in their society and themselves), were radicals in creation. Lawrence Levine's remarkable reappraisal of the historiography of the decade perhaps helps us, more than most historical accounts, to see some of the contextual reasons why this is so: they lived in an environment of transition, of tense dialectic between the forces of the decade.

If, then, one of the ways of exploring the destiny of American literary experimentalism is by focussing on this remarkably creative decade, another is to reconsider our judgment of the decade itself. This is what we have encouraged our contributors to do in this volume. Four of them—Malcolm Bradbury, Lawrence Levine, Henry Dan Piper and Eric Mottram—look at the decade as a decade. The others have been asked to consider, by looking at particular authors, the evolution of American experiment in fiction, the dimensions of American modernism. And the overall aim of this book is to reassess, at a fifty-year distance, the nature and the context of some of the most remarkable writing America has produced.

April 1971

MALCOLM BRADBURY
DAVID PALMER

Acknowledgments

THE editors and publisher gratefully acknowledge permission given by the following to reprint copyright works: Chatto and Windus Ltd., Random House Inc. and the Literary Estate of William Faulkner for extracts from *Sartoris* by William Faulkner (1929), *The Unvanquished* by William Faulkner (1938), *The Hamlet* by William Faulkner (1940), *Go Down Moses* by William Faulkner (1942) and from *Essays, Speeches and Public Letters* by William Faulkner (1953); Jonathan Cape Ltd. and Harcourt, Brace, Jovanovich Inc. for extracts from *Dodsworth* by Sinclair Lewis (1929) and *Babbitt* by Sinclair Lewis (1922); Jonathan Cape Ltd., Viking Press Inc. and the Estate of Sherwood Anderson for extracts from *Winesburg, Ohio* by Sherwood Anderson (1919), *The Triumph of the Egg* by Sherwood Anderson (1921) and *Poor White* by Sherwood Anderson (1920); Michigan State University Press for extracts from essays by Malcolm Cowley and by George Marion O'Donnell in *William Faulkner: Three Decades of Criticism* edited by Frederick J. Hoffman and Olga W. Vickery (1960); Mrs. Elizabeth H. Dos Passos and the Houghton Mifflin Company for extracts from *Three Soldiers* by John Dos Passos (1921), *Manhattan Transfer* by John Dos Passos (1925) and *U.S.A.* by John Dos Passos (1930), copyright © H. Marston Smith and Elizabeth H. Dos Passos; Cornell University Press for an extract from *One Man's Initiation: 1917* by John Dos Passos, © 1969 by John Dos Passos; New Directions Publishing Corporation and Martin Secker and Warburg Ltd. for extracts from *Miss Lonelyhearts* by Nathanael West (1933), © 1960 by Laura Pevelman; New Directions Publishing Corporation for an extract from 'L'Affaire Beano', an unpublished short story by Nathanael West quoted in Richard B. Gehman's introduction to *The Day of the Locust* (1953); McGibbon and Kee (Granada Publishing Limited) and the New Directions Publishing Corporation for an extract from *The Autobiography of William Carlos Williams* by William Carlos Williams (1951).

Note

The best general survey of the history of the American nineteen twenties is William E. Leuchtenburg, *The Perils of Prosperity* (Chicago, 1958), supplemented by the document-collection edited by George Mowry, *The Twenties: Fords, Flappers and Fanatics* (Englewood Cliffs, N.J., 1963). On the changing social structure, see Lewis Mumford, *The Myth of the Machine: Technics and Human Development* (New York, 1968); Louis Wirth, 'Urbanism as a Way of Life', in *American Journal of Sociology* XLIV (1938); Siegfried Giedion, *Mechanization Takes Command* (New York, 1948), and Elting Morison, *Men, Machines, and Modern Times* (Cambridge, Mass., 1966). On modernist style, see Harold Rosenberg, *The Tradition of the New* (New York, 1956); Wylie Sypher, *Rococo to Cubism in Art and Literature* (New York, 1960), and Northrop Frye, *The Modern Century* (Toronto, 1967).

On the response of writers to the nineteen twenties, the best contemporary documents are *Civilization in the United States* edited by Harold Stearns (New York/London, 1922), his *America and the Young Intellectual* (New York, 1921), and his memoir *The Street I Know* (New York, 1935); Joseph Wood Krutch, *The Modern Temper* (New York, 1929); Waldo Frank, *Our America* (New York, 1919; London, 1922); Paul Rosenfeld, *Port of New York* (New York, 1924); Edmund Wilson, *The American Earthquake* (New York, 1958); F. Scott Fitzgerald, *The Crack-Up* edited by Edmund Wilson (Norfolk, Conn., 1945), and Malcolm Cowley, *Exile's Return* (New York, 1934; revised edition, 1951; London, 1961). On the expatriate scene, see Robert McAlmon, *Being Geniuses Together* (1938); Sylvia Beach, *Shakespeare and Company* (1960); Matthew Josephson, *Life Among the Surrealists* (New York, 1962); Harold Loeb, *The Way It Was* (New York, 1959); Samuel Putnam, *Paris Was Our Mistress* (New York, 1947); Morley Callaghan, *That Summer in Paris* (London, 1963); Gertrude Stein, *The Autobiography of Alice B. Toklas* (New York, 1933), and *Americans Abroad: An Anthology* edited by Peter Neagoe (The Hague, 1932). For analysis, see Albert Parry, *Garrets and Pretenders: A History of Bohemianism in America* (New York/London, 1933; revised edition, 1960); Caroline Ware, *Greenwich Village: 1920–1930* (Boston, 1935); R. P. Blackmur, 'The American Literary Expatriate', in *The Lion and the Honeycomb* (New York, 1955); George Hickes, *Americans in Paris, 1903–1939* (Garden City, N.Y., 1969); Elizabeth Stevenson, *Babbitts and Bohemians* (New York, 1967); Arthur Mizener, 'The Lost Generation', in *A Time of Harvest: American Literature, 1910–1960* edited by Robert E. Spiller (New York, 1962), 73–82; Alan Holder, *Three Voyagers in Search of Europe* (Philadelphia, 1966), and Warren I. Susman, 'A Second Country: The Expatriate Image', in *Studies in Literature and Language* III (Summer 1961), pp. 171–83. General studies of the literature of the period are Frederick J. Hoffman, *The Twenties: American Writing in the Postwar Decade* (New York, 1949); Maxwell Geismar, *Writers in Crisis: The American Novel Between Two Wars* (Cambridge, Mass., 1942); Alfred Kazin, *On Native Grounds* (New York, 1942); *After the Genteel Tradition* edited by Malcolm Cowley (New York, 1937); Sean O'Faolain, *The Vanishing Hero* (London, 1951), and John McCormick, *American Literature, 1919–1932: A Comparative History* (London, 1971).

I

Style of Life, Style of Art and the American Novelist in the Nineteen Twenties

MALCOLM BRADBURY

> Perhaps we might be called a transitional generation, bent on enjoying the urban pleasures, but at the same time hunters and fishermen eager to feel the soil instead of ashphalt underfoot. We were radicals in literature and sometimes in politics, but conservative in our other aspirations, looking back for ideals to the country we had known in childhood, where people led separate lives in widely scattered houses; where there were broad fields in which a boy could hunt without fear of No Trespass signs, and big woods. . . . (Malcolm Cowley, *The Faulkner-Cowley File*)

> What about the world, Mr. Cummings?
> I live in so many: which one do you mean?
> (E. E. Cummings, 'Introduction' to *The Enormous Room*)

I

THE AMERICAN nineteen twenties are a paradoxical decade; and part of that paradox is that a decade often defined as one of the most conservative in American history, an era of material and business expansion, was also one of the most remarkable periods of American literary experiment, of radical creative exploration and development, and (while extending much that had gone before) the great founding phase of modern American writing. For those for whom cultural change means explicit political manifestations, and for whom radicalism means intellectual innovation used for action, the decade becomes one curiously lacking in events, a phase of withdrawal into isolationism, and social reaction—an oasis, therefore, between the progressivism of the early part of the century and the political involvement and the social restructuring of the nineteen thirties, even a low, dishonest decade. The nineteen twenties can in fact be neatly separated as a period of illusion between two severe political realities—the end of the First World War, which tarnished liberal idealism and was followed by the Versailles Treaty, which more or less discredited it; and the Wall Street Crash of 1929, which in turn discredited the entire social and political action of the 'Jazz Age'. The moralistic historian can draw an easy lesson: the nineteen twenties were an era in which the political impulse was driven underground and a dangerous ideal of free enterprise America ran unchecked, leading to business expansion and unheeding social hedonism; and it suffered the comeuppance of a society which fails to invigilate its economics, adjust to the human interest, question its illusions. Yet even by this view the nineteen twenties remain a curious cultural mixture. Sometimes reported as an age dominated by Main Street, Prohibition, Red Scare and the Ku Klux Klan, an age of reversion and political reaction, it is also the period in which American life-style totally changed, in which the nation turned from being a production-orientated to a consumption-orientated society, in which the great capitalists gave way to the managerial revolution, in which there was a large-scale movement from the small town to the big city, and in which all of these things were accompanied by a vast acceleration in 'modernity', in emancipated sexual mores, increasing stratification of the generations, an acceleratingly tense pace of life, and an enormous change in moral focus. It is, therefore, a period of tension between past and present, of intensified style: an era of lost orientations, new manners, self-conscious fashions, the exploration of new tastes, a search for personal identity through the quickening flux of modern history. It is, at the level of human consciousness and behaviour, a very radical decade.

The view of the nineteen twenties, then, as a static and conservative period certainly does not account for many of its most striking phenomena;[1] and it certainly does not help us to understand the remarkable efflorescence in literature. To those critics who have seen the decade

[1] For a view of the changing perspectives on historical discussion of the nineteen twenties, see the articles by Henry F. May and Burl Noggle cited in the *Note* to Laurence Levine's article. May profitably stresses the extent to which it should be regarded as a revolutionary decade, in which 'The prophets of mechanization and welfare, the Fords and Edisons who scorned history and tradition, were equally [with the literary rebels] revolutionary. Most revolutionary of all, perhaps, were the prophets of psychology and social science, with their brand new societies full of brand new human

as a period of repressive puritanism and conservatism, the wave of experiment in literature is, of course, best explained by seeing it as a protest, a vast assault on America old and new. This, of course, it partly was. Running through it, or much of it, is a devastating attack on smugness, backwardness, provinciality, small-town values; and we are, after all, confronted in the nineteen twenties with the remarkable spectacle of a large part of the emerging literary generation leaving home and expatriating itself to Paris, in a kind of group withdrawal— a large-scale enactment of Harold Stearns's dictum at the end of his criticisms of civilization in the United States: 'Get out!' Disgust with American materialism and puritanism does run deep; 'puritanism' indeed becomes the great abuse-word to assault the total lack of interest in, the total lack of effective environment for, the creative arts. The element of protest against this and the traditional smug, small-town sensibility that seemed to underlie it—protest, then, against Main Street and an older generation that had not felt the intense experience of modernity, the deep, symbolic wound of the war and the consequent existential exposure—is very much there. But what is also there, in the writing of this generation, is a curious map of feeling, and a far from total protest, a far from complete expatriation. Most of the writers in Paris wrote about America, and not from an improbable distance, the distance of total political disenchantment. They were also ready to think of America not as a static society, but as a rapidly changing one; and their reactions to the change were not always those of cries for more of the same, but rather of desire to reconvert some of the American past into valuable currency, areas of attributed worth. Far from being remote from American culture, they shared its confusions—its attachment to the past, its speedy rush to the future. Then again, their assault on American puritanism and lack of interest in the arts was itself necessarily qualified by the very rapid acceptance received by their own work—an acceptance and recognition remarkable for a generation that regarded itself both as exiled and utterly experimental. And though they regarded Paris as an alternative culture in the absence of any at home, they also had, as American expatriates had long had, a strong feeling of assimilating the arts, the new movements of modern culture, consciousness and sensibility, into American

---

beings.' Levine himself shows how this produces a politically powerful sense of nostalgia.

experience, rather in the spirit of Ezra Pound's dictum: 'There are just two things in the world, two great and interesting phenomena: the intellectual life of Paris and the curious teething promise of my own vast occidental nation.'[2]

Paris, indeed, was not a capital for out-and-out exiles; it was rather a staging post for writers moving fairly readily back and forth, pulled this way by disgust and that way by nostalgia, critical of stability but also critical of change. And what they were close to in Paris was what was also happening in the United States. They sought, above all, style, the literary and emotional economy appropriate to a new age: the search was explicit and part of an essential craft or aesthetic orientation which, for them, made Paris into a kind of *atelier*—an education in style and form conducted, in part, by the experimentalists of the immediately preceding generation in English: Gertrude Stein, Ezra Pound, Ford Madox Ford, James Joyce.[3] But—in most of the countries in the west, certainly, but very especially in the United States—the nineteen twenties were a period of intensified style in life: an era of new manners, self-conscious fashions, exploration of new tastes, a modernized world-weariness, a dedication to a changing, historicist sense of fashion. They were a period of behavioural experimentalism, startling new styles of personality, strong reaction against the parental generation, attempts at new starts and new definitions, of social identity crisis—a period highly 'modern'. One might even say that it was a period of behavioural politics, an age conditioned quite as much by Freud (who had a remarkable acceptance in the United States)[4] as by Ford. Many of the new novelists were immersed in this evolving life-style, the history-as-consciousness of the decade—none more so than Scott Fitzgerald, who pointed out that part of the significance of the American Jazz Age, with all its novelty, febrility and tension, was that it put America in the historical front-line: 'something subtle passed to America, the style of man.'[5] And one result was that it was possible

[2] Ezra Pound, 'The Approach to Paris', *The New Age* XIII (4 September 1913), pp. 551–2. Warren I. Susman comments on this view in his valuable essay 'A Second Country: The Expatriate Image' (see *Note*).

[3] On this see Mark Schorer, 'Some Relationships' in *The World We Imagine* (London, 1969).

[4] Celia Burns Stendler, 'New Ideas for Old: How Freudianism was Received in the United States from 1900 to 1925', *Journal of Educational Psychology*, XXXVIII (April, 1947), 193–206.

[5] Scott Fitzgerald, 'The Jazz Age' in *The Crack-Up* (see *Note*).

for the American writer to set up an alliance between the spirit of modernism in literature and art, and the spirit of modernism in life —between art-style and life-style.

The idea that it is in the behaviour of persons that writers may look for the radical of experiment, that innovatory consciousness is not simply a matter of authorial creation but a matter of social stimulus and report, has undergone some complex developments lately—for example in the work of Norman Mailer, who has asserted himself as a novelist-historian of an age of evolving consciousness. This is not entirely a new proposal—indeed it was the basis of Whitman's explanation of the character of American literary experiment when, speaking of the distinctiveness of democracy, he wrote: 'For all these new and evolutionary facts, meanings, purposes, new poetic messages, new forms and expressions, are inevitable.'[6] And it is indeed one of the striking facts of American life that the nation has possessed the ideal of forging new consciousness, the experimental tone of life. This, of course, gives us a somewhat different mood of modernism from that we are accustomed to in contemplating in the European variant, or even in the slightly earlier generation of American modernists (James, Eliot, Pound) for whom art was the product of the international cosmopolis and for whom America was still, with whatever hopes it raised, a 'half-savage country out of date'. The one writer of this earlier generation who is closest to the spirit of experiment in the nineteen twenties is Gertrude Stein, who claimed that the new, modernist art-forms like cubism were American, because they were the expression of modern history and the new space-time continuum —which is what America, the futurist nation, was. This much more nativist, and much less crisis-centred, view of experiment—the view that William Carlos Williams embodied when he protested that Eliot had not advanced writing but set it back—seems atmospherically very different from the bleak epics of contingency that European modernism produced; it lightens the modernist spirit, claims it for the historical evolution of consciousness, gives it a progressive context. Where in Europe modernism seems largely a crisis of the intellectuals and the social place of the arts, in the United States it can be seen as a manifestation of a democratic-evolutionary society always orientated toward innovation and the future. In short, the experiment of the decade

6 Walt Whitman 'A Backward Glance, O'Er Travel'd Roads', *November Boughs* (1888).

was not simply an expatriate-bohemian manifestation; it was often conducted in close relation to the forces for change in American life, picking up its detail—its new manners, its new people, its machines and skyscrapers—and acting, often, on behalf of a modernist celebration.

This is not to deny the element of crisis in the experimental American writing of the nineteen twenties. It is clearly there, but it tends to come out of the forces of the changing world, rather than simply out of form itself. It is less a crisis of perception and language than a crisis of consciousness, of the strain of living in a modernizing world. Nor is it to deny the element of critique in the great writing of the period, which later essays here explore, though it is to change the terms in which that critique is often viewed. For what many of the writers of the nineteen twenties saw in the America of their time was *not* a stultifying and traditional society, unaffected by war, change, modern experience, nor a total disaster for meaning and language in society. Often they saw a society of change and new forms. The critiques of traditionalism are there, objects of direct (yet still ambivalent) satire in *Main Street* and of psychological criticism in *Winesburg, Ohio*. But the real importance of the latter is surely that it helped to establish in American fiction a level of psychological exploration and notation by which both psychic energy and psychic repression could be caught. It helps to break up the material and naturalistic surface of American fiction, and so lead the way into the writing of the nineteen twenties, with its concern with complexities of consciousness, its desire to penetrate not so much *beyond* naturalism as *beneath* naturalism. What, rather, novelists like Fitzgerald, Hemingway, Wolfe and Faulkner sought to understand was the dangerous drumming of psychic threat that came to man from his intense and contemporary involvement with the times. Dick Diver, in *Tender Is the Night*, immerses himself in the age of breakdown in order to know it; he does not see a crack-up unrevealed to others, for it is there in plain view, and Diver tries to redeem it by living through it. He loses himself in the flux of the urbanized, centralized society, the force of that being greater than his own humanism. Jake Barnes, in *The Sun Also Rises*, similarly shares the universe of the modernized herd and tries to make an economical, personal destiny within it, the real distinction of the book coming not between Jake and Robert Cohn, who as a pre-modernized romantic is an easy target, but between Jake and Brett. What in fact runs through many novels of the twenties is the idea of the distinctive modernity of the times, of Oedipal exposure in the face of a parental generation already overthrown, of an involvement in a speeding historical present in which the symbolic wound of change and exposure, the wound of war which bound a generation, is common property. In the American novelists of the nineteen twenties, in Anderson, Hemingway, Fitz-gerald, Faulkner, we can sense the desperate novelty of a generation feeling the distinctiveness of its own conditions and searching out the emotional and moral terms of a new life, free of provincialism, re-gressiveness, the confining populist embrace.

These writers shared the experimental sense of life that belongs to the times: they also shared something as important in its map of feel-ing—a sense of lost bearings, what Lawrence Levine (chapter 2) calls its 'nostalgia'. One part of their experimental aim is to capture the new consciousness, the new pace, the new relationships. Perhaps the writer in whom this intent is most apparent is John Dos Passos, several of whose novels are novels of the contingent city and the collage of modern experience. His primary techniques—the interfusing of the four basic structural orders of *U.S.A.*, for instance (the stories of a large group of representative individual lives, the factual biographies of public figures, the Newsreel, the Camera Eye), and the related use of stream-of-consciousness presentation both for the flickering collage of contemporary historical event in the Newsreel and for visual and sense-impressions in the Camera Eye sections—are clearly there to present the great city of modern life, the cubism of modern perception. Dos Passos suggests a further reason for the mannerism, however; it is the expression of a loss of language in American society, and hence the loss of historical meaning, so that the structure is itself an implicit critique.[7] There is a quality of artistic ambivalence in the method as a

[7] The critic who has best commented on this is a cultural historian, John William Ward, who in an essay, 'Lindbergh, Dos Passos and History', *The Carleton Miscellany* VI (Summer 1965), notes the common features that link together *The Great Gatsby* and *USA* as follows: 'As far apart as they are in other ways . . . both books at climactic moments project the sense of loss, of failure, of betrayal, through the violation of greenness, of meadows, of open, inviting, unravaged nature.' He goes on to comment on the metaphorical significance of this pattern for the nineteen twenties, analysing the same cultural dichotomy, the green land of individualism versus the technological-corporate impulse, in the rhetoric of reception that acclaimed Lindbergh's flight across the Atlantic in 1927. On his further essay 'The Meaning of Lindbergh's Flight' Lawrence Levine comments valuably in his essay in this volume.

B

result, and in various forms we can see the same ambivalence in other writers of the period—Faulkner, Hemingway, Fitzgerald, West. On the one hand, there is an immense immersion in the times, which are a total condition of existence. On the other hand, there is a primitivist alternative to set against them—the simple howtowns of Cummings, the struggle between man and the moment of claim out of nature in Hemingway, the initiation into the big woods in Faulkner, the green image of the enravaged virgin land and of the American dream in Fitzgerald. As Thomas Wolfe said, you can't go home again; but there was always the metaphor of alternative, the silent, still universe out of history which could be held to restore a sense of direction and give an equipoise and a luminosity to art. This too, because it produces a reaction against a simple realism or naturalism, provokes the complexities of aesthetic experiment. This element of pastoral has been commented on frequently by critics; the best discussion occurs in Leo Marx's brilliant book *The Machine in the Garden*, where he follows out the pervasive relationship between the progressive machine and the timeless garden, once a genuine American historical ideal, through the history of American literature, and locates these conflicting images deep in American culture. What he notes about the treatment of this theme in the American writers of the nineteen twenties is the complexity of form it produced:

> Again and again they invoke the image of a green landscape—a terrain either wild or, if cultivated, rural—as a symbolic repository of meaning and value. But at the same time they acknowledge the power of the counter-force, a machine or some other symbol of the forces which have stripped the old ideal of most, if not all, of its meaning. Complex pastoralism, to put it another way, acknowledges the reality of history. (pp. 362–3)

My suggestion here is more than that these writers acknowledged the reality of history; it is that they saw history in new ways, and found its significance deep in the meanings of the life around them. They saw themselves as the first generation of a new condition of modernity that had come into American life; and it was the relationship of that to the past, to the process of historical evolution *and* to the American past conceived of as a timeless ideal, that concerned them. They lived in the world of the city and the machine, of vast acceleration, of novel experience; and the pastoral was the past in its dimension of pre-inflationary stability, purpose and meaning, a universe on the other side of some essential line drawn across human experience. For some writers, that line was drawn by the war itself: those who had been through its experience, its disillusionments, its realness, its exposure of the 'truth' about human nature, could not, indeed, go home again. For others, it was drawn by other things: the accelerating intrusion of the machine, the bursting forth of new mores and new consciousness.

It is perhaps significant that the great phase of American experimental writing falls not, as it does in Europe, in the prewar period. Admittedly, as we have seen, it was American expatriate writers who helped in that ferment; but it is in the nineteen twenties that experiment becomes so prevalent a style in American writing that it is virtually *the* style—the style of changing America. The American novelists of the nineteen twenties clearly do relate to the general modernist endeavour that runs through the western literatures in the first decades of the century; but their novelty also comes from the situation of modern America. They embody something of the novelty of a fictional experiment which generates formal complexity, encourages the thrust outward from history and into symbolist transcendence —the crisis of the word. But they also embody that novelty of modern awareness and experience, that sense of expansion and exposure, the experiment of history itself: the crisis of the world. One interesting result of this mixture is that the crises moderate one another; this makes their experiment not so much a terminus, a literature of the end of things, as in a good deal of European modernism, but a mode of coping with the continuity of modern experience, so that what they were doing could become an available tradition for their successors. To this extent, in fact, they were consciously making American literature, separating it from its European origins and its provincial situation. And perhaps the best way of illustrating this is to turn to three writers of major importance who seem to me to embody the forces of which I have been speaking—the divergence from and the relationship to European experiment; the involvement with and the reaction against contemporary America—and look briefly at the bases of their experiment. The three are Faulkner, Hemingway and Fitzgerald; very different writers yet with sufficient in common—an intense stylistic concern, an obsession with craft and stance in a context of change—to illuminate many important features of the action of fictional style and structure in the period when America was passing into an utterly novel environment of evolving history.

II

Though there is little dispute today about the seriousness with which his work should be taken, William Faulkner seems to have acquired two divergent reputations. To many critics, he is pre-eminently a Southern novelist, a rooted man, the voice of his place, his society, his history; to others, he is one of the great international modernists, a writer with the range and capacities we associate with Joyce, Proust and Mann, a writer of sophisticated technique, distilling the force of an international tradition, an experimentalist, symbolist, and witness to modern exile.[8] The two views are not incompatible: as Robert Penn Warren says of his 'legend' of the Southern history: 'The legend is not merely a legend of the South, but is also a legend of our general plight and problem. The modern world is in moral confusion. . . .'[9] And if Faulkner's writing is 'backward-looking', then so too is the vision of much of modern and modernist literature. Yet there remains a problem of emphasis: one can see the force of his reputation as an experimentalist—in the sense that his novels use the techniques of time-shift, stream-of-consciousness, errant grammar, collage presentation and dechronicity, and explore the themes of human exposure and alienation that we associate with a good deal of modern writing—while also seeing a curious distance between what he was doing and what other modernist writers were doing. His own view of himself was of a private man, a farmer; of a writer who was a rhetorician of the endur-ing human virtues, honour, endurance, amity, compassion, sacrifice; of an author whose language was bred, as he himself said, 'by Oratory out of Solitude'. This can be taken as a convenient disguise, as in part it was; yet it seems significant that Faulkner's own aesthetic formu-lations, his discussions of his writing, never fully articulate the impulses that drove him to technical convolution and complexity. There is an odd surprise about the fact that, whereas in most modernist careers (Joyce's for example) the works increase in complexity and texture,

8 Compare, for instance, the emphasis of Michael Millgate, *The Achievement of William Faulkner* (1965), which stresses Faulkner's cosmopolitanism and his acquaintance with and relation to the broader literary tradition; and Cleanth Brooks, *William Faulkner: The Yoknapatawpha Country* (1963), which offers as a countervailing balance a stress on Faulkner as a cultural historian and a sociological interpreter of his regional society.

9 Robert Penn Warren, 'Cowley's Faulkner', in *William Faulkner: Three Decades of Criticism* edited by F. J. Hoffman and O. W. Vickery (East Lansing, Mich., 1960).

refining themselves toward the extreme point of experiment and aesthetic consonance, Faulkner's did not; indeed, his most experimental writing comes in the middle of his career, and is frequently regarded by critics as a 'phase'. As one of his critics puts it, Faulkner used such means, since he was aware of his times, but his 'temperament, his genius, his habits of mind, are more congenial to the narrative, the epic, the bardic attitudes in the creation of literature'.[10] His tour de force methods are thus part of a more general barrage of literary skills, and his materials extend beyond the particular means used for their working out. Certainly, for Faulkner, those materials did have an assumed, continuous life beyond the realm of the fictional construct. As Arnold Goldman shows (Chapter 8), they exist somewhere between a status as 'real' objects of imitation, and as imaginative creations; nonetheless, they are part of an assumed social history of the South, partly factual, partly mythical, onto which a variety of literary moods and modes can be projected.

It is, indeed, significant that it is only when the historical dimension enters Faulkner's work that his technical experiments emerge in their full force. In his first two novels, *Mosquitoes* and *Soldiers' Pay*, Faulkner seems consciously to adopt the modes of the cosmopolitan and sophisticated modern writer, to deal with themes concerning the aftermath of war and modern bohemian existence. With *Sartoris*, Faulkner discovered that his materials were not simply contemporary, but had an extended historical and social dimension, emerging from his familiar environment and its past; the special postage stamp of soil began to be populated: 'I discovered,' said Faulkner about his book, 'that writing was a mighty fine thing. You could make people stand on their hind legs and cast a shadow. I felt that I had all these people, and as soon as I discovered it I wanted to bring them all back.' But bringing them back seemed to involve complicated aesthetic introversion, as if the very fact of making his characters part of a larger history and hence part of a vast plan of pluralized narratives compelled this upon him. It is in the work right after *Sartoris*, the work of the end of the nineteen twenties and the nineteen thirties (*The Sound and the Fury, As I Lay Dying, Light in August, Absalom, Absalom!* and some of the stories), that we can feel Faulkner's experimental power at full force. These are works that involve a sense of history, but they

[10] John Lewis Longley, Jr., *The Tragic Mask: A Study of Faulkner's Heroes* (Chapel Hill, N.C., 1963).

are not all historical novels; they reach back in time as they reach
across into the broader society of Yoknapatawpha County, but these
are mostly works about a present burdened with a past. A distinct
if implicit historiography underlies their vision, one that includes a
conspectus of all American history, with special reference to the South,
from the point of settlement in the new land to the contemporary
instant. The history itself is a kind of imaginative fiction, mythically
woven round the facts; it is a very modernizing history, a process
whereby land as spirit yields to land as property, woods to axes,
gardens to machines, aristocrats to carpetbaggers and entrepreneurs,
men of feeling and honour to men of mechanical sensibility and
material ambition, country to city, South to North. It is a sequence
of significant times, frozen instants when the chance of innocence or
freedom is newly offered, but when taint, corruption or rape also
constantly recur. In Faulkner's history there are two recurrent para-
digms: one is the instant of personal renewal, or of wonder, or of
delocalized vision, experienced for example by Ike McCaslin in *The
Bear* and converted into value ('Forever wilt thou love, she be fair');
the other is the Civil War or its surrogates, the simultaneous shock, in
Southern terms, of the industrial revolution and modern war as the
destroyer of values and cultural continuity. And it is the conversion
of this—the flow and the arrest, the process and the transcendence—
into art that creates the peculiar fictional basis of Faulkner's history and
the basis of his experimentalism.

It is clear that time, historical time and interior time, is the essential
theme of Faulkner's work; all he writes raises questions about *when* this
happened, and what sort of relationship exists between one time-layer
and another, so that the handbooks that aid us to read Faulkner must give
us chronological and genealogical maps in order to help us. The relationship between historical time and inner time or consciousness, and the
related structuring of works not according to evolving logics of chron-
icity but according to alternative sequences that substitute for it aesthetic
or symbolistic coherence, are familiar modes in modernism. Such
apocalyptic time is in fact at the centre of the long, prolix Faulknerian
sentence that is at the heart of his style, as in this from *Light in August:*

> Though the mules plod in a steady and unflagging hypnosis, the
> vehicle does not seem to progress. It seems to hang suspended in the
> middle distance forever and forever, so infinitesimal is its progress,
> like a shabby bead upon the mild red string of road. So much is this

so that in the watching of it the eye loses it as sight and sense drowsily merge and blend, like the road itself, with all the peaceful and monotonous changes between darkness and day, like already measured thread being rewound on a spool.

Faulkner's sentences repeatedly work like this one, the grammatical structure being exerted to create not a sense of cause and effect, but motion and stillness, so that the object perceived is held rhetorically static within the development of the narrative. Clauses reach backwards and forwards, coalescing the past and the present, the advancing motion and the still centre, perception and the thing perceived. We can recognize this as being very consonant with modernist aesthetics, even though the result is not at all that 'scrupulous meanness' that Joyce emphasized or Hemingway used, nor the fear of abstractions invoked by Imagism, but a very prolix rhetoric indeed. In fact it is this obvious rhetorical pleasure that makes Faulkner's a very untense species of modernist writing; it lacks the preserved precisions of crisis writing, but delights in its fluid possibilities, which is one reason why Faulkner's style never acquires the intense personal authority of say Proust's or Joyce's in one direction, or Hemingway's in another.

One can also see that the same features extend from being matters of style to matters of structure: the story of Lena Groves puts a timeless frame round the accelerated events of the Joe Christmas story in *Light in August*; Benjy's continuous present offers an arrest to the cause-and-effect world of Quentin and Jason in *The Sound and the Fury*, that work in which all the active agents seem to be in *pursuit* of subjective time. Faulkner's tactics in these more experimental works are very different from book to book, but they have certain distinctive and very Faulknerian features. Again and again the theme, the obsession, is causative history, the ceaseless ticking of the clock of meaning, and the ensuing hysteria it invites. Against this there are the perceptions that precede or are independent of the acts of organized knowing: Benjy's uncausal, because idiot, world, or Joe Christmas's childhood impressions, events moving shapelessly into the unconscious and becoming not interpretations but psychological traumas. On occasion, then, the complexity seems part of Faulkner's quarrel with history; his multiples of consciousness, like Eliot's fragments, are apparently of a piece with the loss of meaning and order that Faulkner sees in his lapsed Eden of the American South, tales full of sound and fury but signifying nothing. But often they become precisely the opposite. For, like

Sherwood Anderson, who was mentor to both him and Hemingway, Faulkner was interested in the creative as well as the distortive dimensions of the psyche. He was interested not just in its disorders but in its plenitude, its sentience and lyricism, its structures and myths. And because consciousness is creative—as it is in the author himself—then time need not destroy; rather it can be relived, passed on from one human being to another. The past is perpetuated, and hence renewable; history has in consciousness a timelessness—is a constantly replayed myth in which second chances are, indeed, given. And so the spirit of the woods, of Eden, endures; the modern lapse is temporary, and its wrongs will be avenged; the doom or the curse is a test of the enduring qualities of human nature. Though the reasons for despair are made evident in his work, and certain of his characters face extremes of disillusion and exposure presented with profound imaginative sympathy, Faulkner is not himself a despairing writer, and certainly not an utterly nostalgic one. The past, the old order, serves as a remote guide; but it, too, operated under the same curse as the present; and history has in itself the ceaseless potential for becoming joyous myth. It is this that maintains Faulkner's language in the world of public language, for it is not finally a language of crisis. Faulkner's style, his structures, and the total sequence that his whole oeuvre makes, all explore discontinuity and despair, but they end up in rescue—a rescue that takes him not simply into the autotelic literary symbol but an encompassing literary rhetoric, what he himself calls 'oratory'. Indeed, given his culture and his vision of its growth and meaning, Faulkner is oddly undespairing—a curiously buoyant version of the modernist impulse, a spokesman of an American optimism.

III

The writer of the nineteen twenties who in fact does embody the strain and crisis of the times as a matter of language is surely Ernest Hemingway. Compared with Faulkner, Hemingway avoids the elaborations of technique that the modernist writers had acquired to present the complexities and disjunctions of modern experience, the loss of value in their interpretation. There is little in his work in the way of those large presentational strategies by which they create the flux and plurality of contemporary consciousness; but there *is* that consciousness. Hemingway's fictional construct is a clean, well-lighted place, a world of the hard, well-registered minimum. There is a specified Hemingway world; it has its own type of terrain, a *paysage moralisé*, its own geography of sanctified places, its special drinks, guns and rods, its distinctive verbal mannerisms. There is also a specified Hemingway hero who is the appropriate tenant, moving through the estate with a certain ease and comfort despite his obvious tension, insomnia and nightmare. The world is a selective fiction, and there is therefore a special discourse for its presentation; Hemingway deftly expresses it at the beginning of *Death in the Afternoon*:

> . . . the real thing, the sequence of motion and fact which made the emotion and which would be as valid in a year or in ten years or, with luck and if you stated it purely enough, always, was beyond me and I was working very hard to try to get it.

The language is the energetic pursuit of a truth. It controls and contains; it functions according to a very pure stylistic economy, in which every word written, every fact or emotion rendered, is traded at the best possible rate of exchange. As the universe and action described is sparse, so the words are limited: adjectives are cut to a considered few: causal connectives, similes and metaphors are reduced; the writing points always towards objects, which function as subdued symbols, hard, energetic instances. The result is a controlled limitation of feeling, an ironic materiality in which a small number of details live starkly in clear juxtaposition. The aim of the language is double—to force attention to the economy of the gesture, the cleanness of the line, the active grace of the doing, and to convey with integrity the thing observed, to get toward some ultimate and authentic experience. Hemingway's writing is not a psychological writing in the familiar sense; it does not get inside. It projects action outward, which is why place is so important and why the terrain must be right. The characters live in a conditioned world exterior to themselves; nonetheless the world is a metaphor for their psychic condition, their human state. And they are located like the writer in a place where craft and integrity is a form of action—a motion toward an ultimate realism.

As a number of critics have pointed out, there is a resemblance between Hemingway's distinctive style, and the modernist doctrines of impersonality and the objective correlative.[11] Hemingway knew

[11] See, for instance, Jackson J. Benson, *Hemingway: The Writer's Art of Self-Defense* (Minneapolis, Minn., 1969). For broader discussions of the character

the resemblance; he went to Paris and sat at the feet of Gertrude Stein, though he consciously rejected bohemia, which could give technique but not material, art but not human value. But Hemingway was the writer as man of action, not man of letters; writing itself was a professional skill directed towards a specified end, and Hemingway modelled the artistic role on three other roles, those of the sportsman, the soldier-of-fortune, and the journalist. All are roles of skill and style which involve a particular encounter, a confrontation with an authentic event. There is a *there*, a select reality to be discovered and faced. The journalist faces it with a notebook, and encompasses it with language; this was Hemingway's way too, except that he did not observe but participate, entering on the battlefield and claiming the red badge of courage as well as reporting it. Hemingway always intruded into his realities; he sought out all the wars of his lifetime and when he found them he entered them as well as wrote about them. In the meantime he found war's surrogates, equally *there*: shark-fishing, big-game hunting, duck-shooting. The integrity of words was testable against the integrity of events and then against the integrity of the self. Style, in writing and life, was a moral encounter; and Hemingway tested it all the way through his life to its tragic end. Language in fact intensely contains the self; it energises the perpetual encounter between man and his surroundings; it is the hard intermediary between consciousness and objects or events, and it covers the savagery and struggle of the encounter. As Edmund Wilson once remarked, the landscapes, the calm and contented surfaces, of the Hemingway world are suffused with suffering, with the 'undruggable consciousness of something wrong'. The purity is shrill; it is suffused with the autobiography, the history and the forms of suffering out of which it has been sought. It is for this reason that we can find it so modern a style, just as we find the experience that validates it modern too.

Hemingway's is a very puritan world. It is a world of the elect, who live in purgatory, and the damned, who avoid purgatory by failing to recognize it. The purgatory is in history; it has its specified place in time, for Hemingway's elect is an elect of modernity. Hemingway makes this clear in *The Sun Also Rises*, called in England *Fiesta*; when

of Hemingway's rhetoric, see Harry Levin, 'Observations on the Style of Ernest Hemingway', in *Contexts of Criticism* (Cambridge, Mass., 1957) and David Lodge, 'Hemingway's Clean, Well-Lighted, Puzzling Place', in *The Novelist at the Crossroads* (London, 1971).

it appeared in 1926, it bore an epigraph from *Ecclesiastes* and another from Gertrude Stein: 'You are all a lost generation.' Gertrude Stein denied having said it, and when it became a cliché Hemingway wanted to remove it. Nonetheless it is not hard to see why he thought it appropriate: Hemingway's fiction, like much of the fiction of the nineteen twenties, is one in which the word 'generation' counts. The novel turns on the assumption that the war drew a large line across history, and that those who had lived through it, been tested by it, and come to maturity after it are bearers of certain kinds of knowledge and certain kinds of trauma and deprivation unknown to their predecessors. The most resonant symbol of all for Hemingway is of course the wound, the red badge he himself acquired on the Italian front and was to suffer time and again in the physical risk-taking of his continuous search for 'the real thing'. The wound of war is an intolerable intrusion into the self; it is the ultimate exposure. But it is also the ultimate realism and hence a genuine possession. What is more, it is, in his writing, an initiation not only into the human condition but into the conditions of history; it is a place in time. It leads to a world of trauma, sleeplessness, loss, risked relationships, awareness of *nada*; it also creates the communal consciousness of a generation. This is the theme of *The Sun Also Rises*, Hemingway's most social novel, which is divided between, on the one side, the lost modern spirits, like Jake and Lady Brett, who share the complicity of being modern, and the romantic spirits, like Robert Cohn, who, having read the wrong writers, liked the wrong countries for the wrong reasons, and operated according to the wrong emotional set, lack the sense of nothingness but became thereby historical strangers. It is those who bear the modern trauma who carry all the weight of significant action. They determine the landscape, provide the modern Baedaker, lead the way in contemporary sensibility; they find the right drinks, use the right meeting places and set the cultural pace.

The Sun Also Rises is not only Hemingway's most social novel, but his most fashionable one, in the Scott Fitzgerald sense. In it Hemingway is consciously concerned with catching the historical mood of the time of writing, by exploring a community self-consciously advanced and aware, the expatriate literary and smart set of the Parisian nineteen twenties. His characters are modern initiates signalling across the uninitiated with styles and languages of their own; their behaviour, their febrility, their sense of shock becomes the essential contemporary state of mind and their wanderings and responses constitute the essential modern landscape. They are a set, and they belong not only to their decade but a particular social and economic strata within it: all more or less young, more or less wealthy, and more or less beneficiaries of the favourable rate of exchange which puts the dollar high against the franc, they are products of the postwar disorder and the moral chaos which invests it. They are urban cosmopolites, freed from their economic and moral roots, and so permitted to explore the pleasures of the time, the consumption of new styles in sexual relationship and conduct, to use the stuff of the modern as a 'damned good time', while at the same time they have the moral onus to redeem it from total chaos. 'I did not care what it was all about,' says Jake Barnes, 'All I wanted was how to live in it.' They seek a purity of line at the point of maximum exposure, and that exposure is central to their natures. Hemingway creates, by external referents, the sense of hell inside them, the way their relationships run along the edge of mental and moral chaos. Jake's wound of impotence and Brett's nymphomania thus became antithetical symbols both of futility and modern heroism. By paradox, Jake's impotence is in fact a basis for his survival; it keeps him in the tight, closed world of male comradeship, of men without women, of things one cannot lose, through which a certain sort of survival is possible. That survival lives in the end outside the social world of the novel, in the glimpse of something more pastoral and primitive glimpsed in Spain and on the fishing trip, offering the basis of a ritual control of self in the presence of a nature the hostility of which is muted to the point of permitting a fighting contact with it, man and the universe battling timelessly on equal terms.

Most of Hemingway's later full-length fiction concentrates on that battle, and the social determinants drop away from direct sight. But if finesse and integrity, craft and style, can yield up something that temporarily staves off the sense of disaster, this happens always in relation to the complex world of the modern which Hemingway states in his first novel. Hemingway appropriately calls one of his collections of short stories (and it is in these that the detail of modernity most persists) *In Our Time*. The shrill psychic underlayer never leaves Hemingway's books, however much these seem to depart from the environmental conditions which shape the peculiar and tense Hemingway consciousness. It is part of Hemingway's developing writerly economy that he leaves the causative behind, only symbolizing the intensity of the psychic depths below—though these can show frighten-ingly through at times, as they do in *Islands in the Stream*. The hero becomes more autobiographical, the landscape more precise, but the shifts and changes of the writing are nonetheless encounters with a developing history, a set of transactions of consciousness between the self and a world of onerous events. Hemingway's political and social interpretations occasionally reassert themselves, though never with any great analytical attentiveness; and, as Irving Howe suggests, his later fiction seems to pass delicately around the urban world of the American mainland from which the entire sensibility and consciousness with which he deals emerges.[12] Nonetheless it is impossible to comprehend Hemingway's economical craft nor his apparent pastoral, his literature of encounter, without comprehending the contingent city out of which it grows, urging his heroes on towards moral and emotional precision and style as short-term redemption against the modern immersion, the growth in stress of contemporary consciousness.

IV

But the writer of the nineteen twenties who most obviously feels the intensity of modern American experience in all its specified and evolving detail is Scott Fitzgerald. The result is that to many of his critics he has seemed little more than a chronicler, a man whose immersion in the social life and commerce of his times, in the prevail-ing ambitions, the shifting life-styles, the fun and the frenzies, the amusements and tunes, the fashionable displays and the current mores, the unwinding detail of history, gave him no real distance with which to stand back and shape or criticize. It is true that Fitzgerald was, more than most novelists, a novelist of immersion; it was the heart of his literary tactic. It was a tactic paid for at high cost; it involved a com-petition for public fame and attention which ran through his personal as well as his public life and cut deep into his marriage and his psyche. Indeed in his essay 'The Crack-Up' Fitzgerald draws a very precise analogy between the historical sequence of America through the nineteen twenties and early nineteen thirties and his own psychological

12 'Of all the writers who began to publish after the war, Hemingway seems best to have captured the tone of human malaise in an era of war and revolution; yet it is noteworthy that, while doing so, he rarely attempted a frontal or sus-tained representation of life in the United States. . . .' Irving Howe, 'The Quest for Moral Style', in *The Decline of the New* (1970).

career: the early euphoria of the decade turning toward a sense of trauma and disturbance and then to Slump is an exact match for the psychic process that takes Fitzgerald through his own early joyous success to his crack-up, his alcoholism and his wife's schizophrenia. The identification could be so precise because Fitzgerald lived it as such; he bound himself tightly to the glossy and wealthy cosmopolitan life which was a species of the decade's experimentalism, and much of his style, in life and in writing, he took from that link. This has often been identified as his weakness; and we can see why it might be thought so. With *This Side of Paradise* Fitzgerald had set himself the task of catching the mood of youth, in a book that while energetic can hardly be thought of as good; its success encouraged him to take on the stance of style-setter for the times, to identify tightly with its emergent moods and fashions; and that identification satisfied many of his crudest ambitions and his obsession with wealth. He caught himself up in the American cosmopolite class at a time when it dominated, by its money and its high consciousness of contemporary fashion, the pace of modern style, substituting for the more rooted social culture of the wealthy in the past a life of flamboyant display, a kind of dream-behaviour. There was obviously something of the parvenu in his involvement, and it was often expressed in the simplest form in his writings, converted into a popular, easy and money-making kind of fiction. It is often supposed that what he acquired, by painful experience and effort, was the power to stand back and criticize; and it is that which explains the quality of his serious fiction. The truth is, I think, that Fitzgerald's creative gift is better understood from a slightly different emphasis; it was not his separation from the frenzied life of the times, but his discovery of the psychic forces which compel it, that made his best work what it is.

Fitzgerald said that his stories all had a 'touch of disaster' in them—a sense of the high emotional cost of human involvement in the times, a sense of the general spirit of psychic over-extension involved in the commitment to youth and glamour, wealth and amusement. Fitzgerald's main characters are deeply immersed in their times, like Dick Diver, who feels compelled to risk his sanity and ordinariness by plunging into the melée of advanced social experience, as if the claims of consciousness and the responsibilities of the human condition demand this. The belief that the writer must know his times and serve in the places where the times are acted out most fully is a familiar literary conviction; it was one Fitzgerald shared with Hemingway. But where for Hemingway the urgent need becomes that of a line of control, a making of style of self and style in writing into protective instruments, Fitzgerald practised the opposite tactic. His style is a mode of involvement, a thrust into the society and psychology of the times. His narrator in *The Great Gatsby*, Nick Carraway, stills the voice of judgment; and by virtue of so doing he explores the complexities of a hero, Gatsby, who at all levels seems morally unsatisfactory. Gatsby is a former bootlegger; he is a parvenu; he is at the service of a vulgar and meretricious beauty. Carraway's peculiar tolerance—partly a condition of his own involvement in a fantastic life in which he, too, is something of a parvenu—is the instrument for a very oblique assessment, which Fitzgerald establishes by an underlayering of subdued symbolism which emerges naturally from the surreal environment of the story, the surreal environment of modern dream-life. *The Great Gatsby* is a novel of the modern city, and it throws up its startling detail in instants and images—in the shifting fashions in clothes and music, the decor of hotel rooms, the movements of traffic, the ashheaps and hearses, that catch Carraway's eye in his mobile way through the varied and populous society of the novel. Through Carraway, too, Fitzgerald establishes a very oblique sense of causality, so that Gatsby, who might well be thought of as the derivative of this world, is gradually distinguished from it and set against it, so that finally he becomes a victim of its contingency. The theme of the novel is the suffusion of the material by the ideal, so that raw stuff becomes enchanted object; and this is not only the basis of Gatsby's peculiar power and quality, but the basis of the writing itself, which manages to invest Gatsby's actions, his parties, his clothes, with this distinctive glow. Fitzgerald's effects are, as I say, surreal, the making bright of evanescent things so that they have the quality of dream; but of course at the end of the novel the dream is withdrawn, and another surreality, the nightmare of the unmitigated mass of material objects, it replaces:

> I have an idea that Gatsby didn't himself believe that it [the phone-call from Daisy] would come, and perhaps he no longer cared. If that was true he must have felt that he had lost the old warm world, paid a high price for living so long with a single dream. He must have looked up at an unfamiliar sky through frightening leaves and shivered as he found what a grotesque thing a rose is and how raw the sunlight was upon scarcely created grass. A new world, material

without being real, where poor ghosts, breathing dreams like air, drifted fortuitously about . . . like the ashen, fantastic figure gliding toward him through the amorphous trees.

Fitzgerald is in fact the great historian of these two interlocking worlds, the world of modern history invested with meaning and the world of that history without it, the modern wasteland, the city of culture and the city of anarchy. The great fact of his work is that he was able, as a young man in his twenties in the twenties, to humanize and internalize his times, to follow out their running sequences, catching the right tunes for the year and the right fashions and tones of voice. As with Hemingway, though with a tighter social detail, he follows out the psychic history of the times, the history of the great gaudy spree, of a 'whole race going hedonistic, deciding on pleasure'. This is a meaningful revolution for Fitzgerald, and he sees the pleasure in it as well as the pain in it. But the flaw is of course inherently there; the Beautiful are also the Damned. And, like Hemingway, Fitzgerald made not only emancipation but neurosis part of his personal history. *The Great Gatsby* is a completed, and is indeed a contained, work; the aesthetic controls are precise, and the way the hero is both valued and distanced involves a complex artistic strategy. But Fitzgerald's great novel of the nineteen thirties, *Tender Is the Night*, a novel coming after his own crack-up ('There was not an "I" any more—not a basis on which I could organize my self-respect . . .'), is incomplete, fully enough written, but open to variants of organization; it is an incompleteness curiously apt to its theme, as in fact is the incompleteness of Hemingway's shrillest and most anguished work, *Islands in the Stream*. The central figure, Dick Diver, is himself shocked out of completeness in the course of the book; choosing, as Fitzgerald chose, to dive into his time, he finds his purity of position, his impersonality, his sanity, compromised by the need to act on the front edges of modern society, and especially with regard to Nicole. His humanism becomes tarnished; a redemptive figure at the beginning of the book, he is unable by the end to perform the trick—once done with elegant ease—of lifting a man on his back while surfing; his pastoral concern for others becomes a breakup of self, and he fades away from significant history at the end of the book. Like Fitzgerald, he becomes an implicated man; the implication draws him into the heart of that disaster, that psychic over-extension, which was to become increasingly Fitzgerald's theme.

By the nineteen thirties, Fitzgerald had come to feel the risks of what he had done, and *Tender Is the Night* is an exploration of those risks; it also takes them again, using once more as its hidden theme the notion that this contemporary and accelerating history might be redeemed, might be made valid. The result is a novel of singular power and force—superior, I think, to that other great expatriate novel, *The Sun Also Rises*, by its comparatively deeper quality of immersion, its attentiveness to the sequence of historical fact, its closeness of registering. But its power lies also in the way in which Fitzgerald, within a method that puts the emphasis on this, traces back causes and reasons, so that, just as Diver's psychic dislocation comes from his concern with the fragility of these front-line modern sensibilities, so in turn those sensibilities, and Nicole's above all, are tracked backwards to their social, cultural and economic roots. The novel becomes an energetic metaphor for the nineteen twenties and their turn into the nineteen thirties; it catches the force of the passion for emancipation and new consciousness, the accelerating tempo, the cultural exploration through shifting sexual morality and sensation-hunting; it is a psychology of all its characters. But the psychology is within a history, and Fitzgerald explains that history. Its awareness is psychological, economic and social at once; man is, so to speak, propelled by history and society into expressive action, but the action itself can come to express the dislocation in society, the energy and the threat of the active modern consciousness. Against the economic history, which he came to recognize as being more or less Marxist, Fitzgerald sought always to establish the alternative—history made luminous by its participants, involvement given meaning and transcendence. Both histories are currents, processes; Fitzgerald would have liked to unite them, as they are united in the great American success stories where American social history serves the American dream.[13] But what he gives us is a world that is both material and dross, a naturalistic world; and a world in which limited meanings can live—the result being neither realism nor autonomous symbolism but a distinctive surrealism. This kind of achievement, because it is not finally an achievement of form organizing matter, is the hardest for us to explore and to value, especially because Fitzgerald uncomfortably possessed the means—he could be a very bad as well as a very

[13] Fitzgerald represents the two currents at the end of *The Great Gatsby*; it is perhaps significant that the directions in which they are moving seem confused, as if Fitzgerald could not determine which is the genuinely progressive force.

good writer—to make them impure. Yet in these two books, as incipiently in *The Last Tycoon*, Fitzgerald shows the enormity of the effort. Indeed of these three writers I have come to find that he wears best of all, and that his reconciliation of the formalism and the historical realism of the novel—those two countervailing attributes of the genre from its beginning—offers a great artistic achievement.

V

One of the legacies that the writers of the nineteen twenties left with us is a strong emphasis on craft and technique; the legacy passed quickly into modern criticism and it has had a strong effect, too, on the character of subsequent American writing. Yet, important as it is for us to recognize that the writers of the nineteen twenties did bring into the novel a radical element of formal discovery and formal attention, it is also important to avoid the assumption that they thereby fled from the history of their times. One cannot help feeling that criticism has sometimes over-used the aesthetic, symbolist emphasis in the discussion of those writers from whom it has indeed partly emanated, and in establishing preferences among them. For this emphasis has helped to encourage the idea that the twenties was a very aesthetic and formalistic decade, in distinction from the thirties, when politics returned and social realism set in again. That the writers who came to notice in the nineteen thirties *were* in many cases more politically orientated, and that by that token they felt they had an accusation to make against their immediate predecessors for their failure to be political and progressive, for their willingness to seek the consolations of art and form, is true. (Likewise it is true that in the nineteen thirties both Hemingway and Fitzgerald felt, in their different ways, pressed to take attitudes more directly political and neo-Marxist, though with very different results: Hemingway turned increasingly to themes of human solidarity, while Fitzgerald increasingly turned to a more ironic view of the broad historical process with which he had identified.) My aim in this article has been to suggest that the style of some of the experimental writers of the nineteen twenties bears a much sharper relationship to, a much more immersed comprehension of, the contemporary history of the American nineteen twenties than is often allowed; and that the urgencies and shapes of form in the decade involve complex responses to its pressures and tensions. This is a question which bears on the responsibility of criticism, which has tended often to categorize novels into life-novels and art-novels and at various times to prefer the one to the other; the aesthetics of the intermediate ground—and these were, I think, the neo-modernist working aesthetics of the American writers of the nineteen twenties— tend to be seriously underexplored. But, if I am right, this is also a question that bears on the responsibility of cultural history. For in cultural history this intermediate ground has a great importance. If, as I take it, cultural history is a form of history concerned not simply with socio-historical process, not with the objective discernment of forces, but is instead concerned with those matters of style and structure, consciousness and culture, which are the lived centre of history, then the concern of writers with behavioural politics is itself illuminating. For the writer's power to mediate between types and structures in history and society and the universe of forms, and to work out that median through the representation of lived and felt life, is itself essential to cultural history. To say that is to touch on many momentous matters which need further exploration;[14] a number of them will recur from point to point in this present volume.

[14] I have explored this general question much more extensively in my essay, 'Sociology and Literary Studies: II, Romance and Reality in *Maggie*', *Journal of American Studies* III(1) (July 1969), pp. 111–21.

Note

William E. Leuchtenburg's *The Perils of Prosperity, 1914-1932* (Chicago, 1958) is the best one-volume synthesis of the nineteen twenties. We lack a comprehensive, scholarly socio-cultural history of the postwar decade; the most informative social descriptions and analyses remain those of contemporaries: Frederick Lewis Allen, *Only Yesterday* (New York, 1931); Robert and Helen Lynd, *Middletown* (New York, 1929); Mark Sullivan, *Our Times: The United States, 1900-1925* volume VI, *The Twenties* (New York, 1935), and *Recent Social Trends in the United States* (2 volumes, New York, 1933). Robert Wiebe, *The Search for Order, 1877-1920* (New York, 1967), Henry F. May, *The End of American Innocence* (New York, 1959), and Richard Hofstadter, *The Age of Reform* (New York, 1955), help to set the stage for many of the decade's cultural developments. *Change and Continuity in Twentieth-Century America; The 1920s* edited by John Braeman *et al.* (Columbus, 1968) has several insightful articles and shows recent scholarly trends. Henry F. May, 'Shifting Perspectives on the 1920s', *Mississippi Valley Historical Review* XLIII (December 1956), pp. 405-27, and Burl Noggle, 'The Twenties: A New Historiographical Frontier', *Journal of American History* LIII (September 1966), pp. 299-314, are good historiographical discussions.

For the quest for ideological homogeneity and the attempt to root out 'alien' doctrines after the First World War, see Paul Murphy, 'The Sources and Nature of Intolerance in the 1920s', *Journal of American History* LI (June 1964), pp. 60-76, Stanley Coben, *A. Mitchell Palmer: Politician* (New York, 1963), and Robert K. Murray, *Red Scare* (Minneapolis, 1955). John Higham, *Strangers in the Land: Patterns of American Nativism, 1860-1925* (New Brunswick, 1955), contains an excellent analysis of attitudes towards and treatment of immigrants during the twenties. For the reaction of the U.S.A. to the Russian Revolution, see Christopher Lasch, *The American Liberals and the Russian Revolution* (New York, 1962) and Peter G. Filene, *Americans and the Soviet Experiment, 1917-1933* (Cambridge, Mass., 1967).

The most perceptive studies of prohibition are those of the sociologist Joseph Gusfield whose work is cited in footnote 6, below, and Andrew Sinclair's comprehensive but hostile *Prohibition: An Era of Excess* (Boston, 1962). The best account of the Ku Klux Klan in the nineteen twenties is David Chalmers, *Hooded Americanism* (Garden City, 1965); also see E. H. Loucks, *The Ku Klux Klan in Pennsylvania* (New York, 1936); C. C. Alexander, *The Ku Klux in the Southwest* (Lexington, 1966); Kenneth Jackson, *The Ku Klux Klan in the City, 1915-1930* (New York, 1967) and Hiram Wesley Evans, 'The Klan's Fight for Americanism', *The North American Review* CCXXIII (March 1926), pp. 33-61, a crucially important inside statement of what the Klan was about. The fullest scholarly study of the fundamentalist movement is Norman F. Furniss, *The Fundamentalist Controversy, 1918-1931* (New Haven, 1954); also see Paul Carter, *The Decline and Revival of the Social Gospel* (Ithaca, 1956); Robert M. Miller, *American Protestantism and Social Issues, 1919-1938* (Chapel Hill, 1958), and Donald Meyer, *The Protestant Search for Political Realism, 1919-1940* (Berkeley, 1960).

American historians have not yet paid sufficient attention to the area of

II

Progress and Nostalgia: The Self Image of the Nineteen Twenties

LAWRENCE W. LEVINE

I

The Dream

AMERICANS have always been comfortable with the idea of progress. The belief that inevitable change brought with it inevitable advancement and betterment fitted easily with, and was reinforced by, the stress on the individual, the belief in human perfectibility, the relative rootlessness and lack of tradition, the unparalleled mobility, the indefatigable optimism, the sense of uniqueness and destiny that has characterized so much of America's history. 'Democratic nations,' de Tocqueville wrote, taking the United States as his model, 'care but little for what has been, but they are haunted by visions of what will

---

popular culture; valuable introductions are Russel B. Nye, *The Unembarrassed Muse: The Popular Arts in America* (New York, 1970), and *Mass Culture: The Popular Arts in America* edited by Bernard Rosenberg and David Manning White (New York, 1957). Specific analyses of the movies and comic strips of the nineteen twenties can be found in the works cited in footnotes 8 and 9, below. Also see Hortense Powdermaker, *Hollywood, the Dream Factory* (Boston, 1950); Martha Wolfenstein and Nathan Leites, *Movies, a Psychological Study* (New York, 1950), and George Perry and Alan Aldridge, *The Penguin Book of Comics* (Harmondsworth, 1967). Twenties' popular music is discussed in Sigmund Spaeth, *History of Popular Music in America* (New York, 1948), and David Ewen, *Panorama of American Popular Music* (Englewood Cliffs, 1957). Newman White, *American Negro Folk Songs* (Cambridge, Mass., 1928), and Paul Oliver, *Blues Fell This Morning* (New York, 1960), give examples of black folk and commercial music. On best-selling novels of the nineteen twenties, see James Hart, *The Popular Book* (Berkeley, 1961); on the decade's humour, see Jesse Bier, *The Rise and Fall of American Humor* (New York, 1968). The transformation of popular images of success and mobility in the twentieth century is analysed in Theodore P. Greene, *America's Heroes: The Changing Models of Success in American Magazines* (New York, 1970), and Richard Weiss, *The American Myth of Success* (New York, 1969).

be; in this direction their unbounded imagination grows and dilates beyond all measure.' Evidence of the validity of de Tocqueville's observation abounds everywhere from Jefferson's assertion, 'The creator has made the earth for the living, not the dead', to Senator Orville Platt's jubilant announcement in the last decade of the nineteenth century, 'We live in a new creation. Literally, the old things have passed away and all things have become new. Human society is full of creators.' When Emerson proclaimed that the one fundamental split in society was between the Party of the Past and the Party of the Future, the Party of Memory and the Party of Hope, and described himself as 'an endless seeker, with no past at my back', he seemed to be speaking for his countrymen in general.

Only recently have scholars come to the realization that the ode to progress, no matter how eloquently composed, was not alone in the land; it was accompanied by a cry of longing for what had been[1]. The compulsion to peer forward was paralleled by an urge to look backward to a more pristine, more comfortable, more familiar time. Nostalgia is beginning to be recognized as an historical force no less prevalent and perhaps no less important than the idea of progress. Nor were its roots dissimilar. The imagery which pictured nineteenth-century Americans as latter-day Adams in an Edenic 'Garden of the World', may have allowed them to visualize themselves as free to rise, favoured as they were by a perfect and completely open environment and untrammelled by the taint of original sin or the heritage of the past, but it also confronted them with the dilemma of whether the roads from Eden could lead anywhere but down. Richard Hofstadter has captured this dilemma perfectly in his ironic comment that 'the United States was the only country in the world that began with perfection and aspired to progress.' Thomas Jefferson served as a paradigm of this dilemma when he assured his country of its destined power and influence at the same time that he urged it to retain its purity and simplicity by remaining a nation of agrarians.

The central paradox of American history, then, has been a belief in progress coupled with a dread of change; an urge towards the inevitable

---

[1] See, for example, Henry Nash Smith, *Virgin Land* (Cambridge, 1950); R. W. B. Lewis, *The American Adam* (Chicago, 1955); John William Ward, *Andrew Jackson—Symbol for an Age* (New York, 1955); Marvin Meyers, *The Jacksonian Persuasion* (Stanford, 1957); Richard Hofstadter, *The Age of Reform* (New York, 1955).

future combined with a longing for the irretrievable past; a deeply ingrained belief in America's unfolding destiny and a haunting conviction that the nation was in a state of decline. This duality has been marked throughout most of America's history but seldom has it been more central than during the decade after the First World War. The force of nostalgia was manifest in the nineteen twenties in three related but distinct forms: a national movement to restore to America a former purity, cohesiveness and national purpose which had been diluted by the introduction of 'alien' elements and ideologies; a cultural schism which saw a large segment of the population alienated from modernity and longing to return, at least symbolically, to a golden past; and a profound ambivalence towards the future which affected the actions and rhetoric of even some of the most fervid apostles of the 'New Era'.

II

The nineteen twenties were ushered in by the failure of a prophecy—specifically, Woodrow Wilson's prophetic assurance to his countrymen that he was leading 'this great peaceful people into war' in order to foster the world-wide adoption of American democratic principles and forms: 'for democracy, for the right of those who submit to authority to have a voice in their own Governments, for the rights and liberties of small nations, for a universal dominion of right.' To enlist the American people fully in this cause, German ideology was converted into the very antithesis of everything America stood for. Prussian militarism had to be contained to ensure the principle of self-determination of all peoples; German materialism had to be defeated if the principles of Christianity which the United States represented were to have any chance of universal application. 'This war,' a member of the Committee of Public Information wrote to George Creel, 'is being fought in the minds of great masses of people as truly as it is being fought on the battle fields of Europe.'

How seriously this missionary impulse was taken is illustrated by the American reaction to the February Revolution in Russia. The United States was the first nation to extend diplomatic recognition to Kerensky's provisional government for, as Wilson put it, the overthrow of Czarist autocracy in Russia now gave America 'a fit partner of a League of Honor'. From the beginning the United States viewed the

Russian Revolution through the prism of American ideology. 'It was the American flag that has brought about the peaceable revolution in Russia,' the *Des Moines Register* concluded on 23 March 1917, 'and it is the American flag that will bring about the revolution in Germany, peaceable or violent, for that revolution is bound to come. It is American ideals that dominate the world.' When Russian determination to fight the war faltered in the Spring of 1917, the United States sent a commission headed by Elihu Root to reassure the provisional government and strengthen its will. After some time spent in travelling through Russia, Root wired Wilson: 'We have found here an infant class in the art of being free containing 170 million people and they need to be supplied with kindergarten material. . . .'

The October Revolution which established Lenin and Trotsky in power, and the Versailles Treaty which indicated that the war aims of the Allies were not in concord with those of Wilson, left the messianic prophecies of the United States everywhere in ruins. The resulting disappointment supposedly impelled a disillusioned American people to turn inward, to abandon their former dreams, to forsake idealism for hedonism. 'Feeling cheated,' Lloyd Morris has written: 'the war generation was cynical rather than revolutionary. It was tired of Great Causes. . . . It wanted slices of the national cake. There resulted the general decision to be amused.'

In fact, the immediate aftermath of the First World War exhibited the opposite tendencies. Americans did not abandon their old verities and values but reasserted them with renewed vigour. The psychologist Leon Festinger and his associates, in their study of prophetic movements, concluded that while there are limits beyond which belief will not withstand disconfirmation, the introduction of contrary evidence often serves not to destroy the belief but rather to strengthen the conviction and enthusiasm of the believers. The dissonance resulting from the clash of a belief-system and facts which tend to discredit it produces anxiety which can be reduced in one of three ways: by discarding the disconfirmed belief; by blinding oneself to the fact that the prophecy has not been fulfilled; by reconfirming the belief and increasing proselytizing in the hope that 'if more and more people can be persuaded that the system of belief is correct, then clearly it must be correct.'[2]

[2] Leon Festinger, Henry W. Riecken, Stanley Schachter, *When Prophecy Fails* (New York, 1964).

Although Americans exhibited all three tendencies during the nineteen twenties, the latter two, and especially the third, constituted by far the most prevalent responses. With respect to Russia, for instance, there was little disposition to recognize that Americans had misinterpreted the direction and meaning of the revolutions of 1917. At first the Bolshevik regime was seen as merely a passing phase in the Russian drive to adopt American ideals. George Kennan predicted that the new regime would fail because it violated 'certain fundamental economic laws', and for two years after the October Revolution the *New York Times* repeatedly (ninety-one times in all) reported that the Bolsheviks were on the brink of defeat. While Wilson joined England and France in an abortive attempt to bring down the new government by sending troops to Siberia, his ultimate response was to deny the existence of the Bolsheviks by withholding recognition; a refusal which the United States persisted in until Franklin Roosevelt took office in 1933.

On the domestic front, too, the defeat of American predictions about the effects of the First World War resulted in a nationwide tendency to reassert the viability and meaning of the very principles and beliefs upon which the failed prophecy had been erected. The full significance of the Red Scare of 1919 cannot be grasped unless it is perceived as an attempt to restate traditional American values, to reconfirm long-standing American images, to purify the nation and call it back to its historic mission by ridding it of intruding ideologies and groups. Stanley Coben, utilizing the anthropological theories of Anthony F. C. Wallace, has likened the Red Scare to a 'revitalization movement' (other examples of which were the American Indian Ghost Dance cults of the late nineteenth century and the Boxer movement in China from 1898 to 1900), which under the spur of intensive social disruption attempts to relieve anxiety by reviving central cultural beliefs and values and eliminating alien influences.[3]

The emphasis upon revivification was omnipresent in the early postwar years: in the national repudiation of every possible form of radicalism; in the reaction against strikes and unionization; in the race riots of 1919 which struck out against the changed image and status of black Americans; in Warren Harding's assurance to his countrymen that theirs was a time for 'not heroics but healing; not nostrums but

[3] Stanley Coben, 'A Study in Nativism: The American Red Scare of 1919–1920', *Political Science Quarterly* LXXIX (March 1964), pp. 52–75.

normalcy; not revolution but restoration'. A substantial portion of the nation faced the new decade not in excited anticipation of what might be or in stubborn satisfaction with what was, but with a nostalgic yearning for what had been. Americans continued to have grandiose hopes for the future, but increasingly their dreams were moulded upon the patterns of the past.

Nowhere was this clearer than in the national attitude toward immigration and acculturation. A heterogeneous conglomeration of peoples, Americans above all other nationalities have had to strive for a sense of national identity and speculate endlessly about the process by which the diverse national and ethnic groups emigrating to the United States became American. The most familiar concept, of course, was that of the melting pot which Crèvecoeur spoke of as early as the seventeen eighties when he wrote 'Here individuals of all nations are melted into a new race of men', and which Frederick Jackson Turner was still celebrating at the end of the nineteenth century when he concluded that 'In the crucible of the frontier the immigrants were Americanized, liberated, and fused into a mixed race, English in neither nationality nor characteristics.' 'America is God's crucible,' the hero of the 1908 play *The Melting Pot* exclaimed. '. . . A fig for your feuds and vendettas! Germans and Frenchmen, Irishmen and English-men, Jews and Russians—into the Crucible with you all! God is making the American.'

The concept of the melting pot was a unique and difficult base upon which to build a sense of identity, since it posited an ever-changing American image dependent entirely upon the ethnic components that were 'melted' down. Indeed, for many Americans the concept was too difficult and, as Milton Gordon has shown, the melting pot was continually confronted by a counter concept—the idea of Anglo-conformity. If immigrants to the United States could not accom-modate themselves to the nation's character, 'moral, political and physical,' John Quincy Adams wrote in 1818, 'the Atlantic is always open to them to return to the land of their nativity and their fathers. To one thing they must make up their minds, or they will be dis-appointed in every expectation of happiness as Americans. They must cast off the European skin, never to resume it.' 'Our task,' an educator asserted one hundred years later, 'is to . . . assimilate and amalgamate these people as a part of our American race, and to im-plant in their children, so far as it can be done, the Anglo-Saxon conception of righteousness, law and order, and popular government. . . .'[4]

A number of reformers during the Progressive Era took the melting pot idea one step further in complexity by arguing for 'cultural pluralism'. The United States, they maintained, should become a 'democracy of nationalities' a 'nation of nations', in which every ethnic group retained many of its identifying characteristics, each living in harmony with the others. While this concept may have come closer to describing the reality of the acculturation process than either of the others, it never took strong hold of the American imagination. The First World War not only made it difficult for ideas like cultural pluralism to take root; it led to the rejection of the melting pot itself. Profoundly disturbed by the sight of German- and Irish-Americans openly calling for the victory of the Central Powers and immigrants from the subject peoples of the Austrian Empire along with English- and French-Americans siding with the Allies, large numbers of Americans, from the President down, reacted against what were popularly called 'hyphenated Americans'. 'When the Klan first appeared,' its Imperial Wizard Hiram Wesley Evans recalled, 'the nation was in the confusion of sudden awakening from the lovely dream of the melting pot. . . . [Nordic Americans] decided that even the crossing of salt water did not dim a single spot on a leopard; that an alien usually remains an alien no matter what is done to him. . . . They decided that the melting pot was a ghastly failure. . . .'

For all his hyperbole, Evans reflected the national mood. In the Americanization movement with its emphasis upon 'One country, one language, one flag', and in the immigration acts of 1921 and 1924 with their national origins formula which reversed the tide of immigration from southern and eastern Europe and Asia in favour of the more familiar northern European countries, this mood was made explicit. Americans in the postwar era were turning away from the idea of the melting pot with its dynamic, future orientated concept of national identity and embracing the notion of Anglo-conformity which looked to the past and took as its model the early Anglo-American. If the term 'melting pot' remained in use, it came to symbolize less and less a crucible which boiled *down* differences into a new composite identity

[4] Milton M. Gordon, *Assimilation in American Life* (New York, 1964), chapter 4. See also chapters 5–6 for incisive discussions of the melting pot and cultural pluralism.

and more and more one which boiled *out* differences into the image of the old American. To be sure, the melting pot concept had been attacked periodically in the nativist movements of the nineteenth century, but not until the nineteen twenties was the reaction strong enough to legislate it out of existence. In their immigration policies, as in so much else, Americans during the nineteen twenties exhibited a national urge to turn backwards in an effort to recapture the images and meaning of their country's youth.

III

It would, of course, be an egregious misreading of the nineteen twenties to maintain that it was *primarily* a backward-looking decade. The 'New Era' deserved its title in many respects. The impact of the new technology, of the automobile, of mass production and consumption, of the radio, the movies and other forms of mass media, of modernist religious teachings in the churches, of the enhanced political and cultural influence of large cities, of the greater emphasis upon science in the schools which now reached far greater portions of the population than ever before in American history, of new moral codes and standards, was very real and constituted what Walter Lippmann called the 'acids of modernity' which were eating into and transforming the entire society.

Historians in emphasizing these developments to the exclusion of all else, however, have been in danger of ignoring the tone and aspirations of a large part of the United States. As I have argued elsewhere at greater length, the tendency to see the nineteen twenties as an age of materialism in which the American people turned their backs upon idealism and reform does not accurately describe a decade which was marked by furious struggles waged over prohibition, religion, the rights of Catholics and Jews, the very nature of the morality and ethos that would define and guide Americans in the years to come. If the term 'idealism' is used to define not merely those movements of which historians approve but any movement that puts forward a set of principles about which people feel strongly enough to band together and fight for, then idealism and crusading zeal were still very much alive throughout the decade.[5]

[5] Lawrence W. Levine, *Defender of the Faith: William Jennings Bryan, The Last Decade, 1915–1925* (New York, 1965), chapters 5–9.

The millions of Americans who joined or at least sympathized with the Ku Klux Klan and fundamentalist movements and who fought for the enforcement of prohibition were an indication that a substantial part of the population greeted the new forces of the nineteen twenties with a sense of loss, frustration and antipathy. They were as alienated from the ethos and developments of the age as the bitterest members of the Lost Generation. They attempted to reverse the trends dominating modern America and return to the moral and ethical code of the past. They longed for the *Gemeinschaft*, the community, which they had been brought up to believe was central to America. They constituted one half of a pervasive sectional and cultural schism that disrupted the prewar progressive coalition, prevented the resurgence of a new political and economic reform movement, rendered the Democratic Party almost impotent, and prevented the nineteen twenties from ever becoming the materialistic, hedonistic age it has been pictured as.

The United States with its heterogeneity, individualism, mobility and success ethic may never have furnished fertile soil for the growth of a true *Gemeinschaft* culture characterized by permanence, intimacy and binding tradition. But the rural, small-town cultures of nineteenth-century America, which Robert Wiebe has called 'island communities', at least approached this ideal in principle if not always in fact. The insularity of these communities was first seriously disturbed by the nationalizing tendencies of the expanding industrial economy after the Civil War. This threat to the independence and integrity of small-town America helped give rise to the reform movements of the late nineteenth and early twentieth centuries which Richard Hofstadter has characterized as efforts 'to realize familiar and traditional ideals under novel circumstances'. By the early decades of the twentieth century the threat had expanded inevitably to the social and cultural spheres. The further Americans were carried from their version of the *Gemeinschaft* the more ideal it seemed to become.

In 1925 a woman in Muncie, Indiana, recalled that

In the nineties we were all much more together. People brought chairs and cushions out of the house and sat on the lawn evenings. We rolled out a strip of carpet and put cushions on the porch steps to take care of the unlimited overflow of neighbors that dropped by. We'd sit out so all evening. The younger couples perhaps would wander off for half an hour to get a soda but come back to join in the

informal singing or listen while somebody strummed a mandolin or
guitar.

By the twenties the citizens of Muncie were besieged by newspaper and
magazine advertisements urging them to buy automobiles and
'Increase Your Weekend Touring Radius'. 'A man who works six days
a week,' a banker was quoted in one such ad, 'and spends the seventh on
his own doorstep certainly will not pick up the extra dimes in the great
thoroughfares of life.' On 4 July 1891, a Muncie merchant noted in his
diary: 'The town full of people—grand parade with representatives
of different trades, an ox roasted whole, four bands, fire-works, races,
greased pig, dancing all day, etc.' On 4 July 1925, Robert and Helen
Lynd found Muncie deserted; its inhabitants had taken to the road.
    The automobile was only the most visible and dramatic symbol of
the new forces that were eroding traditional standards and modes of
action in religion, morality, familial patterns, life styles. The changes
left large numbers of Americans bewildered and alienated. Unlike the
writers and artists of the Lost Generation they could not escape to
Europe or to bohemian enclaves within the United States. Instead they
attempted to contain the forces reshaping America through a series of
movements which, unlike the Red Scare and anti-immigration
movements, were regional rather than national in character. It is
important to understand that the cultural regionalism exemplified by
prohibition, fundamentalism and the Klan was psychic and not purely
geographic in character. All three movements had supporters in large
cities as well as in small towns and rural communities, but it would be
a mistake to deduce from this that they were therefore urban as well as
rural in tone and purpose. The large numbers of urban migrants from
rural, small-town America faced a difficult, often impossible, cultural
adjustment which left them bereft of identity. They, perhaps even
more than those who remained behind, craved a lost sense of community and longed for a reassertion of the old moral values. Though
they were technically urbanites—inhabitants of the *Gesellschaft*—they
were psychically attuned to the cultures from which they had emi-
grated. They supported prohibition, fundamentalism and the Klan
precisely because these movements promised a real or symbolic flight
from the new America back to the familiar confines of the old.
    The fate of the prohibition experiment provides an excellent
example. Prohibition came into being as a movement during the

reform ethos of Jacksonian America and retained its reformist overtones right down to the nineteen twenties. It won the support of a large segment of the nation's progressives and was passed in the form of a constitutional amendment during the Progressive Era itself by reformers who could see nothing more reactionary in deciding that man for his own good must not drink alcoholic beverages than in ruling that he must not eat impure beef or work in dangerous and unhealthy surroundings. 'Those who labour for prohibition,' William Jennings Bryan declared, 'are helping to create conditions which will bring the highest good to the greatest number without any injustice to any, for it is not injustice to any man to refuse him permission to enrich himself by injuring his fellowmen.' To dismiss prohibition as simply a reform that failed is to miss the importance of what occurred to it during the twenties. As an *institutional* reform its impact was significant. In spite of lax and inefficient enforcement, the consumption of alcohol during the nineteen twenties was from thirty to fifty per cent lower than it had been during the period 1911–1915. If this was not reflected in the image of the nineteen twenties it was because prohibition had the greatest impact upon the beer-drinking working classes and was least effective among the wealthier professional classes who could afford bootleg liquor and who set much of the tone and style of the decade. Nevertheless, sharply decreased rates of arrests for drunkenness, hospitalization for alcoholism and the incidence of such diseases as cirrhosis of the liver, all attest to the relative effectiveness of the reform.

Prohibition failed in the twenties not because it was institutionally impossible but because it was more than an institutional reform. It was in addition, as Joseph Gusfield has argued so convincingly, a 'symbolic reform' which gave recognition and legitimacy to the norms and values of rural, Protestant America. It existed as a national symbol of the work habits and morality of the old America; it clearly told every immigrant and every urbanite what it meant to be an American; it attempted to make the American Protestant ideal of the good life national by enshrining it in law. 'The hope of perpetuating our liberties,' an advocate of prohibition maintained, 'is to help the foreigners correct any demoralizing custom, and through self-restraint assimilate American ideals.' This cultural imperialism, perhaps even more than the material effects of the reform, infuriated the urban, industrial, immigrant populations who constituted the chief opponents of prohibition. As the decade progressed, prohibition was transformed from a complex reform movement into an essentially cultural crusade which cut through the lines of reform. Increasingly it lost many of its reformist supporters and forged natural alliances with the multitude of other movements which had as their aim the nostalgic reassertion of a fading life style.[6]

The very defensiveness of these movements in the face of the new developments of the twenties forced them into an aggressive posture. Their fears and aspirations were evident in the rhetoric of the Klan's leader, Hiram Wesley Evans, who lamented in 1926 that 'the Nordic American today is a stranger in large parts of the land his fathers gave him.' Traditional Americans, Evans complained, were beset by confusion and hesitancy 'in sharp contrast to the clear, straightforward purposes of our earlier years'. They were plagued by futility in religion and a general moral breakdown: 'The sacredness of our Sabbath, of our homes, of chastity, and finally even of our right to teach our own children in our own schools fundamental facts and truths were torn away from us. Those who maintained the old standards did so only in the face of constant ridicule.' Robert Moats Miller has argued that the Klan of the twenties was a genuine counterrevolutionary movement. Certainly, under Evans's leadership it sought to combat and defeat the entire host of evils threatening its countrymen. The Klan, Evans warned, would be satisfied with no less than 'a return of power into the hands of the everyday, not highly cultured, not overly intellectualized, but entirely unspoiled and not de-Americanized average citizen of the old stock.'

In the final analysis, however, the movements for which Evans spoke were less counterrevolutionary than defensive; movements on the run which were struggling vainly to stay off the erosion of their cultures and life style—but not at the price of giving up all of the advantages of modernity. It is this that explains why they were so often content with the symbols rather than the substance of power. By the middle of the decade the fundamentalists had begun to stem the tide of the modernist advance within the churches and, through local pressure and intimidation, had made serious inroads upon the teaching

---

[6] Joseph Gusfield's important analyses of the prohibition movement can be found in his study, *Symbolic Crusade: Status Politics and the American Temperance Movement* (Urbana, 1963) and his article, 'Prohibition: The Impact of Political Utopianism', in *Change and Continuity in Twentieth-Century America: The 1920's*, edited by John Braeman *et al.* (Columbus, Ohio, 1968).

of evolution in the schools. But this was not enough. They demanded such statewide laws as the Tennessee Anti-Evolution Act of 1925 not because they really desired to overturn modern education in the states and the nation, but because they craved the comfort of statutory symbols which would settle the question of whose version of the good society was legitimate. The Governor of Tennessee recognized this when, after signing the bill into law, he told the legislature: 'After a careful examination, I can find nothing of consequence in the books now being taught in our schools with which this bill will interfere in the slightest manner. Probably the law will never be applied.' All that the framers of the bill intended, he insisted, was to lodge 'a distinct protest against an irreligious tendency to exalt so-called science, and deny the Bible in some schools and quarters. . . .'

The extent to which symbols became paramount was manifest in the trauma and fear induced by Al Smith's campaign for the Presidency in 1928. It was not Smith's political programme which in many respects met the economic needs of rural, small-town America better than that of the Republican Party, nor even his Catholicism which activated these feelings, but his urban background, his appeal to the polyglot populations of the big cities, his very speech, dress and manner. Al Smith, the Anti-Saloon League's journal observed, 'is different from any candidate of either party within the knowledge of the present generation. . . . He is not in harmony with the principles of our forefathers.' The southern Democratic editor, George Fort Milton, warned that Smith's primary appeal would be to the aliens, the Negroes, the Catholics, the Jews, 'who feel that the older America, the America of the Anglo-Saxon stock, is a hateful thing which must be overturned and humiliated', and called upon 'the Old America, the America of Jackson and of Lincoln and Wilson' to 'rise up in wrath' and defeat them. Although the nationalizing and standardizing forces of large-scale industry and the mass-media were more deeply entrenched in the Republican Party of Herbert Hoover, Smith's defeat was greeted with widespread rejoicing. America, the *St. Paul Pioneer Press* announced jubilantly,

> is not yet dominated by its great cities. Control of its destinies still remains in the small communities and rural regions, with their traditional conservatism and solid virtues. . . . Main Street is still the principal thoroughfare of the nation.

D

IV

Had nostalgia in the nineteen twenties been confined to the national tendency to reassert traditional values and images following the failed prophecies of the First World War and to the past orientated movements of the culturally alienated, it could be treated as an important force but one still on the periphery of a decade that seemed so dedicated to and enamoured of change. The most pervasive manifestation of nostalgia in the twenties, however, took the form of the ambivalence I discussed at the outset of this essay. In 1914 Walter Lippmann wrote of Woodrow Wilson's 'inner contradiction': 'He knows that there is a new world demanding new methods, but he dreams of an older world. He is torn between the two. It is a very deep conflict in him between what he knows and what he feels.' This inner contradiction ran like a thread throughout the decade.

No one has seen this more perceptively or illustrated it more brilliantly than John William Ward in his study of the reaction to Charles Lindbergh's flight across the Atlantic in 1927. Lindbergh had not been the first to conquer the Atlantic. Almost ten years before his flight a British dirigible had crossed the ocean and in 1919 two planes, one manned by a crew of five and the other with two aboard, repeated the feat. But Lindbergh did it *alone*. '. . . no kingly plane for him,' an American bard rhapsodized. 'No endless data, comrades, moneyed chums; / No boards, no councils, no directors grim— / He plans ALONE . . . and takes luck as it comes.' In a technological age of growing organization, complexity and facelessness, Lindbergh symbolized the self-sufficient individual of the past. Compared to Robinson Crusoe, Daniel Boone, Davy Crockett, he was a reminder of America's own uncomplicated beginnings; a product not of the city but of the farm, not of schools and formal training but of individual initiative and self-contained genius.

There was, of course, something jarring in all this. Lindbergh had not been alone. He was enveloped in a plane which was the product of the city, of technology, of organization. In spite of their odes to individualism, Americans really never lost sight of this. Lindbergh himself recognized it when he paid tribute to the industries that had created his plane and entitled the volume describing his flight, *We*. President Coolidge proudly pointed out that over one hundred companies had furnished material and services in the plane's construction.

Thus on the other side Lindbergh's flight was recognized as the triumph of modernity. As another American poet put it: 'All day I felt the pull / Of the Steel Miracle.' In these two reactions Ward has documented one of the basic tensions in American life. The crucial point is that this tension was not merely present in the antithetical reactions of different groups but *within* the responses of the same groups and individuals. Americans were still torn between the past and the future, the individual and society.[7]

It is difficult to find any aspect of American culture in the twenties that did not exhibit this tension. Motion pictures, which came into their own as a popular art form during the decade with 100,000,000 people attending 20,000 theatres weekly by 1926, seem on the surface to have been one long celebration of the new woman, the new morality, the new youth, the new consumption patterns that marked postwar America. Films with such titles as *Forbidden Fruit, Flapper Wives, Week-end Wives, Parlor, Bedroom and Bath, Madness of Youth, Children of Divorce, Modern Maidens, Dancing Mothers, Love Mart* were advertised as featuring 'Brilliant men, beautiful jazz babies, champagne baths, midnight revels, petting parties in the purple dawn, all ending in one terrific smashing climax that makes you gasp.' The reality fell short of the promises. As uninhibited as they might have been, the movies of the twenties rarely failed to conclude without a justification of the moral standards of the past. Flappers and 'It' girls married at the end of the film and entered a life of middle-class respectability. Faithless husbands and wives mended their ways and returned to patient, forgiving mates. The new woman may have been depicted as tough but, as David Robinson has put it, their toughness was used to protect their purity, not to dispose of it. The widespread popular revulsion against the excesses of the first wave of postwar movies forced Hollywood to resort to the cliché of the happy and moral ending; a standard which never marked European movies to the same extent and which made them seem, to movie critics at least, less artificial and more realistic.[8]

[7] John William Ward, *Red, White, and Blue: Men, Books, And Ideas in American Culture* (New York, 1969), chapter 3.

[8] Here and in much of what follows on the movies of the twenties, my interpretations have been heavily influenced by Arthur Knight, *The Liveliest Art* (New York, 1959); David Robinson, *Hollywood in the Twenties* (New York, 1968); Lewis Jacobs, *The Rise of the American Film* (New York, 1939, 1968); Gilbert Seldes, *The Seven Lively Arts* (New York, 1924, 1957). (See *Note* at beginning of chapter.)

The career of Cecil B. DeMille is instructive. After attempting to make the bathroom and bedroom national shrines in his series of postwar sexual comedies, DeMille turned to the public for suggestions for new films. Impressed by the number of requests for religious themes, DeMille hit upon a new formula in his widely popular films, *The Ten Commandments* (1923) and *The King of Kings* (1927). Sex and orgies were still prominent but they were now placed within a religious framework with a moral message. 'Better than any other director of the era,' Arthur Knight has written of DeMille, 'he seems to have apprehended a basic duality in his audiences—on the one hand their tremendous eagerness to see what they considered sinful and taboo, and on the other, the fact that they could enjoy sin only if they were able to preserve their own sense of righteous respectability in the process.' This was the result not of hypocrisy but of the kind of tension manifest in the response to Lindbergh. Just as Americans could accept the fruits of modern technology only if they could assure themselves that the potency of the individual was enhanced in the process, so they could enjoy the freedom of the new morality only by surrounding it by the verities of the past.

The continued popularity of the comedy film throughout the twenties provided an outlet for the disquiet the decade produced in many Americans. Charlie Chaplin, Buster Keaton, Harold Lloyd, the Keystone Kops, did not celebrate the new age, they satirized it; they did not worship order and stability, they emphasized surrealistic anarchy and mayhem; they did not deify the products of a consumer society, they destroyed them with wilful abandon; they did not bow down to the image and manners of the new middle classes, they parodied them with hilarious accuracy. They focussed not on the strong but on the weak, not on the confident man on the make but on the bewildered man whose direction and goals were uncertain.

Even more indicative of the difficulty Americans had in embracing the new was the increased popularity of the Western film which reached its classic stage in the twenties. The West continued to be a place of regeneration. In *The Mollycoddle* (1920), a young man brought up amid the decadence and over-civilization of France returned to his native West and regained the latent virility which enabled him to throw off his effete manners and emerge as a hero. Above all, the West continued to be the centre of virtue and morality. The Western heroes of the nineteen twenties—Tom Mix, Buck Jones, Hoot Gibson—were strong, clean-living, uncomplicated men who needed the help of neither institutions nor technology in defeating darkly clad villains and urban scoundrels. They were living embodiments of the innocence, freedom and morality which Americans identified with and longed to regain if only vicariously.

The desire to escape from the complexity of their own time led American moviegoers back beyond the history of their own West. In the immensely popular films of Douglas Fairbanks—*The Mark of Zorro* (1920), *The Three Musketeers* (1921), *Robin Hood* (1922), *The Thief of Bagdad* (1923–4), *Don Q., Son of Zorro* (1925), *The Black Pirate* (1926), *The Gaucho* (1927), *The Iron Mask* (1929)—and in the desert epics of Rudolph Valentino, Americans were transported to a world in which moral issues were clearly delineated and the ability of the individual to influence his own destiny was undiluted by modernity. This search for simplicity accounts also for the surprising success of such anthropological documentary films as *Nanook of the North* (1922) and *Moana* (1926) as well as the literary vogue of Harlem and the fascination with Negro folklore throughout the decade. In these recreations of Arctic Eskimos, South Sea Islanders, urban and rural blacks, Americans of the twenties were able simultaneously to feel superior to those who lacked the benefits of modern technology and to envy them for their sense of community, their lack of inhibitions, their closer contact with their environment and with themselves.

During the nineteen twenties the newspaper comic strip, like the movies, became a regular feature of American popular culture with tens of millions of readers daily by 1924. Like the movies, too, the comic strip had its anarchic side. *Mutt and Jeff, Bringing Up Father, Abie the Agent, Barney Google, Moon Mullins, Krazy Kat* laughed at propriety, order, romantic love, the sanctity of money and position. It was through the medium of nostalgia rather than satire, however, that the strips had their greatest impact. 'If historians of the next century were to rely upon the comic strip,' Stephen Becker has written, 'they would conclude that we were a peaceful lot of ruminant burghers from 1920 to 1929, with only occasional flashes of inspired insanity, and that our social conflicts and national crises were settled by family conferences at the dinner table.' *The Gumps* and *Gasoline Alley*, which first appeared in 1917 and 1919 respectively, were typical of an entire genre of family centred comic strips which constituted one of the most popular forms of mass culture in the nineteen twenties. The characters inhabiting these strips were distinguished primarily by their lack of distinction: decent, plain-looking, dependable, unexciting, independent but community-orientated people who were destined to live out their lives among neighbours just like themselves. Their very normality, the strips seemed to be saying, made them worth celebrating and emulating. Their virtues were those of the old America and when they strayed from these (for as normal people they had foibles) they were brought to account sharply.

A striking feature of the comic strips of the nineteen twenties was their almost total lack of heroic figures. The central males in *Toots and Casper, Tillie the Toiler, Betty, Fritzi Ritz*, and ultimately *Blondie*, were ineffectual, usually diminutive men whose entire lives revolved around the statuesque, beautiful women for whom the strips were named. It was from their wives or sweethearts (e.g., their present or potential families) that they derived meaning and purpose. The financial tycoon Daddy Warbucks of *Little Orphan Annie* was one of the decade's few prototypes of the incredibly powerful heroes who were to proliferate in the comic strips of the Great Depression. But in spite of the great wealth of her capitalist benefactor, Annie's triumphs in situation after situation were due, more often than not, to her own inner qualities and the innocence, goodness and old-fashioned virtues of the average people who were always on hand to help her. The comic strips of the nineteen twenties, with their quiet resignation, their emphasis upon steadiness, their celebration of the average, might appear to have been incongruous additions to newspapers whose front pages heralded the new, advertised the spectacular achievements of uncommon men, and called for endless change and progress. But they were a necessary addition, for they comprised the other half of the cultural equation that characterized the United States throughout the decade.[9]

V

This web of ambivalence must be unravelled in order to reveal the meaning of any aspect of American culture in the twenties. Serious

[9] My analysis of the comic strips of the twenties follows the interpretations of Stephen Becker, *Comic Art in America* (New York, 1959); Coulton Waugh, *The Comics* (New York, 1947); Pierre Couperie, Maurice C. Horn, *et al.*, *A History of the Comic Strip*, translated from the French by Eileen B. Hennessy (New York, 1968). (See *Note* at beginning of chapter.)

artists and musicians attempted to come to terms with modern forms of painting and music at the same time that they were returning to the themes and sources of an earlier America: the art of the Shakers, the Indians and the colonial primitives, in painting; the tribal chants of the Indians, the spirituals of black slaves, the songs of cowboys and the Anglo-American folk, in music. Ernest Hemingway spoke for many members of his literary generation when he recalled that avant-garde Paris was a good place in which to think and write about his native Michigan. During the twenties Americans found it far easier to come to terms with the new if it could be surrounded somehow by the aura of the old.

In their accounts of the 'galloping materialism' of the nineteen twenties, historians have made much of the secularization of American religion during the decade and the penchant Americans had for incorporating within the religious message the vulgarizations of American business rhetoric and ideology. The advertising executive Bruce Barton in his best-selling *The Man Nobody Knows* (1925), transformed Jesus into a twentieth-century hustler, 'the most popular dinner guest in Jerusalem' who 'picked up twelve men from the bottom ranks of business and forged them into an organization that conquered the world'. Comparisons like these were ubiquitous but the reasons for them may not be quite as simple as we have assumed. It is entirely possible that modern businessmen were led to this rhetoric not out of supreme confidence in their standards and vocation but, on the contrary, because they were defensive and needed the ideals of Christ to justify and sell themselves to the American people. After announcing his aphorism, 'The business of America is business', President Coolidge was quick to add this strained and obviously defensive analogy: 'The man who builds a factory builds a temple, the man who works there worships there, and to each is due not scorn and blame but reverence and praise.' 'Would Isaiah be writing more Bibles if he were here today,' Henry Ford asked, and answered self-consciously, 'He would probably be gaining experience; living down in the shops among workingmen; working over a set of blueprints; . . . There is no reason why a prophet should not be an engineer instead of a preacher.'

Statements like these, when placed beside the rhetoric of businessmen who more often than not sounded like figures out of nineteenth-century McGuffey Readers or Horatio Alger novels, indicate the need

American business spokesmen still had for some noble purpose which stretched beyond mere material reward; they continually manifested the inability to accept the practices of modern business and technology purely in terms of practicality and efficiency. When Henry Ford declared, 'I am more interested in people than I am in profits. . . . I don't give a hang for money as such, only as it helps me to help people with it', and when Herbert Hoover studded his speeches and writings with such words as 'salvation', 'devotion', 'service', 'dedication', 'liberty', 'vision', 'courage', 'faith', they were not derided by a cynical, materialistic generation but enshrined as two of the chief icons of America's business civilization. The production techniques of Amercan business in the twenties may have been new, but the images used to justify them were old and hallowed.

To stress the force of nostalgia and the presence of ambivalence is not to deny the realities of change. The desire to have things both ways—to accept the fruits of progress without relinquishing the fundamentals of the old order—explains many of the tensions in American life, but it has never led to complete paralysis. In spite of the persistent lag between actuality and perception, there has been a gradual acceptance of changes and a reordering of desires, expectations and action throughout American history. Americans in the twenties, as before and since, tended to turn to the past in their ideology and rhetoric more than in their actions. Still, the existence of this dualism between a past and future orientation is important for if it has not prevented action it has certainly impeded and shaped it. 'The health of a people,' Alfred North Whitehead has observed, 'depends largely on their ability to question their inherited symbols in light of contemporary actualities, to keep them fluid, vibrant, and responsive.' The nineteen twenties had begun with the failure of President Wilson's prophecy concerning the First World War. They were to end with the failure of President Hoover's prophecy that the United States was on the threshold of abolishing poverty and ensuring the promises of the American dream to all its citizens. The confused and ambivalent symbols and images with which the American people emerged from the nineteen twenties made it all the more difficult and painful for them to cope with the material and psychic traumas that lay before them.

Note

General Studies

The best full-dress discussion of twentieth-century American prose writers, including the novelists of the twenties, in their social and intellectual setting, is still Alfred Kazin's *On Native Grounds: An Interpretation of Modern American Prose Literature* (New York, 1942). It is comprehensive rather than selective; we still lack an analytical discussion of the relations between the major writers of the twenties and the social and intellectual background comparable to F. O. Mathiessen's study of the major writers of the eighteen fifties, *American Renaissance* (New York, 1941). Frederick J. Hoffman's attempt in *The Twenties: American Writing in the Post-War Decade* (New York, 1955) is interesting but overly systematic. Some other general books about the novelists of this period, most now out of date, are Joseph Warren Beach, *American Fiction: 1920–1940* (New York, 1941) and Maxwell Geismar, *Writers in Crisis* (New York, 1942) and *The Last of the Provincials* (New York, 1947).

The best guide to changing critical opinion over the last several years is *American Literary Scholarship: An Annual*, 1963— edited by James Woodress (Durham, North Carolina, 1965—): each annual volume, containing a series of essays reviewing the year's scholarship and criticism, treats major writers in special chapters; it is noteworthy that the only novelists after Henry James to rate such special attention are Faulkner (the subject of an entire chapter), Hemingway and Fitzgerald (regularly combined in another chapter). Additional chapters deal with 'Fiction: 1900-1930', and 'Fiction: 1930 to the Present'.

Studies of Individual Authors. Some idea of the increasing attention now being given to the social criticism of Faulkner, Hemingway and Fitzgerald can be seen in the collections of critical essays now being published on them: among the most recent and perceptive are those in the *Twentieth-Century Views* series— *F. Scott Fitzgerald: A Collection of Critical Essays* edited by Arthur Mizener (Englewood Cliffs, New Jersey, 1963); *Faulkner: A Collection of Critical Essays* edited by Robert Penn Warren (Englewood Cliffs, New Jersey, 1960); and *Hemingway: A Collection of Critical Essays* edited by Robert P. Weekes (Englewood Cliffs, New Jersey, 1963). Four excellent essays by one critic who is unusually perceptive about both aesthetic and social values are Malcolm Cowley's introductions to the *Viking Portable Faulkner* (New York, 1946), to the *Viking Portable Hemingway* (New York, 1948), to *The Stories of F. Scott Fitzgerald* (New York, 1950), and to his edition of Fitzgerald's *Tender is the Night* (New York, 1953).

Considerable discussion of the major novelists of the twenties as social critics will be found in the following recent studies of special aspects of American literature: Michael Millgate, *American Social Fiction, James to Cozzens* (New York, 1964); Leslie A. Fiedler, *Love and Death in the American Novel* (New York, 1960; revised edition 1966); Wright Morris, *The Territory Ahead* (New York, 1957), Charles Child Walcutt, *American Literary Naturalism: A Divided Stream* (Minneapolis, Minnesota 1956).

Social Criticism in the American Novel in the Nineteen Twenties

HENRY DAN PIPER

The creation of tragedy demands of its author a mature understanding of the relation of the individual to society and, more especially, of the nature of good and evil. He must have a coherent grasp of social forces, or, at least, of man as a social being; otherwise he will possess no frame of reference within which to make actual his dramatic conflicts. For the hero of tragedy is never merely an individual, he is a man of action in conflict with other individuals in a definite social order. (F. O. Matthiessen, *American Renaissance*)

Man does improve, since the only alternative to progress is death. . . . Man has improved. (William Faulkner to students at the University of Virginia, 15 February 1957, *Faulkner in the University*)

I look out at it and I think it is the most beautiful history in the world. It is the history of me and my people. And if I came here yesterday like Sheilah I should still think so. It is the history of all human aspiration—not just the American dream but the human dream and if I come at the end of it that too is a place in the line of pioneers. (F. Scott Fitzgerald in a note found among the MS pages of *The Last Tycoon* after his death in 1940)

I

ALTHOUGH it was published back in 1942, Alfred Kazin's *On Native Grounds* is still the best-written and most intelligent assessment we have had of earlier twentieth-century American fiction in its social and intellectual setting. But critical opinion has changed a great deal since then. *On Native Grounds* today is more important for us as a record of the opinions of a brilliant twenty-five-year-old critic who had recently come of age during the worst economic and social crisis in the nation's history. In Kazin's chapters on the twenties, the writers to whom he gave the most attention were Sherwood Anderson, Sinclair Lewis, Willa Cather, Ellen Glasgow and Theodore Dreiser, whose *An American Tragedy* he considered the outstanding novel of the decade. Similarly, for Kazin, Steinbeck's *Grapes of Wrath* was the most important social novel of the thirties. He discussed the fiction of James Branch Cabell, Carl Van Vechten and Elinor Wylie at great length in a chapter entitled 'The Exquisites'. Hemingway and Fitzgerald were lumped together with E. E. Cummings and Dos Passos in another chapter, 'All the Lost Generations'. Faulkner was sandwiched in with Henry Miller and Thomas Wolfe in another chapter, 'The Rhetoric and the Agony'. Richard Wright, today one of the most widely read protest-novelists of the thirties, was dismissed by Kazin as 'sinister' because of his slickness and his disturbing manipulation of the emotion of terror. Nathanael West was not mentioned at all.

Looking back now at the beginning of the nineteen seventies we can see more clearly than Kazin could that a sharp break separated the novelists of the twenties from the older generation. Age was one factor; just as important was the shared experience of having reached the age of twenty-one during or immediately after the First World War. The writers of the twenties were literally children of the century: William Faulkner, F. Scott Fitzgerald, Ernest Hemingway, Hart Crane, Malcolm Cowley, John Steinbeck, John Dos Passos—all of them were born after 1896. By contrast, Sherwood Anderson, Theodore Dreiser, Willa Cather, Edith Wharton, Ellen Glasgow, T. S. Eliot, Ezra Pound, Robert Frost, Eugene O'Neill—even Sinclair Lewis—had been born in the eighteen-seventies or early eighties. They had come of age, indeed had outgrown their youth, well before the beginning of the First World War.

Of the novelists of the twenties, Faulkner, Fitzgerald and Hemingway are the most widely read and studied today. One especially important reason for this has been the influence of the so-called New Criticism, whose emergence Kazin viewed with such misgivings in 1941 when he was writing *On Native Grounds*. By 1950 that preoccupation with problems of form and technique which had been so popular in the criticism and study of poetry was now being applied with increasing skill to the evaluation of American—as of all modern—fiction, notably by Lionel Trilling, Malcolm Cowley, Arthur Mizener and Robert Penn Warren. Another influential factor was the belated American revival of interest after 1944 (the year of his centenary) in the fiction of Henry James. No less important was a growing recognition of the fact that the works of Faulkner, Hemingway and Fitzgerald were exercising a more important continuing influence on contemporary American fiction than any American writers since James and Mark Twain. From Robert Penn Warren, Norman Mailer and J. D. Salinger to William Styron, Ralph Ellison, Carson McCullers, John Updike, Saul Bellow and Bernard Malamud, every postwar American novelist had felt it necessary to come to terms in some way with these three predecessors from the twenties. Today their influence may be diminishing. Nonetheless, during the past thirty years no younger novelist has yet emerged of comparable stature. According to a recent *New York Times* survey of American paperback sales, Faulkner and Hemingway are today the most widely read American novelists of the twentieth century, and *The Great Gatsby* is the single most widely read paperback novel.

How different this is from 1920, when the most vital native literary tradition in fiction was the 'new realism' (or 'naturalism'—the two terms are really indistinguishable). Theodore Dreiser and his protégé, Sherwood Anderson, were the two novelists most admired by the younger writers then just coming of age. So far as this new postwar generation was concerned, Dreiser's *Sister Carrie* (1900) and Anderson's *Winesburg, Ohio* (1919) were the two most influential works in American fiction to have been published since *Huckleberry Finn*. Every American writer who emerged between the two great wars would have to come to terms with the naturalistic tradition represented by these two books: either by adopting and refining it—as in the case of John Dos Passos, Richard Wright, John Steinbeck and so many other 'Protest' novelists—or by incorporating or transforming it into a more tragic form, as did Faulkner, Fitzgerald and Hemingway. But regardless of these differences, what Anderson and Dreiser shared with all these younger writers was the belief that it was the writer's responsibility to expose and hopefully to correct the shortcomings and injustices of contemporary American society. Any account of the social criticism in the fiction of the twenties must begin by describing the tremendous importance of Dreiser and Anderson to these younger men.

II

Dreiser, the poor weaver's son from Terre Haute, Indiana, was America's first proletarian novelist. By 1920 he, more than any other living American, represented for the postwar generation of younger writers the triumph of that native literary tradition of social protest and criticism that had its origins in the fiction of Flaubert and Zola, as well as in the methodology of the new quantitative social sciences of economics and sociology. It is not necessary to rehearse here the history of the rise of American naturalism in the fiction of Stephen Crane, Harold Frederic and Frank Norris, nor Norris's role in arranging for the publication of Dreiser's first novel, *Sister Carrie*, in 1900. *Sister Carrie* was not, as Dreiser's own story had it, suppressed by the first publisher as immoral, but it was disliked and unwillingly promoted, and only gradually emerged to notice, largely through its English reception; it would not be widely read until some years later. By 1902 Crane, Norris and Frederic were dead, their youthful promise cut short. But Dreiser persisted and survived. By 1920, thanks to the championship of the influential critic, H. L. Mencken, he had finally won a hearing. When his *An American Tragedy* appeared in 1925, its spectacular success marked the belated triumph of the naturalistic method. *An American Tragedy* was not only a widely read novel but also a successful Broadway play and a popular Hollywood film. By the laborious, powerful accumulation of factual detail, Dreiser's fiction revealed the tragic contradictions lying beneath the prosperous surface of American life. Reading *An American Tragedy* or the artistically superior *Sister Carrie*, the untutored American reader experienced something of the shock of recognition aroused in the young European of any earlier generation by Marx's *Das Capital*. No one was surprised when Dreiser decided shortly before his death to become a member of the American Communist Party.

Although Anderson was only five years younger than Dreiser, his development as a writer took place much later. Indeed it was Dreiser who was responsible for finding a publisher for Anderson's first novel in 1916. Where Dreiser was primarily the novelist of urban industrial culture, Anderson wrote about the loneliness and frustrations of the outsider and non-conformist in small-town Puritan America; his subject was the wounded psyche. Where Dreiser in his vague way embodied the spirit of Marxism, Anderson introduced into American fiction the new psychology of individual behaviour best exemplified by the writings of Sigmund Freud. Just as Marx and Freud between them provided a new way of seeing the relationship between the individual and society, so the fiction of Dreiser and Anderson suggested, to the writers beginning after the First World War, provocative new ways of organizing and expressing their experience in fiction. Where Marx and Freud agreed particularly was in their conviction that the ills of contemporary society were the result of the expansion of middle-class industrial capitalism. To the young writer of the twenties this mutual agreement had special meaning since, as far as he could see in any direction, American society, far more than the society of Europe, was unrelievedly middle-class.

Anderson added an important artistic element to the naturalism of Dreiser. Where Dreiser's fiction demonstrated a way of organizing successfully the larger surfaces of American society, Anderson introduced a further dimension through his probing of his characters' psychic depths. Anderson was also a more conscientious stylist than Dreiser. But he could only write short stories centred around a central character. He was unable to cope effectively with the structural demands of longer fiction. He never wrote a really first-rate novel. Despite Dreiser's lumbering style, he was much more accomplished as the architect of naturalism, as Anderson generously acknowledged. 'If there is a modern movement in American prose writing,' he wrote in an introduction to a volume of Dreiser's collected stories, 'a movement toward greater courage and fidelity to life in writing, then Theodore Dreiser is the pioneer and hero of the movement. . . . We are rapidly approaching the old French standard wherein the only immorality for the artist is in bad art and I think that Theodore Dreiser, the man, has done more than any living American to bring this about.'

In 1929 when the Wall Street Crash and the ensuing Depression of the thirties disclosed more grimly than ever before the degree of suffering and degradation in American life, the naturalism of Dreiser and Anderson became the dominant literary tradition. Novelist after novelist emerged to adapt it to his fictional revelations of social injustice in the coal fields, in the mines, the ghettos, the factories, the farms, the slums. Most novelists added little artistically to the examples of Dreiser and Anderson, and their fiction is unread today. John Dos Passos attempted in U.S.A. to relieve the monotonous journalistic narration of naturalism with various lyric and graphic devices borrowed from newspaper headlines and the cinema, but they failed to disguise the shortcomings of his imagination. The most successful naturalistic novel after *An American Tragedy* was Steinbeck's *The Grapes of Wrath* in 1939. Steinbeck had learned from Frank Norris as well as from Dreiser, from Anderson as well as from Anderson's pupil, Ernest Hemingway. *The Grapes of Wrath* confronted the plight of the dispossessed tenant farmer with Dreiser's ruthless honesty as well as Anderson's tender concern with rural America, and his lyric simplicity of style. The starker, more journalistic and more limited techniques of naturalism can be seen in James Farrell's three-decker novel of Irish-Catholic Chicago, *Studs Lonigan*, and in Richard Wright's bitter account of the brutal treatment of Black Americans in Chicago, *Native Son*.

The Second World War and the boredom and anguish of military conscription provided fresh grievances for the naturalistic novelist during the nineteen forties. It was the usual form by means of which the novelist beginning after the Second World War organized his personal experience of the war into a first novel, as in Norman Mailer's *The Naked and the Dead* (1948); John Horne Burns's *The Gallery* (1947); Saul Bellow's *Dangling Man* (1944); and James Jones's *From Here to Eternity* (1951). The pervasive popular influence of naturalism from the nineteen twenties onwards was also reinforced by its gradual triumph in the American theatre, first in the naturalistic plays of Eugene O'Neill (*Desire under the Elms*, 1924; *Strange Interlude*, 1928) and of Clifford Odets (*Waiting for Lefty*, 1935; *Golden Boy*, 1937), as well as Arthur Miller's *Death of a Salesman* (1949) and Tennessee Williams's early successes (*The Glass Menagerie*, 1945; *A Streetcar Named Desire*, 1947) just after the war.

But today the American naturalistic tradition, so long ago departed from Europe fiction, seems to have reached a dead end. Its greatest vitality lay in its propagandistic uses as a literature of social reform. Here it has gradually been replaced by the camera—notably by the film and television documentary, the cheap picture book and photomagazine. The dilemma of the present-day writer who wants to dramatize in fiction the grievances of an unjustly exploited social group, but for whom naturalism is no longer a vital tradition, can be seen in the plight of such American Black writers as James Baldwin, Ralph Ellison and LeRoi Jones. Each in his own way has rejected the limitations of naturalism, notably the example of the most successful of all American Black protest novels, Richard Wright's *Native Son*. After deliberately rejecting Wright's practice, Ralph Ellison introduced the techniques of surrealism and expressionism into *Invisible Man* (1953). But Ellison's subsequent failure to find a more satisfying form and to complete a second novel (at least to date) suggests the artistic problems faced by the novelist of protest for whom naturalism is no longer a viable form. James Baldwin continues to search out ways of extending the form, but with less and less success. LeRoi Jones, the most talented of the next generation of American Black protest writers, has turned far away from naturalism in his difficult but important so-called 'novel' of protest, *The System of Dante's Hell,* based on the structure of the *Inferno*. Meanwhile the experiments of Mailer, Styron, Bellow, etc., to go beyond naturalism, continue on and on.

Thus, it is against this fifty-year history of the popular triumph and decline of naturalistic fiction that the continued vitality of the novels of Faulkner, Fitzgerald and Hemingway stands out most vividly today. Hemingway was the first of the group to attain an extensive American following. The first sympathetic reviews of his fiction date from 1923; by 1929 he was already exercising considerable stylistic influence on such writers as Dashiell Hammett, Raymond Chandler and John O'Hara. But Faulkner would not enjoy as large a public in the United States as in France until he won the Nobel prize in 1950. And the revival of interest in Fitzgerald's novels dates from around the same time. But, as for Hemingway, critical interest in Faulkner and Fitzgerald has been primarily concerned with matters of technique and form. Literally dozens of essays have been published about them dealing with problems of structure, texture, imagery, symbolism, patterns and narrative points of view. But no critic since Alfred Kazin has yet given us a full-dress analysis of the social implications of their work as a whole. The closest anyone has come has been Malcolm Cowley in his important but still uncollected introductory essays to his *Viking Portable* anthologies of selections from Faulkner (1946) and Hemingway (1948), and to his editions of Fitzgerald's *Short Stories* (1950) and *Tender Is the Night* (1953). The present essay is thus an attempt to break new ground.

III

From what has been said so far, it is not surprising that Dreiser and Anderson were powerful shaping factors in the development of Faulkner, Fitzgerald and Hemingway. Each of these younger writers

E

had to come to terms with at least one and perhaps both of these two predecessors before he could go on to forge his own distinctive style. What all five writers retained in common, despite their many differences, was a mutually-shared belief that the novelist must be not only a responsible artist, but also a responsible critic of society. I propose to show in the rest of this essay that Faulkner, Fitzgerald and Hemingway differed from other novelists of the period between the wars, 1920–1940, to the extent that they turned to the unfashionable form of tragedy as a means of dramatizing the eternal conflict between the individual and society, and that by so doing they attained in their fiction a more complex and more satisfying form for social criticism—and a far greater artistic distinction—than that to be found in the naturalistic tradition. Until now, the brilliance of their technical accomplishments has blinded critics to the no less brilliant insights these novelists have given us about the nature of American society. They explored more fully in their fiction than any other twentieth-century American novelists the implications of Henry James's comment, that to be an American is a tragic destiny. It is this intellectual achievement, even more than their remarkable artistry, that explains the continuing passionate interest in their fiction.

It was not Dreiser's lumbering style so much as his honesty and sense of responsibility as a practising writer that explains Fitzgerald's tremendous reverence for him at the beginning of his own career. *This Side of Paradise*, which Fitzgerald began writing in 1917 as a Princeton senior, was modelled on the lyric sentimentalities of two recent undergraduate discoveries—Compton Mackenzie's *Youth's Encounter* and, less importantly, H. G. Wells's *Tono Bungay* and *The Research Magnificent*. It was not until 1919, just as Fitzgerald was rewriting *This Side of Paradise* for the third and last time, that he discovered the tradition of American naturalism dating from the eighteen nineties. 'I had never read Zola and Frank Norris or Dreiser. . . ,' he said in 1921. 'No one of my English professors in college ever suggested to his class that books were being written in America. Poor souls, they were as ignorant as I.'

As a result, a great deal of his next novel, *The Beautiful and Damned*, was consciously modelled on the fiction of these native naturalists, notably Norris's *Vandover and the Brute* and Dreiser's *The 'Genius'*. Their influence is especially evident in Fitzgerald's protrayal of the sordidness of American business and the frustrations of army life. But before long he realized that he was temperamentally unsuited to the conventions of naturalism. He was too much of a poet. Soon after finishing *The Beautiful and Damned* he discovered Conrad's *Lord Jim* and *Youth* and Willa Cather's *My Antonia* and *A Lost Lady*. He found there a more satisfying way of organizing his imaginative experience around the device of a detached but emotionally involved first-person narrator. He told his editor that he had decided it had been a mistake to try to write *The Beautiful and Damned* in the 'vein of realism'. Although at first he had adopted the naturalistic point of view of the third-person narrator in his plan for *The Great Gatsby*, he now discarded it in favour of a new plan, using a first-person narrator named Nick Carraway.[1]

But even though he was rapidly moving away from the conventions of naturalistic realism, Fitzgerald continued to admire Dreiser, and even to see him as a serious artistic rival. One thinks of the well-known story of Fitzgerald's uninvited appearance at Dreiser's apartment one evening in 1922 and his reverent gift to the embarrassed Dreiser of a bottle of wine as a token of his admiration. Later in 1925, when Fitzgerald was planning *Tender Is the Night*, which he hoped would be the great American tragedy, he was on tenterhooks until Dreiser's own new novel of that name was published, because he was afraid that Dreiser's *An American Tragedy* might make his own novel redundant. Actually, Clyde Griffiths, the hero of Dreiser's story is more like Jimmy Gatz in *The Great Gatsby* than Dick Diver of *Tender Is the Night*. The difference between Clyde Griffiths and Gatsby is not so much in conduct as in the artistic treatment. Where Clyde Griffiths's history is one of un-relieved dehumanization and waste, *The Great Gatsby* is a vision of tragic affirmation. *(note first para.)*

Another affinity Fitzgerald shared with Dreiser was their mutual interest in the life of the modern metropolis. He took less interest in the work of Sherwood Anderson, because Anderson was so much more concerned with rural, small-town America. When Fitzgerald started reading Anderson in 1923, his problem was not so much how to write sentences (he had been practising that for ten years) but rather how to organize his material into a more capacious and complex form. That was Anderson's problem too. But although Anderson had less to teach Fitzgerald than Dreiser, Fitzgerald saw more quickly than many of Anderson's admirers that the older writer was by no means the guile-less, spontaneous cracker-box philosopher and story-teller that he often

[1] See my *F. Scott Fitzgerald: A Critical Portrait* (1966); also my 'Frank Norris and Scott Fitzgerald', *Huntingdon Library Quarterly* XIX(4), pp. 393–400.

pretended to be, 'an inarticulate fumbling man bursting with ideas,' as Fitzgerald wrote in a 1923 review of Anderson's *Many Marriages*. Rather, he said, Anderson was 'the possessor of an almost inimitable prose style and scarcely any ideas at all'. Anderson, who was indeed a painstaking literary craftsman like Fitzgerald, was delighted when this shrewd bit of insight appeared in print and promptly wrote Fitzgerald telling him so.

Anderson was much more important for Faulkner and Hemingway than for Fitzgerald, both as a friend and as a writer. Even if American literature began with *Huckleberry Finn*, as Hemingway claimed, Anderson's *Winesburg, Ohio* was proof that the idiomatic style of the former was capable of expressing a more complex and profound vision of life than that of a fourteen-year-old river boy. In Hemingway's Nick Adams stories and in others like 'My Old Man' and 'Fifty Grand', he amply demonstrated his stylistic debts to Anderson. But, before long, stories in this style came too easily for him (as he wrote in an unpublished letter to Fitzgerald). Anderson's usefulness to Hemingway had come to an end. He was now more aware of Anderson's weaknesses— his sentimentality, his dependence on personal experience, and his inability to go beyond the limits in his fiction of the short story of character revelation. Yet so great was Hemingway's debt to Anderson that he had to exorcize him by cruelly making fun of him in 1926 in his first published novel, *The Torrents of Spring*, written in haste after *The Sun Also Rises* but released (by Scribner's) before it. Yet despite this brutal declaration of independence on Hemingway's part, Jake Barnes, Frederick Henry, Robert Jordan and Nick Adams all bear marked family resemblances to the George Willard of *Winesburg, Ohio* as well as to their more obvious progenitor, Huckleberry Finn.

Faulkner's debts to Anderson were as crucial as Hemingway's, but of a somewhat different order. In an essay, he has left affectionate testimony of the shaping influence of the older writer whom he met in 1925 in New Orleans and whom he credits with having been more responsible than anyone else for his decision to become a writer. At that time the twenty-seven-year-old Faulkner had published only a slender volume of uninspired verse. Anderson not only encouraged him to write prose fiction but arranged for the publication of his first novel, *Soldier's Pay*. At this time Faulkner was still very much under the influence of the literary wits of the era—James Branch Cabell, Aldous Huxley, Thomas Beer. It would be several years yet before he would recognize his unsuitability for this kind of efflorescence and turn to subject matter he knew, and find the style that suited it best. But when he finally saw the light, he said that it was Anderson who had turned it on for him.

'You have to have somewhere to start from: then you begin to learn,' he told me. 'It don't matter where it was, just so you remember it and aint ashamed of it. Because one place to start from is just as important as another. You're a country boy; all you know is that little patch up there in Mississippi where you started from. But's that's all right too. It's America too; pull it out, as little and unknown as it is, and the whole thing will collapse, like when you prize a brick out of a wall.'
'Not a cemented, plastered wall,' I said.
'Yes, but America aint cemented and plastered yet. They're still building it. That's why a man with ink in his veins not only still can but sometimes has still got to keep on moving around in it, keeping moving around and listening and looking and learning. That's why ignorant unschooled fellows like you and me not only have a chance to write, they must write. All America asks is to look at it and listen to it and understand it if you can. Only the understanding aint important either: the important thing is to believe in it even if you don't understand it, and then try to tell it, to put it down. It won't ever be quite right, but there is always next time; there's always more ink and paper, and something else to try to understand and tell. And that one won't probably be exactly right either, but there is a next time to that one, too. Because tomorrow America is going to be something different, something more and new to watch and listen to and try to understand; and, even if you cant understand, believe.'[2]

Like Hemingway, the young Faulkner was so hypnotized by Anderson's personality that he had to free himself by publicly ridiculing him, as he did good-humouredly in his introduction to a book of caricatures by his friend William Spratling, *Sherwood Anderson and Other Famous Creoles*. But Faulkner's permanent debts to Anderson can be seen in his decision to make his home town, Oxford, Mississippi, the subject of his major work, just as Anderson had immortalized his own home town of Clyde, Ohio, as Winesburg, Ohio, in *his* best-known book.

[2] William Faulkner, 'Sherwood Anderson: An Appreciation', *Essays, Speeches and Public Letters* (New York, 1953), reprinted in *'Winesburg, Ohio': Text and Criticism* edited by John H. Ferres (New York, 1966), pp. 491-2.

Faulkner's adolescent heroes, Ike McCaslin in *Go Down Moses*, Lucius Priest in *The Reivers*, Quentin Compson in *Absalom, Absalom!*, Chick Mallinson in *Intruder in the Dust*, young Bayard Sartoris in *The Unvanquished*, like Hemingway's adolescents, also share conspicuous affinities with Anderson's George Willard as well as with Huckleberry Finn.

The great shortcoming of the naturalistic tradition represented by Dreiser and Anderson and their followers was that it failed to allow room for the romantic aspirations of the individual as well as for the restrictive forces in society that limited them. This is readily understood, since nineteenth-century American naturalism emerged as a necessary corrective to that fatuous optimism with which the popular literary romance celebrated a simple-minded philosophy of material success. Booth Tarkington was one of the most skilful purveyors of this kind of magazine pabulum. In many respects Scott Fitzgerald shared more in common with the cosmopolitan Tarkington than the uncouth Dreiser. Yet it was characteristic of the attitude of the new postwar generation that Fitzgerald revered Dreiser and said in a review of one of Tarkington's latest *Saturday Evening Post* pot-boilers, 'It is a pity that the man who writes better prose than any other living American was brought up in a generation that considered it a crime to tell the truth.'

But naturalism, in a negative way, merely emphasized how deeply the myth of success lay at the heart of the American experience. Where the Horatio Alger romance of the rise of the poor country lad in the big city expressed the aspirations of the average American, the naturalistic novel of social protest assumed unconsciously the validity of this dream, and then proceeded to show how various political, economic or social institutions stood in the way of its being realized by the average American. Reform these undemocratic institutions, the naturalists implied, and the hero of the novel of protest would then be free to succeed and realize his dreams. Dreiser's first novel, *Sister Carrie*, is by far the best of his novels because Carrie Meeber shares so many of its young author's confused and ambiguous feelings about his relationship to American society. Dreiser portrays Carrie as both the pathetic victim of society, and the modern career woman burning for success and self-realization. In his later novels—*Jennie Gerhardt*, *The 'Genius'*, *An American Tragedy*—his heroes are pathetic victims, 'little men', and their stories are tedious and thin. Sherwood Anderson suffered from a similar relationship to the myth of success. He disliked it so intensely that, unlike Dreiser, he could not even use its negative aspects as a means of organizing his imaginative experience into something larger than a character sketch. As a result he could not write a successful full-length novel, nor find another myth to replace the myth of success. 'I hardly know what I can teach,' he complained to his brother, 'except anti-success.'

By 1929, naturalistic truth had gained so many adherents among the younger generation, in a swing away from the vulgarized nineteenth-century romance, that it seemed to some onlookers as though Americans were merely substituting one rather simple-minded view of the nature of things for something not much better. In *The Modern Temper* in 1929, Joseph Wood Krutch called for a return to a more complex and tragic vision of life. 'If the plays and novels of today deal with little people and less mighty emotions, it is not because we have become interested in commonplace souls and their unglamorous adventures but because we have come, willy-nilly, to see the soul of man as commonplace and its emotions as mean.'

What Krutch could not see in 1929, what indeed would not be discernible to criticism for some years yet, was the fact that at this moment Faulkner, Fitzgerald and Hemingway were independently engaged in an attempt to go far beyond the limits of both the nineteenth-century romantic tradition in American fiction and the more recent complementary tradition of naturalism, and create new forms capable of expressing the tragic nature of the individual's relation to his society. That is, they were engaged in a venture that no American novelist had undertaken since James and Mark Twain, and before them, Hawthorne and Melville. From the evidence available, it seems unlikely that the examples of Hawthorne and Melville played much of a direct role in this phenomenon. The rediscovery of Melville was itself a parallel development of the twenties; and Hawthorne's genteel idiom made him increasingly remote as a fruitful literary source. Hawthorne's other virtues—his amazing structural inventions in literary form, his exploitation for the first time in American fiction of the theories of puritanism and the American cultural dependence on Europe—were more directly accessible from Hawthorne's great disciple, Henry James. But even James was less of a direct influence on Faulkner, Fitzgerald and Hemingway than James's more recent disciples, Joseph Conrad, Willa Cather and Edith Wharton. No less important was the example of *Huckleberry Finn*, the first American novel of stature to be expressed in a native literary idiom.

A parochial genealogy of this sort obviously fails to account for the importance to these younger novelists of the experiments in the European fiction of Balzac, Flaubert, Dickens, Hardy, Turgenev, Dostoievsky, Tolstoi, Joyce, Proust, Mann. But it does make it possible, from another point of view, to see the fiction of Faulkner, Fitzgerald and Hemingway as the culmination of the literary traditions of naturalism and romance, of the idiomatic style of Mark Twain and the formal experiments of James and his English and American disciples, resulting in a tragic vision of the American experience that had been unequalled in American fiction since the so-called 'American Renaissance' of the eighteen fifties and the novels of Melville and Hawthorne.

IV

Let us turn first to the example of Fitzgerald. As we have seen, he worked his way through the naturalism of *The Beautiful and Damned* to the more complex and Conradian form of *The Great Gatsby* that allowed him to affirm the power and vitality of Gatsby's dream as well as the shabby moral limitations of the society in which Gatsby sought to realize that dream, and thereby destroyed himself. But Gatsby himself is so victimized by the meretriciousness of his world that he exists primarily as an abstraction—a Platonic idea. He lacks the capacity for tragic recognition, he hardly exists as an individual outside of Nick Carraway's imagination. And Nick himself, lacking Gatsby's capacity for heroic action, can only retreat at the end to the safety of the *status quo*.

Dick Diver in *Tender is the Night* is a more representative American middle-class hero than Gatsby. He embodies all the aspirations of the cultivated, dominant American Establishment. The son of a poor but honest parson, Dick has successfully garnered all of the badges of bourgeois success—not money and power themselves, but the means for possessing them and enjoying them: scholarships to the best preparatory schools and to Yale, a Rhodes Fellowship to Oxford and then another for medical studies at Johns Hopkins, capped by a post-doctoral grant to study with the leading Viennese psychiatrists. As a psychiatrist he is an acknowledged priest as well as a member of the highest paid profession in American society. Money and power come naturally in their train as he marries the daughter of a Chicago millionaire and settles down to the beautiful life of the French Riviera.

Where Gatsby's commitment remained an abstract idea to the end, Fitzgerald narrowed Dick's purpose to the care and cure of his lovely patient, and to the creative social leadership of a colony of rich expatriate Americans. When the inherent limitations of this commitment reveal themselves, Dick has no spiritual resources to sustain him and disintegrates both as a personality and as a tragic hero. The significance of Dick's ordeal lies in the objective meaning it has for the sympathetic onlooker whose humanity is aroused by witnessing this tragic action. In *The Great Gatsby* this was the necessary role of Nick Carraway. In *Tender is the Night* it is the reason for Rosemary Hoyt. Once Fitzgerald sheds Rosemary's controlling point of view, Dick Diver loses his heroic qualities and becomes the pathetic victim of a corrupt society.

This is why *The Last Tycoon*, even in its unfinished state, is such a fascinating novel. Here Fitzgerald successfully imagined an objective tragic commitment for his hero, Monroe Stahr, that sets him apart from Gatsby and Dick Diver. The tragic destiny that finally overwhelms and destroys Stahr is not the result of a mistaken judgment about people. It is inherent in the nature of his heroic achievement. Singlehandedly he has created a new economic institution which has also been of considerable social benefit. He has surpassed all the other studios in the production of artistically and commercially successful motion pictures. But his very success breeds dissension and a conspiracy to replace him by a less paternalistic, more rationalized and consequently less creative and imaginative management. Stahr struggles desperately to resist the forces that finally overwhelm him. Celia Brady, from whose point of view Fitzgerald tells Stahr's story, is not only a necessary means for artistic control; she is desperately in need of an affirming vision. Like Stahr, she too is both the product and the victim of the film industry. She has been spiritually as well as physically damaged by the murderous forces of American business. She is telling Stahr's story from a hospital, and seeks in her recapitulation some positive reason for living. In *The Last Tycoon*, far more consciously than in any of his previous works, Fitzgerald was attempting to come to terms with an important aspect of American society as a tragic experience. The measure of his success can be gauged by comparing *The Last Tycoon* with Nathanael West's surrealistic novel of protest about Hollywood, *The Day of the Locust*.

We can observe a parallel movement from naturalistic to tragic form going on in the novels of Faulkner, beginning with *Sartoris*, which he started writing in 1927 and concluding with *Absalom, Absalom!*, the last of his great tragedies, which was published in 1936. In one experimental novel after another Faulkner sought to reconcile in tragic terms the heroic, positive virtues of the South with its self-defeating limitations. Only from such a reconciliation, he felt, could the forces emerge that would allow the South to fulfil its 'peculiar' destiny in American society.

Bayard Sartoris, the hero of *Sartoris* (which he first called *Flags in the Dust*) embodies the romantic virtues of aggressiveness and vitality which Faulkner celebrates in all his work. But Bayard is incapable of harnessing them in any positive way and so they finally destroy him. The straightforward naturalistic form that Faulkner used to suggest Bayard's plight and the burden of the Southern past did not allow him to express the tragic nature of Bayard's fateful destiny. He is more convincing at the naturalistic level as a postwar Hollow Man than as the heroic embodiment of the South's predicament.

In the great novels that followed, in *The Sound and the Fury*, *As I Lay Dying* and *Light in August*, Faulkner's radical experiments with technique are so dazzling that we can be blinded to the fact that in these novels he was groping for a more satisfying form to express his tragic vision. In both *The Sound and the Fury* and *As I Lay Dying* he succeeded in creating tragic heroes of compelling power simply by avoiding all naturalistic representation of them and—in the case of Caddy Compson and Addie Bundren—suggesting the heroic power of their characters through its effects on the actions and feelings of others. In *Light in August* he generalized and broadened the social implications of such heroic behaviour by reducing his 'hero' to two abstractions—Joe Christmas, the male element of force and vigour who is dehumanized and finally extinguished by society, and Lena Grove, the passive female element that survives by living naturally apart from society. Together, Joe and Lena affirm the values by which the South—and humanity—must live if it is to endure. Because Joe is so conspicuously the victim of society, Faulkner treats him with a naturalistic detail that contrasts effectively with his more lyric, symbolic treatment of Lena.

Absalom, Absalom!, Faulkner's last great novel, is important because here finally Faulkner created a tragic form embodying that vision of the South first suggested in *Sartoris* but now fully realized in the legend of Thomas Sutpen. Sutpen shares with Bayard Sartoris and Joe Christmas that aggressive, violent energy and force essential for individual fulfilment. This is why Faulkner devotes so much space at the beginning of this novel to describing Sutpen's superhuman physical attributes. Where Bayard Sartoris existed entirely in the present, Sutpen partakes of the legendary attributes of General Compson, General Sartoris, and Faulkner's own celebrated great-grandfather. Quentin Compson, on the other hand, shares with young Bayard the sensitive, responsible young Southerner's sense of alienation and despair, trapped in a defeated civilization where the old values no longer seem relevant. But where Bayard sees no alternative but to destroy himself, the Quentin Compson of *Absalom, Absalom!* engages in a desperate inquest in the hope of finding something positive and life-giving in the story of Sutpen's downfall. This he finally achieves by a powerful effort of will and imagination. In the process of probing the hidden truth behind Sutpen, Quentin reveals the blindness of first Miss Coldfield's and then his own father's interpretation of the mystery. It is only in cooperation with his room-mate Shreve, a Canadian completely detached from the American experience, that Quentin finally wins through to a tragic understanding of the Sutpen legend, as well as of the society that produced Sutpen. By this vicarious effort of the imagination, Quentin is able to share the vigour and thrust of Sutpen's dream, and to understand the social forces that destroyed him. For the South was the source of the racism that brought about Sutpen's downfall, as well as the snobbish complacency that could not absorb and make constructive use of his tremendous energy. It is important to note that in 1929 Faulkner destroyed Quentin Compson in *The Sound and the Fury* just as he destroyed Bayard Sartoris that same year in *Sartoris*. Neither young man was capable of sustaining a tragic vision and enduring. Both were the naturalistic victims of society from which they felt entirely alienated. But by 1936 Faulkner would rewrite Quentin's story in *Absalom, Absalom!*, the last of his great tragedies. And the implication now was that there was something to be affirmed and celebrated in the Southern experience. Later, when Faulkner was asked which of his characters he regarded as the most tragic, he passed over Quentin and Bayard and listed, instead, Dilsey and Caddy Compson from *The Sound and the Fury*, and Thomas Sutpen.

In comparing Faulkner's and Fitzgerald's parallel developments towards the recovery of the tragic form in their fiction, one cannot help being struck by the fact that, once again, the American dream of success is the controlling myth around which they organize the narrative elements in their novels. It is the basis of American popular romance, of the countervailing naturalistic tradition, the tragic vision of Melville's *Pierre* and Henry James's *The American*, Fitzgerald's novels, and Faulkner's last important novel, *Absalom, Absalom!* Sutpen is the familiar poor boy whose tragic destiny is set in motion by his determination to realize the democratic dream. Because of its racism and its antidemocratic bias, the society of Jefferson—and by extension, the South—denied itself the benefits of energy and leadership released in Sutpen by that dream. Here for the first time a Southern novelist of stature joins hands with the novelists of the North and reaffirms the continuing vitality of that dream as a source for the realization of the nation's still unfinished business.

V

Elsewhere I have pointed out that Fitzgerald can be seen as the tragedian of the Forty-Second Parallel, that arterial highway stretching from New York to Pittsburgh, through Cleveland, Chicago and Denver to San Francisco, along which pumps the lifeblood—the liquid cash—of contemporary American society.[3] Here are concentrated most of the population, the cities, the money, the banks, the industry, the universities and other instruments of power and culture. Not only is this concentration increasing but it is reaching out to include London and Paris to the east, and Honolulu and Tokyo at its western extremities. Its standards are the familiar middle-class values of success, popularity and material well-being. The central tenet of its faith is that a man's value is measured by his ability to rise in the world—indeed, it is his moral duty to do so. Its hero is the self-made man.

In the seventeenth and early eighteenth century the Southern colonists were as romantically imbued with this Renaissance, Anglo-Saxon dream of capitalistic success as their partners to the North. Both shared a common admiration for the story of Dick Whittington. But after the invention of the cotton gin, as slavery became increasingly the basis of Southern economic prosperity, southern mythmakers abandoned the myth of entrepreneurial success and substituted instead the myth of aristocratic stable feudalism. Although the South's defence of slavery lacked conviction, nonetheless by its very self-conscious detachment from the values of the industrial North, it was able to criticize fruitfully the shortcomings of the North's headlong rush after 1800 towards the

[3] See my *F. Scott Fitzgerald: A Critical Portrait* (1966), pp. 292–5.

creation of a chaotic, mechanized, industrialized urban society. During the years prior to the Civil War, John Calhoun, the long-time senator from South Carolina and the South's leading political theorist, foresaw the dangers of an uncontrolled industrialism and warned of their consequences with the passion of a Karl Marx. The defeat of the South silenced the Calhouns, and the nation as a whole paid a price for the loss of this corrective criticism. Faulkner describes the corrupting consequences of unregulated commercialism in such characters as the Snopes, Jason Compson and Popeye. But he also reaffirms the importance of the democratic dream of individual success in the legend of Thomas Sutpen. The reconstruction of the South depends on its ability to accept and recognize and make use of the energy and leadership of men like Sutpen, instead of rejecting and destroying them through its fear of mixed blood and democratic enterprise.

In Hemingway's case, the development of his novels from naturalism to the tragic vision is the most conspicuous of all. The characters in his first two novels are the innocent victims of a shabby war and stupid peace, where the only solution is to withdraw from society at large and preserve one's integrity as an individual. One can struggle to maintain a small group of friends by sharing a common rigorous code, as Mike and Brett and Jake Barnes hope to do in *The Sun Also Rises*; one can find a companion like Catherine, as Frederick Henry does for a time in *A Farewell to Arms*. But in the end even one's friends and loved ones die. Man is ultimately left alone. The individual can only steel himself to a stoic endurance, as the peasants of Spain seem to do, and as the matador and artist must. Looking back, we can now see the tragic elements inherent in Hemingway's early fiction, but it is not surprising that the critics of the twenties quickly labelled him a naturalist.

To Have and Have Not is hardly a novel. But in this series of disconnected episodes in which Hemingway describes Harry Morgan's desperate and unsuccessful struggle to survive and take care of his family during the depths of the American Depression, Harry reaches the conclusion that survival by oneself is no longer possible. Men must join hands and destroy the old institutions that are no longer capable of providing people with the simple necessities of life. Harry's last words as he dies are: 'One man alone ain't got. No man alone now. . . . No matter how a man alone ain't got no bloody fucking chance.' 'He had told them,' Hemingway says, 'but they had not heard. . . . It had taken him a long time to get it out and it had taken him all his life to learn it.'

For Whom the Bell Tolls is the most tragic of all Hemingway's novels in form and it is also the most affirmative. It begins where Harry Morgan's death-bed conversion to brotherhood ends. Robert Jordan has come to Spain to join with the Spanish peasants and workers whom Hemingway admires, and with their Socialist government, in defending the brotherhood of man against the Fascist, capitalistic system that threatens to engulf it, and ultimately the western world. It is through Jordan's commitment to this ideal, and his readiness to give his life to defend it, that the heroic nature of his tragic commitment is fully conveyed. By now Hemingway himself was personally so deeply committed to the value of the tragic view of life that in his final novel, The Old Man and the Sea, he would strip away all social relevance and write a brilliant and moving allegory that by its very purity revealed the limitations of tragedy as a literary form. For tragedy is not a way of life. It is merely a means whereby the imaginative writer orders and makes meaningful certain fundamental aspects of life. In The Old Man and the Sea Santiago demonstrates courage over overwhelming odds and proves his right to be called a man. But life involves much more than proving one's courage. The effort to fulfil one's responsibilities to the society of which one is inescapably a part, and also to oneself as an individual, especially when these responsibilities conflict, is also tragic. Robert Jordan's struggle to make a better world by fighting for a cause which fails and brings about his destruction, and the necessity of his reconciling himself to this consequence, is a more compelling subject than Santiago's attempt to land a big fish. For Whom the Bell Tolls is Hemingway's most impressive tragedy.

Even more than Fitzgerald or Faulkner, Hemingway was a representative of the American bourgeoisie. He was born and raised in the prosperous Chicago suburb of Oak Park, Illinois, the son of a respected physician and his public-spirited wife. A member of the Oak Park High School Football team, editor of the school paper, president of the high school graduating class, he embodied the virtues and aspirations of the all-American boy. Ineligible for the army because of an eye injury, he volunteered as a Red Cross ambulance driver and went off to the European war, over the protests of his parents, blithely looking for thrills and adventure. 'I was an awful dope when I went to the last war,' he later said, 'I can still remember thinking that we were the home team and the Austrians were the visiting team.'[4]

4 Carlos Baker, Ernest Hemingway: A Life Story (New York, 1969), p. 38.

Three months later he was almost killed in a mortar barrage on the Italian front and spent many painful weeks in an Italian hospital. When he returned to his family after less than a year's absence it was as though to an unfamiliar world. He had been wounded psychically and spiritually as well as physically and would never feel at home again. The rest of his life would be devoted to revenging himself on the middle-class world of Oak Park, Illinois, which had prepared him so poorly for the realities of a world at war, and left him so vulnerable. Instead, in his fiction, he would celebrate the values of a way of life which is best described as the polar opposite of life along the Forty-Second Parallel. In contrast to Oak Park, to which he now rarely returned, he preferred the values of the older, Catholic, primitive, rural Mediterranean civilization where he had first confronted evil—Italy, Spain and Cuba. This is the burden of one of his early and most important short stories, 'The Doctor and the Doctor's Wife'. There Nick Adams, Hemingway's alter ego, deliberately rejects the simple-minded optimism of his Christian Scientist mother. He chooses instead to go with his Catholic, henpecked father whose sense of evil is beyond Mrs. Adams's comprehension.

It is ironic that Hemingway's first-written novel, *The Sun Also Rises*, should have been adopted by his American readers as a guide to Paris and a better life. For in that novel the Paris of the expatriate Americans stands for everything Hemingway hated about Oak Park. It is not the Paris of Harry's New York Bar that Hemingway celebrates in this story but rather the values of primitive Spain, symbolized by the ritual of the bullfight. At the beginning Jake Barnes is humorously resigned to his life in Paris and the camaraderie of his spoiled, self-centred American friends. But in Pamplona he has an opportunity to compare the disciplined dignity of rural Spain with the dangerous irresponsibility of his undisciplined companions from Paris, and to see their destructive power. On his way back to Paris, after he crosses the border, he is compelled to return to Spain, where he washes away the contamination of Biarritz. It is not France, but rather the contagion of the expatriate Paris to which he must return, that he is trying to wash away. Long before the hubbub over *le défi Américain*, Hemingway foresaw the encroachment of Oak Park, Illinois, into the affairs of Europe. The Forty-Second Parallel is the home of all those overdressed, undersexed, sterile, spoiled, loud-talking American housewives and their businessmen husbands, who clutter the trains, beaches and bullfights in Hemingway's fiction, bringing with them nothing except boredom or trouble. When Robert Jordan goes to fight in Spain it is to protect the simple peasants and workers against the insensitive, irresponsible, capitalistic, Fascist powers of the Oak Parks of the world.

But it is easy to be put off by all this anti-Americanism in Hemingway's work. The truth is that when we look more closely at his heroes, they also bear a striking resemblance to the members of the Oak Park High School Class of 1917. One is reminded by them of another heroic American who was especially popular with young people at that time— Theodore Roosevelt, the spokesman for 'the strenuous life'. Everyone in Hemingway's generation knew about Teddy Roosevelt, the shy East Coast weakling who had made a man of himself by learning to ride and to box, and then went west and became a cowboy. No wonder that he later won the Spanish-American War single-handed by leading a charge up San Juan Hill. As the youngest president of the United States he then straightened out American foreign affairs by seizing Panama and building the Canal, and sent down his bankers and troops to put the rest of South America on a sound financial basis. When a clique of effete businessmen and politicians betrayed him and failed to administer the government to his satisfaction while he was shooting lions in Africa, Roosevelt returned, organized a new party in opposition to the two major parties, wrote a platform so radical it frightened the old guard, and almost got himself re-elected to the presidency. Later, when the European War broke out Roosevelt asked for a general's commission so that he could lead a volunteer regiment overseas and end the war. But President Wilson, the pedantic college professor who had won the election, told Roosevelt that he was too old to fight. Many people believed that as a result of this rejection Roosevelt died of a broken heart.

Frederick Henry and Robert Jordan are classic examples of the American soldier abroad—a type with which the world has become increasingly familiar. It is worthwhile taking a closer look at them. Superficially, Frederick and Robert seem to be opposites—one quits the war and runs away with his girl; the other sends his girl away and dies heroically with his gun in his hands. But these differences are only apparent. Both are good technicians who are happy so long as they can do their job. When the Italian army collapses and Frederick no longer has a function to perform, and is about to be shot, he cuts and runs. Jordan on the other hand is free to blow up his bridge. With character-

istic initiative and enterprise he organizes the guerrillas, isolates and dis-
arms Pablo the trouble-maker, and carries out his impossible mission,
although it costs him his life. Under similar circumstances, we feel
Hemingway's other heroes would have done the same thing.

Because Hemingway's heroes work out their various destinies in
foreign countries, often on foreign battlefields, they have a greater
interest for us than ever before. It was quite proper for Jordan to volunteer to participate as a private individual in the civil conflict of another
nation. But during the past thirty years it has become the official policy
of his country to involve itself in so many foreign conflicts of one kind
or another—the Second World War, Korea, Guatemala, Lebanon,
Cuba, the Dominican Republic, Viet-Nam—that Jordan's exploits take
on a new significance. What is he doing in Spain? Why is is he fighting?
Jordan is an earnest, courageous young college professor and should be
able to instruct us.

The irony is that he really doesn't know why himself. He went off
from America to join in the Loyalist cause because he loved the primitive peasants of Spain and hated to see the Socialist government they
supported wrecked by the forces of conservative reaction. These forces
consisted not only of the Spanish aristocracy, industrialists, churchmen
and military, but their Fascist allies in Germany and Italy and in Oak
Park as well. If the Fascists succeeded in Spain, they would be that
much stronger everywhere, Jordan feels, including America. On his
arrival in Spain he accepts the rigorous discipline of the Marxist leaders
and enjoyed 'the feeling of consecration to a duty toward all the op-
pressed of the world'. But after a year of fighting, he becomes increasingly disillusioned as he sees the chaos, inefficiency and waste in the
Socialist army. He loses faith in the leaders of the cause for which he is
fighting. 'He believed in the Republic as a form of government but the
Republic would have to get rid of all that bunch of horse thieves that
brought it to the pass it was in when the rebellion started. Was there
ever a people whose leaders were as truly enemies as this one?' Finally
he decides that the only solution is not to think about questions of this
kind. 'The first thing was to win the war. If we did not win the war
everything was lost.'

This is his attitude at the beginning of the novel, when he arrives at
Pablo's encampment to blow up the bridge. But as his plans go awry,
and he falls in love with Maria, doubts continually recur. Why doesn't
he take her and run, as Frederick Henry had so many years earlier with

F

Catherine? One reason is his loyalty to the American Dream. 'You're not a Marxist and you know it. . . . You believe in life, Liberty, and the Pursuit of Happiness.' Then, there is the reason that he has come there to collect material for a book he is planning to write. But most insistent of all is simply the fact that he enjoys the thrill and carnage of killing. 'This was the greatest gift he had, the talent that fitted him for war: that ability not to ignore but to despise whatever bad ending there could be. . . . Stop making dubious literature and admit that you liked to kill as all who are soldiers by choice have enjoyed it at some time whether they lie about it or not. . . . Hunters kill animals and soldiers kill men.'

Obviously, thinking and fretting about why he is there will not get the job done. So Jordan goes back to non-thinking. 'I have fought for what I believed in for a year now. If we win here we win everywhere. The world's a fine place and worth fighting for, and I hate very much to leave it.'

Wounded and alone at the end, he realizes that if he is to escape torture or a messy death he will have to kill himself. 'I don't want to do that business my father did,' he thinks, remembering his own father's suicide. 'I will do it all right but I'd much prefer not to have to. . . . Don't think about it. Don't think about it at all.' Since he must die, at least he might as well take along with him as many of the bloody enemy as possible. On the last page, his life blood ebbing away, he heroically sits waiting for the end. His machine gun is at the ready, one last bullet marked with his own name.

It is all very fine and brave and thrilling. And it is easy for Hemingway to laugh at the absurdities of Oak Park, Illinois. But despite his apparent rejection of the values of middle-class American society, Robert Jordan bears a terrifying resemblance to the present governmental representatives of that society in their confused efforts to explain why American soldiers are fighting and dying today in Viet-Nam. As a social critic, Hemingway reveals more about American society in his fiction than he knowingly realized.

VI

I have purposely narrowed this account of the social criticism of American novelists of the twenties to a discussion of the work of Faulkner, Fitzgerald and Hemingway because all three shared a tragic sense of life that set their work above the other writers of this period, not only because of its artistic brilliance but also because they dealt in a more complex and perceptive way with the limitations as well as the positive values of contemporary American society. All three writers shared much in common. But where society was the source of the tragic limitations that circumscribed the aspirations of Faulkner's and Fitzgerald's heroes, Hemingway's heroes were, far more than their creator realized, the victims of their own confused lack of tragic insight. In any case, the attempt by these novelists to treat the conflict between the individual in tragic terms, and to reveal not only the shortcomings of society but also the value of individual effort and imagination is, I believe, the reason for the continuing vitality of their novels today—even more than the brilliance of their respective styles.

Note

Life and Writing

Sinclair Lewis was born at Sauk Centre, Minnesota, in 1885. After graduating from Yale in 1908 he held a variety of jobs, mostly connected with publishing, before his first novel *Our Mr Wrenn* appeared in 1914. He wrote four more novels before reaching an international audience with *Main Street* (1920), the book that auspiciously inaugurated the decade in which he produced his best and most characteristic work: *Babbitt* (1922), *Arrowsmith* (1925), *Elmer Gantry* (1927) and *Dodsworth* (1929). The effect of these writings, in the words of E. M. Forster, was 'to lodge a piece of a continent in our imagination', and in 1930 Lewis received the Nobel Prize for Literature, the first American writer to be so honoured.

His later novels are for the most part unmemorable; collectively they testify to a melancholy decline in his creative powers. Among these works published in the last twenty years of his life are *Ann Vickers* (1933), *It Can't Happen Here* (1935), *Bethel Merriday* (1940), *Gideon Planish* (1943), *Cass Timberlane* (1945), *Kingsblood Royal* (1947) and (posthumously) *World So Wide* (1951). For many of these years Lewis travelled extensively, perhaps compulsively, in the United States and Europe. He married—and was divorced—twice. After his death in Rome in 1951 his ashes were returned to Sauk Centre whose values he satirized but never completely escaped.

Lewis wrote twenty-three novels (including a work for juveniles published in 1912), some of which are still in print. (*Main Street*, *Babbitt* and *Dodsworth* were conveniently collected in 1951 as *Lewis at Zenith*.) *Selected Short Stories* appeared in 1935; Mark Schorer edited *I'm A Stranger Here Myself and Other Stories* (1962). Other selections are: *From Main Street to Stockholm: Letters of Sinclair Lewis, 1919–1930* edited by Harrison Smith (New York, 1952), which draws upon the files of Lewis's American publisher; and *The Man From Main Street: Selected Essays and Other Writings* edited by Harry E. Maule and Melville H. Cane (New York, 1953).

Biography and Criticism. Mark Schorer, *Sinclair Lewis: An American Life* (New York, 1961) is an exhaustive biography; interesting reflections on its writing are included in the same author's *The World We Imagine* (New York, 1968). The story of Lewis's life with Dorothy Thompson is told in Vincent Sheean, *Dorothy and Red* (Boston, 1963); in *With Love From Gracie* (New York, 1955) Grace Hegger Lewis gave her version of Lewis's first marriage.

Mark Schorer has edited *Sinclair Lewis: A Collection of Critical Essays* (Englewood Cliffs, 1962). It should be supplemented by Sheldon Norman Grebstein, *Sinclair Lewis* (New York, 1962) and D. J. Dooley, *The Art of Sinclair Lewis* (Lincoln, 1967). Robert J. Griffin edited *Twentieth Century Interpretations of Arrowsmith* (Englewood Cliffs, N.J., 1968).

IV

Sinclair Lewis and the Drama of Dissociation

HOWELL DANIELS

I

IT HAS long been a critical commonplace that Sinclair Lewis's novels
are seriously and sometimes irredeemably flawed. The quality of his
prose is generally poor, he wrote too much and too quickly, and no
writer of this century with claims upon our attention can have published so many short stories of such little consequence. The internal
organization of his works frequently appears arbitrary or simple. His
characters are often approximations to humanity, blue-prints for
human beings with the complexities of motive and behaviour reduced
to the minimal outlines consistent with an effective credulity. Cumulatively, it may be held, his writings testify to an emotional immaturity,
an intellectual imprecision and a moral fuzziness. Yet the best of his
novels continue to find new readers, and since the publication of Mark
Schorer's monumental biography critical interest has quickened.

Lewis was a baffling and often unappealing figure whose savage
pilgrimage in the United States and Europe now commands more
sympathy than it once received. Sherwood Anderson early detected
in his writings a man 'who, wanting passionately to love the life about
him, cannot bring himself to do so . . .'[1]; even in the last year of his
life Lewis could say that he loved America still for its promises but
he did not like it.[2] His personal appearance tended to confirm his
symbolic status as an exile both from his society and from the normal
affections of the heart. His eyes, we learn from Malcolm Cowley,
were those of a fairy-book hero, who is 'taken for an idiot, and mis-
treated by his elder brothers, and sent bare-handed into the world to
seek his fortune, but he proves the wiliest of them all'.[3] Although

[1] Sinclair Lewis: An American Life, p. 281. (Where full bibliographical
information is omitted from the footnotes, see Note at beginning of chapter.)
[2] Sinclair Lewis: An American Life, p. 810.
[3] Sinclair Lewis: An American Life, p. 316.

Lewis achieved a remarkable success and exercised a wholly dis-
proportionate influence—John Dos Passos has referred to him as 'a
sort of folk hero of the time'—personal happiness eluded him. His
biographer, entirely appropriately, was to discern in Lewis indications
of the official cause of his death in Rome: paralysis of the heart. As a
major writer, however, his career had been over for some time, for
if ever a novelist defined a decade and in turn was defined by it
then that novelist was Sinclair Lewis and the decade the nineteen
twenties.

II

In the 1920 census it was revealed that for the first time the majority
of Americans now lived in cities. The United States had become an
urban nation. The succeeding decade saw the arrival of megalopolis
and a phenomenal growth in suburban living brought about as a
direct result of the impact of the motor car upon American life. A
phase of historical development if not the myths associated with it
had come to an end. In his Nobel Prize speech Sinclair Lewis could
criticize those writers who 'chant that the America of a hundred and
twenty million population is still as simple, as pastoral, as it was when
it had but forty million . . . that, in fine, America has gone through
the revolutionary change from rustic colony to world-empire without
having in the least altered the bucolic and Puritan simplicity of Uncle
Sam.'[4] But in his own fiction, which presented the national lineaments
transformed, Lewis was unable to escape completely from the prevail-
ing mood of cultural nostalgia. For, in response to increasing urbaniza-
tion, a defensive ideology had come into being which ascribed to the
natural state a value that was metaphorical or spiritual rather than
economic. Inevitably, too, as a result of the high proportion of foreign-
born Americans in the larger cities, this pastoral impulse contained
within it a strong element of ethnic nostalgia. It is a theme that appears
but tangentially in Lewis's writings, but in this respect, too, he reflects
the spirit of his age. In making his vague affirmations in favour of
nature, it is obvious that Lewis is participating in a general reaction
against the complexities of life in an industrialized society. Within two
years of the publication of Dodsworth a group of Southerners was to
offer new articles of belief in I'll Take My Stand, but this agrarianism

4 The Man From Main Street, pp. 6–7.

had been preceded by the diffusion of a pastoral nostalgia among the urban middle classes.[5]

The one specific work in which this nostalgia is empirically tested is *Mantrap* (1926), the feeblest of all Lewis's novels during the decade if we exclude the five-finger exercise *The Man Who Knew Coolidge* (1928). Very loosely based on his own trip to Canada with his elder brother Claude, it is the account of a New Yorker who escapes from the mounting horrors of urban life to the last frontier:

> The long trail. A dim path among enormous spruces. Overhead gold-green light slipping through the branches. Lost lakes, reflecting as ebony the silver of birch groves. The iron night, and in the vast silence more brilliant stars. Grim wordless Indians, tall and hawk-nosed, following for league on league the trail of a wounded moose. A log cabin, and at the door a lovely Indian princess.

The dream is, in fact, the 'most blatant of all our American myths: roughing it in the woods!' The Indians appear as 'undersized Sicilians', and at the door of the log cabin is not the princess but an ex-manicurist. As a result of his amatory and other experiences, however, Ralph Prescott achieves some sort of self-knowledge before he returns, renewed, to New York; but the most interesting development is the nature of his companionship with Joe Easter, his guide, who quite explicitly informs him that no woman 'that ever loved is worth giving up a real friendship for'. Even in the wilderness, it seems, masculine fidelities are threatened by the female. The situation is but one of several such examples of male chauvinism. In *Babbitt* Paul Riesling and the hero sneak off to Maine in advance of their wives and, of course, in *Arrowsmith* Terry Wickett and Martin finally pursue in the depths of the woods the scientific truths to the attainment of which woman is apparently an impediment.

Whatever we make of this particular scenario, in Lewis's writings there is certainly evidence of that recoil from the problems of life in a complex civilization that Leo Marx had noted, but the direction of the recoil leads not to the creation of a pastoral regionalism but to a strange and, with rare exceptions, quite unconvincing internal fantasy world devoid of any value except that of exoticism. Dissociation tends to take the place of a nostalgic impulse unable to find its correlatives in

[5] See Peter J. Schmitt, *Back to Nature: The Arcadian Myth in Urban America* (New York, 1969).

a particular region at a particular time. From the biographical evidence available we know that Lewis's childhood and youth at Sauk Centre was a time of loneliness, that he was denied kindness, that his physical appearance brought him unhappiness, and that he turned increasingly to romantic literature for compensation. The conclusion of his short article 'The Long Arm of the Small Town', written for the fiftieth anniversary of his old school's annual, is apparently merely another example of its author's endless capacity for self-deception:

> Indeed, as I look at these sons of rich men in New England with their motor cars and their travel, it seems to me that they are not having one-tenth the fun which I had as a kid, swimming and fishing in Sauk Lake, or cruising its perilous depths on a raft (probably made of stolen logs), tramping out to Fairy Lake for a picnic, tramping ten miles on end, with a shotgun, in October; sliding on Hoboken Hill, stealing melons, or listening to the wonders of an elocutionist at the G.A.R. Hall. It was a good time, a good place and a good preparation for life.[6]

Although he returned regularly to Sauk Centre, it was the town's prejudice, ignorance and meanness that he chose to commemorate.

Instead of the concrete remembered values of childhood, Lewis's characters proffer the vaguenesses of a fantasy world that is often the adjunct of youth. When Lewis began writing verse his subject—in Fenimore Cooper's terminology—was the castle rather than the corn-field; as a student at Yale his literary contributions were suffused with a thin, post-romantic medievalism; and even in his correspondence with the woman who was to become his first wife he cast himself in the roles of Jacques the Jester and Francois the Troubadour.[7] In the introduction to *Selected Short Stories* (1935) Lewis could disclose that 'he, who has been labelled a "satirist" and a "realist", is actually a romantic medievalist of the most incurable sort.'[8] If he was not quite accurate in his assessment of himself as 'essentially a story-teller', there is no reason to doubt the truth of his acknowledging, in a self-composed obituary of 1941, that 'Mr. Lewis smote—or tries to smite—sentimentality because he knew himself to be, at heart, a sentimentalist, a romanticist. . . .'[9]

[6] *The Man From Main Street*, p. 272.
[7] *With Love From Gracie*, p. 8. One of Lewis's 'Tennyson-and-water verses' is reproduced at p. 84.
[8] *The Man From Main Street*, p. 219.
[9] *The Man From Main Street*, p. 105.

The effect of this persistent romantic strain in Lewis's imagination is that characters, who generally speaking have no sense of history, must resort to fantasy in order to come to terms with or escape from their society. They tend to be individuals continuously in a state of self-creation, seeking a humanity which their creator is perhaps incapable of providing. It is, therefore, not surprising that Sinclair Lewis has sometimes been criticized for failing to establish a dynamic relationship between a character and the society against which he or she is in revolt; instead, it is argued, there is substituted an 'outward acquiescence and inward rebellion that is the death of drama'.[10] But this condition of dissociation has always existed as a permanent feature of American life; its obverse is that urge to conformity in a nation populated, after all, by immigrants who underwent the most drastic form of dissociation when they crossed the Atlantic. At this point it may be useful to turn to Mary McCarthy's essay 'America the Beautiful' in which she maintains that the 'openness of the American situation creates the pity and the terror; status is not protection; life for the European is a career; for the American it is a hazard.' She goes on to state that all attempts to introduce a concept of the 'little man' have failed, for a national passivity should not be confused with abjectness:

> Americans will not eat this humble pie; we are still nature's noblemen. Yet no tragedy results, though the protagonist is everywhere; dissociation takes the place of conflict, and the drama is mute.[11]

It is this mute drama of dissociation that is central to Lewis's best works of the nineteen twenties—*Main Street*, *Babbitt* and *Dodsworth*—and it is with these three novels that this essay is primarily concerned.

III

The little man does, however, make an appearance in Lewis's first novel, *Our Mr Wrenn*, which is interesting for the way in which it anticipates the essential pattern of Lewis's better-known works—discontent, escape, compromise or defeat. Initially bludgeoned into acquiescence by his environment, the Wellsian title figure can only resort to his imagination to justify his dreary existence. Then, with the aid of a legacy, there is a physical escape—to Europe, as it will be in

[10] *Sinclair Lewis: A Collection of Critical Essays*, p. 117.
[11] *On the Contrary* (New York, 1961), p. 17.

Lewis's last and posthumously published novel *World So Wide*. The dream landscape possesses the usual ogres; the head foreman on the cattle boat is known as Satan and there is one Pete, who 'was very evil'. The *princesse lointaine* is Istra Nash, an exotic creature who, as so often in Lewis's fictional world, succeeds in depriving a sexual relationship of meaning by reducing it to an infantile level. She refers to Wrenn as 'Mouse' and to them both as babes in the wood. In a manner similar to that adopted by Sharon in *Elmer Gantry* and Fran Dodsworth, when this type of association is in any way threatened by more elemental feelings it is quickly restored by means of a special vocabulary. One is tempted to locate the motives for these extraordinary reductions of adult relationships in Lewis himself, but the presence of the same phenomenon in the writings of some of his contemporaries, including Hemingway and Fitzgerald, suggests a larger explanation should perhaps be looked for. In *Our Mr Wrenn* fact finally triumphs over fantasy, and the book ends with the successful hero striding into a Babbitt-like future:

> 'Gee!' he moaned, 'it's the first time I've noticed a sunset for a month! I used to see knight's flags and Mandalay and all sorts of stuff in sunsets.'
> Wistfully the exile gazed at his lost kingdom, till the October chill aroused him.

For all its flights of fancy *Our Mr Wrenn* is set in a visible and verifiable world; *The Innocents* (1917) makes no pretence to realism. Lewis described it as 'a flagrant excursion, a tale for people who still read Dickens and clip out spring poetry and love old people and children'. In fact, the novel is even more sentimental than the author's summary of it, as the elderly Applebys wander across rural America (and in the process become folk-heroes) before achieving happiness and prosperity in a small Indiana town. It is a fairy tale, pure and simple, an attempt to recreate in American terms the Golden Age mentioned by Lewis in his introduction. Lewis's other novels to appear before 1920 were *The Trail of the Hawk* (1915), *The Job* (1917) and *Free Air* (1919). All are variants on the quest theme set forth in *Our Mr Wrenn* and all, in varying degrees, hover between the depiction of the realities of American life and a contrary tendency, seen in characterization and structure, to indulge in the familiar rhetoric offered by the possibilities of romance. Of these the most realistic is *The Job*, an account of a young woman's survival and success in the business world of New York, and perhaps the most interesting *Free Air*, in which Gopher Prairie is introduced for the first time. Where a number of years and several hundred pages were necessary for Carol Kennicott to come to an understanding of the town, here one night only is required. What appears to be insupportable rudeness in the evening is seen in the morning to be genuine friendliness. In this novel, however, and in its predecessors, despite a similarity of themes, there is nothing to indicate that with the publication of *Main Street* Lewis would acquire an international reputation and add a new phrase to the language.

Main Street appeared in 1920, and is the great romantic satire of its decade. Its heroine, Carol Kennicott, is, like Isabel Archer, an absolutist of the imagination; they both exemplify what T. S. Eliot has called *bovarysme*, the adoption of an aesthetic rather than a moral attitude towards life. Instead of the airless study in Albany we are offered the cliffs above Mankato where the valley held in and made coherent the dreams that in the prairie 'go flying off into the big space.' This essential element in Carol's thought is made quite plain as the train bears her to Gopher Prairie and is dramatized later in a conversation with Vida Sherwin in which Carol claims:

> The civic improvements which I'd like the Thanatopsis to advocate are Strindberg plays, and classic dancers—exquisite legs beneath tulle—and . . . a thick, black-bearded, cynical Frenchman who would sit about and drink and sing opera and tell bawdy stories and laugh at our proprieties and quote Rabelais and not be ashamed to kiss my hand!

Her romantic imagination derives its stimuli from and operates in respect of two areas: the Europe of fiction, poetry and painting and the natural grandeur of the prairie with its associated memories of the frontier. Between these conflicting principles for human development Carol is caught in the frozen historical moment represented by Gopher Prairie. In the opposition between her and the environment she in turn invokes first one and then the other of these imaginative possibilities, either in order to escape temporarily from the stultifying society of Gopher Prairie or to impose upon it the values that to her mind it conspicuously lacks.

Her reading of Yeats brings 'the flutter of twilight linnets, the aching call of gulls along a shore to which the netted foam crept out of darkness', but the prosaic reaction of her husband ensures that this is her last attempt 'to buy the lilies of Avalon and the sunsets of Cockaigne in tin cans at Ole Jensen's Grocery'. Indeed, so committed is the novel to Carol's point of view that we can only guess that her imperfect understanding of 'culture'—a fin-de-siècle mixture of Yeats' poetry, Chinese masquerade costumes, Japanese obi, Dunsany plays and dreams of Venice and Mentone—reflects a similar limitation in Lewis himself. When, finally, she gives up the struggle and decides to dissociate herself and her son completely from the world of Gopher Prairie the fantasy, appropriately, transcends the actual and locates itself in the never-never land of faery:

> We're going to find elephants with golden howdahs from which peep young maharanees with necklaces of rubies, and a dawn sea coloured like the breast of a dove, and a white and green house filled with books and silver tea-sets.

But the major role in the novel is played by the myth of the frontier. *Main Street* is haunted by the consciousness of the past and a confidence for the future. It begins and in one sense may be said to end with meditations on empire. The classical opening—a figure in a landscape —sets the scene in the present but it is a present heavy with memories of a recent past, too near for nostalgia. Where Chippewas had camped two generations earlier, Carol expectantly stands: 'The days of pioneering, of lassies in sunbonnets, and bears killed with axes in piney clearings, are deader now than Camelot; and a rebellious girl is the spirit of that bewildered empire called the American Middlewest.' Towards the end of the novel Carol, having seemingly made her peace with the town, is conscious that the prairie is no longer the empty land she had once thought it but a 'living tawny beast which she had fought and made beautiful by fighting'. Across the continent it stretches, 'a dominion which will rise to unexampled greatness when other empires have grown senile'. The alternative possibilities can be expressed in social and political terms: if Carol cannot have the formal ballroom she prefers the puncheon floor and the dancing fiddler; she is unable to conceive of the future except in similar polarities:

> A future of cities and factory smut where now are loping empty fields? Homes universal and secure? Or placid châteaux ringed with sullen huts? . . . The ancient style inequalities, or something different in history, unlike the tedious maturity of other empires?

But Gopher Prairie is neither Europe nor the heroic frontier, and it resists alike the crude sophistication and false simplicity that Carol attempts to impose upon it.

There is even a certain amount of attitudinizing in her reaction to the natural landscape in which, intermittently, she finds the dignity and greatness that elude her in the town. Although Lewis in elegiac mood can evoke successfully the passing seasons of a distinctive regional landscape, the nostalgic impulse is blurred by rhetoric when it attempts to move beyond nature into history. One or two sharply defined images, such as those the Kennicotts encounter at Mendato, scarcely compensate for the basic failure of historical insight.

A similar indecision permeates Lewis's conception of his heroine's character, and this in turn derives from his own ambivalent attitude towards the civilization represented by Gopher Prairie. Although the book is certainly a venomous indictment of the stupidities and banalities of the small town, it is necessary to remember that the novelist and his wife originally explained that the work was intended to illustrate Carol's learning 'the great secret of life in being content with a real world in which it is never possible to create an ideal setting'.[12] The epistemology of the novel is suspect. At one level the double standard is illustrated in the deliberate juxtaposition of the conflicting points of view of Carol and her future maid as they both survey the town for the first time: for the one it is a bleak nightmare, for the other a glamorous dream. At another level Carol's somewhat belated recognition on her return to Gopher Prairie that not individuals but institutions are the enemies would seem to invalidate the truth of many of her earlier criticisms of the town. It is, however, one of the ironies of history that the harsh angularities of Gopher Prairie, which so appalled Lewis's heroine, have softened with time and, with all the detail of an Andrew Wyeth painting, the novel now recalls a vanished innocence.

IV

'He is the typical T.B.M.,' wrote Lewis, 'the man you hear drooling in the Pullman smoker; but having once so seen him, I want utterly to develop him so that he will seem not just typical but an individual.' To his publisher he added that Babbitt was meant to represent 'all of

12 *With Love From Gracie*, p. 147.

us Americans at 46, prosperous but worried, wanting—passionately—to seize something more than motor cars and a house *before it's too late*'.[13] In his desire to make his character both an individual and yet representative of a larger group, Lewis seems to have been caught in a dilemma; since, as Edith Wharton (to whom the novel was dedicated) put it in a letter to him, 'Babbitt is in and of Zenith up to his chin and over',[14] it might seem difficult for Lewis to endow him with traits or quirks that do not reflect back upon or indeed take their distinguishing features from his immediate environment. He succeeds in his intention as a result of the decision to offer us two Babbitts: the gregarious realtor and the asocial dreamer, the complacent conformist and the ageing man who hears dimly the same voice that will whisper to Saul Bellow's Henderson. It may be a limited achievement but it is Lewis's only complete success.

Babbitt is the sole major figure in Lewis's novels of the nineteen twenties who appears immediately before us in the full panoply of the self. During the course of the novel we learn something of his past life but in the opening chapters he is susceptible to a larger freedom of interpretation than Carol Kennicott, Martin Arrowsmith, Elmer Gantry or Sam Dodsworth, all of whom are in varying degrees introduced in terms of their background. Established at once, also, is Lewis's point of view. Zenith is presented as an enchanted city, a living organism, proud of its towers, disdaining its past:

> The towers of Zenith aspired above the morning mist; austere towers of steel and cement and limestone, sturdy as cliffs and delicate as silver rods. They were neither citadels nor churches, but frankly and beautifully office buildings.
>
> The mist took pity on the fretted structures of earlier generations: the Post Office with its shingle-tortured mansard, the red brick minarets of hulking old houses, factories with stingy and sooted windows, wooden tenements coloured like mud. The city was full of such grotesqueries, but the clean towers were thrusting them from the business centre, and on the farther hills were shining new houses, homes—they seemed—for laughter and tranquillity.

The one unconfident note—'they seemed'—hinting at a reality yet to be revealed is repeated in the last phrase of this opening section: 'a city built—it seemed—for giants.' The panoramic sweep then narrows to

---

[13] *From Main Street to Stockholm*, p. 59.
[14] *With Love From Gracie*, p. 221.

focus on the podgy citizen-hero, Babbitt, uneasily suspended in sleep between the two worlds represented by the dream child and the morning noises of Floral Heights: 'There was nothing of the giant in the aspect of the man who was beginning to awaken on the sleeping-porch of a Dutch Colonial house. . . .'

In these opening paragraphs the sentience attributed to the city and to the limousine that 'fled' over the bridge is reflected later in the resistivism of objects which Babbitt encounters in his daily routine: the new razor blades that are misplaced, the oiled envelope that will not unwrap as it should; a bedroom which, released of its occupants, 'settled instantly into impersonality'. The list can be extended: Babbitt's office becomes his pirate ship and his car 'the perilous excursion ashore'; the office itself is part of the Reeves building serviced by 'little unknown people' who 'were in no way city dwellers' but mere 'rustics'; a nickelled cigar lighter becomes 'treasure' and the car for which it is destined 'an aspiration to knightly rank'. Although these examples suggest the nature of the relationship between Babbitt and his environment, his attitude is made explicit as he drives home from Eathorne's house, where the chairs are 'gently supercilious':

> The air was shrewd, the snow was deep in uncleared alleys, and beyond the city, Babbitt knew, were hillsides of snow-drift among wintry oaks, and the curving ice-enchanted river.
> He loved his city with passionate wonder.

And in some ways Zenith is as much the hero of this book as the resident whose job it is to serve the city by extending and populating it.

It is this capacity for wonder, admirably sustained in a prose which moves easily between Babbitt's world of fact and world of fantasy, that is the key to his individuality. In himself a curious mixture of aggressive and regressive tendencies, Babbit's domain is essentially that defined in the work of Lewis's contemporary, James Thurber, where man, menaced by organizations, machines and women, must resort to irrational forms of compensation in order to preserve his identity. Indeed, one of the reasons for the superiority of *Babbitt* over its immediate predecessor is that the solemn Carol attempts to inflict upon the community a programme of eminently rational compensation. Babbitt, whether in his pirate ship or facing unknown dangers with the fairy child or imaginatively transforming the plump business-man into a skilled frontiersman, is triumphantly Mitty-like in his lonely but persuasive irrationality. At the end of Babbitt's first day, for instance, we find him in his tub:

The drain-pipe was dripping, a dulcet and lively song: dripetty drip drip dribble, dripetty drip drip drip. He was enchanted by it. He looked at the solid tub, the beautiful nickel taps, the tiled walls of his room, and felt virtuous in the possession of this splendour.

He roused himself and spoke gruffly to his bath-things. 'Come here! You've done enough fooling!' he reproved the treacherous soap and defied the scratchy nail-brush with 'Oh you would, would you!' He soaped himself, and rinsed himself, and austerely rubbed himself; he noted a hole in the Turkish towel, and meditatively thrust a finger through it, and marched back to his bedroom, a grave and unbending citizen.

There was a moment of gorgeous abandon, a flash of melodrama such as he found in traffic-driving, when he laid out a clean collar, discovered that it was frayed in front, and tore it up with a magnificent yeeeeeing sound.

The extravagant language is obviously employed for satiric purposes in drawing to a close this hyperbolic description of the Babbitt day; but at a deeper level the responses evoked tend to contradict the ironic drift for they complicate our reaction to Babbitt himself in so far as a warm affection for him is both reflected and generated.

For Babbitt is trapped in the conflict between his private and public self, between on the one hand the demands of his business and an oppressive feminism ('a restricted region of wives and stenographers, and of suggestions not to smoke so much') and on the other a deeply-felt if unarticulated need to express his concealed self. The opportunities for this are few, but one such occurs when the Zenith delegation makes its bid for the next realtors' convention:

At the head [of the procession] was big Warren Whitby, in the bearskin and gold-and-crimson coat of a drum-major. Behind him, as a clown, beating a bass drum, extraordinarily happy, was Babbitt.

Babbitt is the facsimile of an adult. The objects in his suit, which to him 'were of eternal importance, like baseball or the Republican Party', confirm his status but the manner of presentation suggests they are indices to a reality of which he is never quite sure:

They included a fountain pen and a silver pencil (always lacking a supply of new leads) which belonged in the right-hand upper vest pocket. Without them he would have felt naked. On his watch-chain were a gold pen-knife, silver cigar-cutter, seven keys (the use of two of which he had forgotten), and incidentally a good watch. Depending from the chain was a large, yellowish elk's tooth— proclamation of his membership in the Benevolent and Protective Order of Elks. Most significant of all was his loose-leaf pocket note-book, that modern and efficient note-book which contained the addresses of people whom he had forgotten, prudent memoranda of postal money-orders which had reached their destinations months ago, stamps which had lost their mucilage, clippings of verses by T. Cholmodeley Frink and of the newspaper editorials from which Babbitt got his opinions and his polysyllables, notes to be sure and do things which he did not intend to do, and one curious inscription —D.S.S.D.M.Y.P.D.F.

His theology is as confused and boyish as the contents of his pockets. After his rebellion is over Babbitt cautiously checks on the prospects of salvation, but this is hardly surprising since to him heaven was 'rather like an excellent hotel with a private garden'.

The act of dissociation assumes different forms in the novel. Babbitt, as the point of view makes clear, is in one sense already at a remove from the 'realities' of Zenith; he exists in a state of perilous equilibrium between himself and his environment. Throughout the book, too, the woods of Maine occur as a leitmotif. There, with Paul Riesling, Babbitt 'revelled in a good sound dirtiness' as in a mood of truancy he exposes his body and troubled spirit to a conventional immersion in nature. Even after the wives have appeared, bringing with them matriarchal prohibitions and restrictions, he feels as though 'he had cleansed his veins of poisonous energy and was filling them with wholesome blood'. But the solution is temporary; Maine eventually fails him and Babbitt has one of his rare moments of insight when he realizes that he cannot run away from himself. Dissociation then becomes open revolt as he rebels against the tyranny of marriage and the despotism of the standardized beliefs that he had earlier defended in his speech to the Zenith Real Estate Board. There is, however, another more private form of withdrawal available to him.

The creation of the fairy child whom Babbitt meets in his dreams has often been criticized for its intolerable whimsy. At one level she obviously represents an escape from the oppressive realities of the day:

Instantly he was in the magic dream. He was somewhere among unknown people who laughed at him. He slipped away, ran down the paths of a midnight garden, and at the gate the fairy child was waiting. Her dear and tranquil hand caressed his cheek. He was gallant and wise and well-beloved; warm ivory were her arms; and beyond perilous moors the brave seas glittered.

While it is certainly true that the language used to describe Babbitt's encounters with the fairy child may be duplicated in *Our Mr Wrenn* and *Main Street*, here the dissociative impulse and its product are located firmly in Babbitt's unconscious mind. Approaching fifty, worried about smoking too much, strangely discontented with his in many ways enviable lot, Babbitt may seem an admirable metaphor of urban man; but he is fully aware of the passing of time, of youthful dreams not realized, and in one way or the other—by immersing himself in the juvenile tribal rites of his masculine clubs or by cultivating his dream child—he seeks to return to the clear, unambiguous and timeless world of childhood. Indeed, we may postulate an implicit relationship between the fairy child and his younger daughter. Among his family Tinka (the nickname is perhaps deliberately reminiscent of J. M. Barrie's creation) is the one person Babbitt genuinely loves; as yet she is still promises, she has not in Housman's phrase been eaten by the grizzly bear, whereas Verona and Ted as extensions of himself have grievously disappointed. Consequently, the father together with his mirror-image in the shape of his idealized daughter can retreat, freed from the tribulations of the circumstantial, into a fantasy world in order to enact the values denied them by their society. Both the concept and the language in which it is realized are artistically justifiable.

Some commentators have taken exception to the two Babbitts. Frederick J. Hoffman, for example, maintained that there is a parody Babbitt and 'a sensitive humane Babbitt, who in his person and in his behaviour cancels the validity and nullifies the success of the other'.[15] But we do not have to choose between two versions because no distinction is made between them in the controlling point of view. The persistent strain of the mock-heroic and the hyperbolic in the narrative ensures that we follow the vicissitudes of its hero with interest and amusement but not necessarily with any great involvement. Occasionally, Lewis will introduce a sentence such as the following: 'Then round the swimmer, bored by struggling through the perpetual surf of family life, new combers swelled. . . .' In this metaphor he detaches himself from his creation and, simultaneously, evokes some degree of

[15] *The Twenties* (revised edition, New York, 1962), p. 414.

sympathetic response. The most common technique, however, is that of comic inflation: parking a car becomes a 'virile adventure'; in order to stop smoking Babbitt 'did everything, in fact, except stop smoking'; his preparations for leaving the office 'were somewhat less elaborate than the plan for a general European war'. The tone of such observations is remarkably consistent and, paradoxically, in view of the satiric intent they cumulatively serve to create an affinity between the reader and the comic anti-hero at war with his inherited world.

One of the fascinations of *Babbitt* is that Lewis's stylistic and conceptual limitations here become strengths. Georgie or, alternatively, George F. Babbitt, according to the role demanded of him, functions for much of the novel as an image of ursine amiability familiar only in juvenile literature. The choice of verbs to illustrate his actions is illuminating. We learn, for instance, that he 'ambled up to Verona's room', 'humming and grunting' as he examines her books; that he roars, rumbles, growls, lumbers, snarls, blunders, and even on occasion squeals and yelps. He snuffs the earth, emits soft grunts. Indeed, at one point, when confronted by the officials of the Good Citizens' League, his primitive reaction is not unlike that of Bongo, a bear in Lewis's pallid little story of that name published in *Cosmopolitan*: 'Something black and unfamiliar and ferocious spoke from Babbitt.' Of course, a similar vocabulary is introduced into other novels, most notably in *Elmer Gantry* and in *Dodsworth*, where Sam and his wife indulge in their bear and rabbit fantasies; but it is the frequency and consistency of this type of presentation that one remarks here, even in such happenings as the strange tribal noises and gestures indulged in by Babbitt and his companions. Taken in conjunction with the mock-heroic technique, the consequence of this distinctive point of view is to condition the reader's reaction and awaken a favourable atavistic response which has the effect of neutralizing Babbitt as a moral being. He becomes a powerful generic symbol into which ethical lapses such as hypocrisy and financial chicanery are comfortably absorbed.

Babbitt is a wry, sad and amusing novel with a special tone and unity unique among Lewis's work. Despite the prompt appropriation of the title into popular speech, the book, as Lewis wrote to H. L. Mencken, is 'not altogether satire'. He added:

I've tried like hell to keep the boob Babbitt from being merely burlesque—hard tho that is at times, when he gets to orating before the Boosters' Club lunches. I've tried to make him human and individual, not a type.[16]

Like Carol Kennicott Babbitt finally returns to the world he knows best. But he is not quite the same man. Although he seems to transfer his dissociative tendencies to his son and in spite of the fact that he continues in a similar pattern of life, we learn that Babbitt's moral fibre 'had been so weakened by rebellion that he was not quite dependable in the more rigorous campaigns of the Good Citizens' League nor quite appreciative of the church. . . .' He is not and never will be one of the real villains of Zenith—which, as the radical lawyer Seneca Doane puts it, is a 'better place to live in than Manchester or Glasgow or Lyons or Berlin or Turin'. The process of apotheosis, which will culminate in the figure of Fred Cornplow, has begun.[17]

V

Dodsworth was Lewis's last novel to be published during the decade and, while the book in some ways reflects his own travel and marital experiences, it continues the exploration of the American character in a traditionally American setting: Europe. The theme obviously recalls James's writings, but the stress on the degradation of the artistic impulse in a mechanized society together with the resolution in terms of the land is oddly reminiscent of Sherwood Anderson.

In seeking to present the story of a human relationship, Lewis by means of his setting complicates and enlarges his subject by examining also an historical and cultural relationship. The Europe of earlier individual fantasies is here offered in a much more circumstantial manner, though it is still, in Jamesian terms, very much the continent seen by the financially privileged outsider. Yet the novel is still the record

[16] Quoted in *Sinclair Lewis: An American Life*, p. 291.

[17] One might add that for all Lewis's satire of the Boosters such organizations were necessary and to a certain extent approved in the nineteen twenties. Jesse D. Nichols, an internationally known town planner and a prominent figure in the real estate industry, told an audience of businessmen in 1921: 'City planning . . . is based on love, ambition, and profit. . . . If you are ambitious for the growth of your business, your institution or your city, if you believe in its future growth, you plan for healthy expansion.' (Quoted in *Change and Continuity in Twentieth-Century America* edited by John Braeman, Robert H. Bremner and David Brady [Columbus, Ohio, 1968], pp. 428–9.) And, whatever the motives for its acquisition, Zenith presumably gets the symphony orchestra that Chum Frink so passionately advocates to the Boosters.

of an education and attempts to trace, in an admittedly rather unsubtle fashion, the growth of an individual consciousness as a result of the frustration between ideas and their translation into action.

Dodsworth has achieved his position as the result of an early and profitable recognition of the concept of functional beauty, that cars 'ought to get away from imitating carriages'. For him the prospect of designing and manufacturing automobiles is deeply fulfilling: 'all the while he dreamed of motors like thunderbolts, as poets less modern than himself might dream of stars and roses and nymphs by a pool.' But with the absorption of his company by the U.A.C. his individuality can find no means of expression, and in a new cultural setting the problem is heightened. Like Anderson, Lewis seems to be suggesting that the industrial process depersonalizes and that it erodes the creative talent; fundamental questions of identity of necessity are raised, including that of sexual identity. According to Edith Cortwright, Fran, as a symbol of American womanhood, represents 'fear and death'; it presumably falls upon her to complete the re-education of Dodsworth, begun by Nande Azeredo in Paris. But the vicious sentimentality with which his marriage has been suffused survives in the form of guilt.

The dissociation here is from the former self and the way of life that defined it, although the closing words of the novel would suggest that the process can never be complete. *Dodsworth* displays the classic Lewis ambivalences in other ways too, most notably in the stress on the essential decency of Sam and other mid-Westerners such as A. B. Hurd, Matey and her husband Tub Pearson, despite the latter's Pocockian reaction to Paris. At the dinner given by Hurd the dilemma is made explicit as Sam attempts a definition of the nation he and the others have left in terms of the picturesque:

> New York on a winter night, with the theatres blaring and the apartment-houses along Park Avenue vanishing up into the wild sky rosy from a million lights. Vermont on an autumn afternoon, with the maples like torches. Midsummer in Minnesota, where the cornfields talked to themselves, and across miles of rolling wheatland, dimpling to the breeze, you saw the tall red wheat-elevators and the spire of the German Catholic Church. The grave silence of the wilderness: plateaus among the sacred peaks of the Sierra Nevadas, painted buttes in Arizona, Wisconsin lakes caressing in dark waters the golden trunks of Norway pines. The fan-lights above serene old Connecticut doorways in Litchfield and Sharon. Proud cold sunsets

in the last five minutes of the Big Game at Thanksgiving-time. . . . Cities of a quarter of a million people with fantastic smoky steel works, like maniac cathedrals, which had arisen in twenty years upon unpeopled sand-barrens. The long road and a rather shaggy, very adventurous family in a squeaky flivver, the new Covered Wagon, starting out to see all the world from Seattle to Tallahassee, stopping to earn their bacon and bread and oil by harvesting; singing at night in tourist camps on the edge of wide-lawned towns—

But these multiple meanings no longer hold; 'except for half a dozen homesick souls, each of them admitted that he was going to go on loving, boosting, and admiring America, and remain in Europe as long as he could.' The bases of this nostalgia are later transformed when, after experiencing the horrors of New York life, Ross Ireland advances to a receptive Dodsworth the suggestion that the real, the true American now lives abroad. The process of dissociation is seemingly complete.

But Lewis continues to weigh and assess the two types of society. Among the flaws of the novel are the unashamed and lengthy debates on the respective merits of Europe and America. They are oddly reminiscent of the colloquies that Fenimore Cooper with a similar purpose in view inserted into his fiction of the eighteen thirties. Another fault is that the Europe which we are here offered is still very much that of the outsider. Dodsworth may be a latter-day, pragmatic passionate pilgrim but, as he himself realizes, this de luxe Cook's tour of London, Paris, Berlin, Madrid, Rome and Florence isolates him from the other Europe of which he has glimpses only. His involvement with the Sans Souci development therefore becomes an attempt to bridge the Atlantic in personal and architectural terms.

The final choice for America, however, is not made until the closing chapters. It is dependent upon Sam's recognition of the truth of Edith's assertion:

Here, we may have ruins and painting, but behind them we're so much closer to the eternal elements than you Americans. You don't love earth, you don't love the wind . . . That's the strength of Europe—not its so called 'culture', its galleries and neat voices and knowledge of languages, but its nearness to earth.

And the weakness of America, correspondingly, is its detachment from the romantic virtues associated with the land. This passage represents a neat inversion of a tradition which goes back to at least the eighteenth century; it may be said to fuse in the values it advances the twin nostalgias for frontier and Europe. Although the reconstructed Dodsworth promptly begins to dream of an 'authentic farm', the final compromise is characteristic of the author: Sam and Edith are to return to the United States to 'experiment with caravans', an action that will satisfy his vaguely creative impulses and, at the same time, provide his fellow-countrymen and women with an opportunity to recover that which has been lost from the national life. While admirably democratic, the proposal is hardly the cosmopolitan solution which has been tentatively suggested in earlier pages and it does not acknowledge that the presence of motorized caravans in the wilderness can only succeed in destroying it.

It is an oddly factitious solution expressed in embarrassingly self-conscious prose. Europe, then, is in traditional American fashion tested and rejected in favour of America—though in Lewis's last novel, *World So Wide*, the Dodsworths re-appear as permanent expatriates in Florence. Against Fran's brittle extoleation of European culture Sam can only offer 'the tradition of pioneers pushing to the westward, across the Alleghenies, through the forests of Kentucky and Tennessee, on to the bleeding plains of Kansas, on to Oregon and California, a religious procession, sleeping always in danger, never resting, and opening a new home for a hundred million people'.[18] In the last months of the decade, however, before the crash of October 1929, this vision could mean nothing except a sentimental gesture towards the American past; it was impossible for Lewis—despite such attempts as the setting up in *Arrowsmith* of reverberations in terms of its opening paragraphs—to translate the virtues of an heroic age into contemporary terms. He could offer only an increasingly idealized series of portraits of the American middle class until in *The Prodigal Parents* (1938), for the benefit of an audience to whom his faded iconography meant nothing, he announced the triumph of the American businessman.

VI

In his essay 'Materialism and Idealism in American Life' Santayana discusses the symbolic American who

can be made largely adequate to the facts; because if there are immense differences between individual Americans—for some Americans are

[18] In the context of the novel it is implied that secession from these natural rhythms of the land leads to a destruction of confidence in the man and allows woman to abrogate her function: the land is equated with the good sexual life.

black—yet there is a great uniformity in their environment, customs, temper, and thoughts. They have all been uprooted from their several soils and ancestries and plunged together into one vortex, whirling irresistibly in a space otherwise quite empty. To be an American is of itself almost a moral condition, an education, and a career. Hence a single ideal figment can cover a large part of what each American is in his character, and almost the whole of what most Americans are in their social outlook and political judgements.[19]

The source of Lewis's power as a novelist seems to lie in his iconic transcriptions of American life where, it might be argued, the icons are made largely adequate to the facts. His achievement rests on his ability to identify the new social dimensions of the vortex and, as a result, his emblematic fictions examine, albeit obliquely, the implications of the moral condition to which Santayana alludes. He is America's first distinctively urban as opposed to city novelist. In *Main Street* he analysed the patterns of a static small-town community; in *Babbitt* he focussed his attention on the problems of urban living and in Babbitt produced his single great creation; in *Dodsworth* he may be said to study by implication some of the consequences of life in a post-industrial society. For Dodsworth, endowed with time and money and released from the functional definition of the self, is able to find in Europe a larger and freer identity than he has known before.

In the nineteen twenties Lewis's sociological fictions made their primary appeal through the satiric observation of phases of contemporary life. Often, however, his novels possessed a special quality that elevated them above the level of mere destructive comment on contemporary folly; this dimension was early recognized by Constance Rourke who pointed out that for all the striking immediacy of his writings Lewis was essentially the fabulist of an older American tradition, a maker of images, who first appropriated and then imaginatively transformed an aspect of national life. He identified and dramatized for his readers certain primary truths concerning the nature of the American character. In so doing he created a fictitious Middle America with its own geography and history and, if he did not develop (at least in his novels) his created region as systematically as Hardy or Faulkner elaborated theirs, in becoming its official mythographer he gave to the world a fable which it welcomed as fact. Even in his best decade the quality of Lewis's work is uneven, illustrating the often

[19] *Character and Opinion in the United States* (New York, 1920), p. 168.

remarked ambiguity of his relationship to his material. It is this uncertainty that excludes Lewis's novels from consideration as a primitive pop art, though at times they certainly seem to belong to that category. *Elmer Gantry*, for example, the most pungent and un-remitting of all Lewis's castigations of American life, is finally a novel that it is difficult to take seriously. Written with considerable energy and gusto, it contains some of Lewis's wittiest prose; but Elmer himself in the final stages of his progress towards the dictatorship of world morality so conclusively disappears into caricature that he ends as an almost medieval illustration of lechery and hypocrisy incarnate.

The attitudes expressed in the three novels examined here would suggest that of the two types of pastoral impulse discerned by Leo Marx Lewis was closer to the popular variety than to that higher, complex pastoralism that distinguishes much American literature. Indeed, in *Arrowsmith*, an excessively schematized variant on the quest theme, the response produced by the closing pages is one of em-barrassment at the simplistic solution and the sentimentality of the prose in which it is expressed. Similarly in both *Main Street* and *Dodsworth* the final resolutions in terms of idealized landscape are uneasy and, ultimately, unconvincing. The resonance that we associate with the genuine work of art is present only in *Babbitt* where Lewis develops the interior landscape of wonder. In these novels the drama is mute; that 'capacity for moral heroism' commemorated by nine-teenth-century American authors is here reduced to the act of dissocia-tion as the self seeks an identity in and commensurate with urban society. A similar search is reflected in Lewis's own paradigmatic life. The hotel rooms and rented houses of two continents suggest that the most permanent form of dissociation is to be found not in his writings but in Sinclair Lewis himself.

Note

Life and Writing

Anderson was born in Camden, Ohio, in 1876. The family, dogged by his father's business failures, moved from one small town to another, finally settling at Clyde, Ohio, in 1884. Anderson's youth was deeply marked by his mother's early death in 1895, and by ambivalent feelings towards his father. He left high school without graduating, and did a variety of odd jobs at Clyde, before leaving for Chicago in 1896, where he worked in a factory. He served briefly in the Spanish-American War in Cuba, without seeing action. On his return, he became an advertising copy-writer, and was soon contributing inspirational articles about business to *Agricultural Advertising*. In 1904, he married the daughter of a wealthy Ohio businessman. He began to write poetry and fiction, and the conflict between these activities and his business responsibilities came to a head in 1912, when he suffered a mental collapse which entirely altered his life. He abandoned his business interests, left his wife, and settled as a writer in Chicago. Gertrude Stein's work began to influence him greatly, and other Chicago writers such as Floyd Dell, Carl Sandburg, and Margaret Anderson became his friends.

His first novels, *Windy McPherson's Son* (1916) and *Marching Men* (1917), were followed by *Winesburg, Ohio* (1919) which established him as a leading writer of the day. This was followed by three further short story collections, *The Triumph of the Egg* (1921), *Horses and Men* (1923), and *Death in the Woods* (1933), and a number of novels: *Poor White* (1920) which is by far the best, *Many Marriages* (1923), *Dark Laughter* (1925), *Beyond Desire* (1932) and *Kit Brandon* (1936). His autobiographical works, of which *A Story-Teller's Story* (1924), *Tar* (1924), and *Sherwood Anderson's Memoirs* (posthumous, 1942) are the most important, are extensions of the art of story-telling rather than attempt to tell the unvarnished truth. There is a selection of the *Letters of Sherwood Anderson*, edited by Howard Mumford Jones and Walter B. Rideout (Boston, 1953).

Anderson was at the height of his fame in the early nineteen twenties, when he exerted a decisive influence over such writers as Hemingway, Faulkner and Dos Passos. At this time he and his second wife lived in New Orleans and travelled extensively on the Continent. Once the initial impact of his work had worn off, however, his reputation declined sharply, and he died in almost complete neglect in 1941. Much of his work remains scattered in periodicals, although some of this material was collected in *The Sherwood Anderson Reader* edited by Paul Rosenfeld (Boston, 1947). There are a number of American editions of *Winesburg, Ohio* and *Poor White*, but most of Anderson's work is out of print and hard to obtain. *Sherwood Anderson: Short Stories* edited by Maxwell Geismar (Hill and Wang, New York, 1962) is however an excellent selection of stories from the four volumes (including the *Reader*) which followed *Winesburg, Ohio*.

Criticism. A good short general survey is provided by Brom Weber: *Sherwood Anderson, University of Minnesota Pamphlets in American Literature* 43 (Minnea-

V

Sherwood Anderson

BRIAN WAY

I

THE ELUSIVE quality of Sherwood Anderson's best work, and, equally, the vague incoherence of his worst, both reflect a writer caught at a moment of transition. He grew up in the last years of the nineteenth century, and his first major work *Winesburg, Ohio* (1919) was a seminal influence on the new literature of the nineteen twenties. In these years when Anderson's artistic consciousness was growing towards maturity, both American society and American literature were undergoing the most fundamental changes that had occurred since the early national period. Anderson lived through the industrialization of the mid-West, one of the most dramatic phases in the shift from a predominantly rural to a mainly urban civilization. He saw puritanism degenerate into the business ethic. As an advertising copy-writer and journalist, he was forced to participate in the first large-scale debasement of American popular culture by the mass media. And as an artist he helped to bring about both the first sexual revolution and the rejection of the genteel tradition in American literature. He experienced that painful emergence from a provincial consciousness which one also sees in Gertrude Stein, Carl Sandburg, Sinclair Lewis and Willa Cather.

The peculiar interest of Anderson's case is that, where his contemporaries usually felt themselves forced to make choices—to uphold a tradition, like Edith Wharton, or to demand a new American literature, like William Carlos Williams—he made the atmosphere of transition itself his subject and his concern. He examined American

polis, 1964), and there are stimulating essays by Lionel Trilling in *The Liberal Imagination* (London, 1951), and by Maxwell Geismar in *The Last of the Provincials* (Boston, 1949). Useful full-length studies are Irving Howe: *Sherwood Anderson* (New York, 1951), James Schevill: *Sherwood Anderson: His Life and Work* (Denver, 1951), and *The Achievement of Sherwood Anderson* edited by Ray Lewis (Chapel Hill, 1966).

civilization in the process of transforming itself almost out of recognition, and he scrutinized himself in order to understand what was happening to the American consciousness. He tried, through a subtle art of evocation and suggestion, to convey the loneliness, the confusion, the anxieties, the sense of liberation and the sense of loss experienced by the emergent American provincial.

Although there has been a more adequate sense recently of Anderson's true worth, his reputation still suffers from two misconceptions. He is too often thought of merely as a historical landmark and an influence on other writers, and, even by those who concede his intrinsic merits, he tends to be treated as a one-book writer. I shall try to meet the first objection through a study of his best work. For the second, I hope it will become apparent that, fine as *Winesburg, Ohio* is, he continued to develop, and such stories as 'Unlighted Lamps', 'The Sad Horn-Blowers', and 'Death in the Woods', are better than anything in his first collection. What matters most is, not that he was a vital influence on Hemingway, Faulkner, Dos Passos, Nathanael West, Flannery O'Connor, and Malamud, but that he is one of the great masters of the American short story.

II

Anderson's imaginative sympathies are most deeply aroused by the loneliness of provincial Americans. Often, such people are lonely because they are inarticulate: they fail to communicate even with those they love, at bottom, perhaps, because of a characteristic American fear of betraying personal feeling, Anglo-Saxon and puritan in its cultural roots. The character-narrator of 'The Man Who Became a Woman' (*Horses and Men*) says of his closest friend—

> To tell the truth, I suppose I got to love Tom Means, who was five years older than me, although I wouldn't have dared say so then. Americans are shy and timid about saying things like that, and a man here don't dare own up he likes another man, I've found out, and they are afraid to admit such feelings to themselves even. I guess they're afraid it may be taken to mean something it don't need to at all.

Such inhibitions have bred a culture in which the people have no vocabulary for communicating with each other or for analysing themselves.

Anderson's great book of loneliness is *Winesburg, Ohio*. It has an artistic unity not possessed by any of his other works, partly because of this central theme linking the stories, and partly through the character of George Willard. George grows into maturity by dis-covering loneliness—his own, and that of the people around him. Early in the book, Anderson's stress is on the isolation his characters already experience in the rural small-town mid-West, but by the end it becomes clear that this society is itself breaking up. Everyone in Winesburg takes it for granted that an active young man must go away if he is to make anything of his life. In the last story 'Departure', George leaves home: he must sever even the slender connections he has, and try to find himself in exile—in the double loneliness of the big city.

He is the town's newspaper reporter, and at first sight this would seem to put him in touch with everything that happens. People even tell him their life-stories, feeling that a newspaperman's interest, factitious as it is, is preferable to the general indifference. All this apparent contact, however, leaves him somewhat in the position of Whitman's noiseless patient spider, spinning filament out of itself, making fragile connections with distant points in the vacant vast sur-rounding, but remaining, nevertheless, on its little promontory, isolated.

One of the simplest and most poignant tales in *Winesburg, Ohio* is 'Mother'. Elizabeth Willard has been a woman of beauty and imagina-tion in her youth, but now she has sunk into a drab middle age, weakened by illness, neglected by her husband, and out of touch with her son. An index of the terrible futility of her life is given by the savage battles she is forced to watch from her window, between Abner Groff the baker and a grey alley-cat which tries to slink in at the back of his store. She has become a kind of mid-Western Emma Bovary, driven half-mad by suppressed passions and thwarted creative impulses. One evening, she overhears her husband urging George to 'wake up' and embark on a business career. She is filled with overwhelming rage and hatred for the man who she feels has stifled her own life, and now threatens her son. Before she got married she had wanted to be an actress, and she determines to murder her husband in the grand tragic manner of a Lady Macbeth or Tosca. But she finds she does not have the strength for this role, and, in conversation with George a few minutes later, finds herself helplessly repeating the platitudes that had made her want to kill her husband. Her tragedy is not merely that she has been unable to live her own life, but that she cannot tell her son about her failure, so that he may perhaps avoid it.

Elizabeth Willard's loneliness is due primarily to her inarticulateness: she does not have a language in which she can express her deepest feelings, or communicate with those she cares for most. It is also caused by the complete suppression of any kind of creative or imaginative life. The important point here is not that the world may have lost a great actress, but that Elizabeth Willard herself has never been given the opportunity to find out what she is capable of. Her imagination, which might have enriched her life, is driven underground where it breeds pitiful and self-destructive fantasies, like her plan to stab Tom Willard with a pair of sewing scissors. Almost all the stories in *Winesburg, Ohio* are explorations of one or other of these insights into the nature of loneliness.

In 'Adventure', Anderson is particularly successful in finding ways of evoking the isolation caused by failures to communicate. Alice Hindman has been deserted by her lover, but she goes on imagining that one day he will write to her. She takes a job in a dry-goods store, where she lives like Bartleby in a kind of dead-letter office of her own. Eventually she realizes her lover will never send for her, and one fall night, distracted by loneliness and frustrated sexual desire, she undresses and runs out into the rain, trying to speak to the world through her naked body. But when an old man passes in the street, she realizes that even that language will not speak in a society starved of the natural responses to sex and the body.

Alice Hindman is one of many of Anderson's characters whose loneliness is made unbearable by the ways in which a puritan society obstructs the expression, and even the understanding, of sexual desire. One of the finest of such stories is 'The Untold Lie'. In it Anderson examines not only what is restrictive and life-denying, but also what is worthwhile in the provincial mid-West puritan tradition. The conflict is explored partly through the contrasting figures of two farmhands, and partly through the way in which each is trying to resolve a difficulty in his own mind. Ray Pearson is middle-aged and tamed—harnessed to a life of toil, a nagging wife and half-a-dozen children. His friend Hal Winters is young, strong, and free—a fighter, a drinker, a woman-chaser, an unbroken man. As they are husking corn one day, Hal suddenly asks the older man for advice. He has got a girl into trouble, and is trying to decide whether to marry her or remain free. Ray is profoundly disturbed, and, unable to answer, walks away. According to all Ray's moral training, Hal should marry the girl, but the beauty of the fall day has made him restless, and he broods rebelliously over the imprisonment of his own marriage.

Anderson presents the conflict from another point of view through the story of Hal's father, Windpeter Winters. He was an unbroken man to the last: he was killed one night driving home along the railroad tracks, forcing his team deliberately into the path of an oncoming locomotive. His kind of freedom is crazily self-destructive, and yet the boys of the village see a wild and flamboyant colour in his drunken courage which they do not find in the slow ageing and decline of ordinary people.

When Ray gets home, his shrill wife nags him intolerably. He goes out and runs across the fields to tell Hal to stay free, but by the time he overtakes him he has begun to remember other things—pleasant evenings spent by the stove with his children. Whatever advice he gives Hal will be a lie, and since he cannot resolve the conflict in his mind he is forced to remain silent.

In two rather weak stories—'An Awakening' and ' "Queer" '—this inarticulateness produces physical violence. Ed Handby, the lover, and Elmer Cowley, the would-be normal and well-integrated young man, try to make up for their lack of words by using their fists. Much of the violence described in American literature can be traced to this source: it has led to the creation of characters as different as Billy Budd and Joe Christmas.

These failures in communication, which take away so many of the satisfactions of life, are especially destructive for the artist, and it is significant that the story in *Winesburg, Ohio* which actually bears the title 'Loneliness' is about a painter. Enoch Robinson goes to live in New York, where other artists admire his pictures and become his friends. But when they discuss his work, he finds that he has not succeeded in communicating what he feels. When his New York friends look at his Ohio landscapes, and talk 'about line and values and composition', he wants to tell them:

'. . . the picture you see doesn't consist of the things you see and say words about. There is something else, something you don't see at all, something you aren't intended to see. . . . The dark spot by the road that you might not notice at all is, you see, the beginning of everything. There is a clump of elders there such as used to grow beside the road before our house back in Winesburg, Ohio, and in among the elders there is something hidden. It is a woman, that's what it is. She has been thrown from a horse and the horse has run away out of sight. Do you not see how the old man who drives a cart looks anxiously about? That is Thad Grayback who has a farm up the road. He is taking corn to Winesburg to be ground into meal at Comstock's mill. He knows there is something in the elders, something hidden away, and yet he doesn't quite know.

'It's a woman you see, that is what it is! It's a woman and, oh, she is lovely! She is hurt and is suffering but she makes no sound. Don't you see how it is? She lies quite still, white and still, and the beauty comes out from her and spreads over everything. It is in the sky back there and all around everywhere. I didn't try to paint the woman, of course. She is too beautiful to be painted. How dull to talk of composition and such things! Why do you not look at the sky and then run away as I used to do when I was a boy back there in Winesburg, Ohio?'

'Loneliness' is a poor story, and this passage has a strained, vague quality which reflects Anderson's difficulties as much as Enoch Robinson's. The sense of insurmountable difficulties is precisely what makes it interesting, however. This kind of art involves its creator in an intense effort to realize and define what he knows best. Enoch Robinson feels it is vitally necessary to 'place' the clump of elders, the farmer, the mill where he is taking his corn. Still more important is his desperate assertion that a buried world of inexpressible beauty and suffering is, like the injured woman, hidden in this unspectacular rural scene. This is what Enoch Robinson is trying to say, but his friends see only agreeable provincial landscapes and genre paintings. In view of what Anderson himself was trying to do, it is impossible not to see this passage as a piece of disguised self-analysis.

There are several other tales in *Winesburg, Ohio* which, although they are not specifically about artists, explore similar situations. In 'Hands', 'Paper Pills' and 'Respectability', we are shown sensitive natures, creative minds, fine impulses, hidden in personalities which are, on the surface, eccentric, grotesque or repellent. A sentence from 'Paper Pills' epitomizes what Anderson feels about such people: 'Winesburg had forgotten the old man, but in Doctor Reefy there were the seeds of something very fine.' All three are among Anderson's best stories, but 'Paper Pills' has particular distinction as a work of art because of the poetic richness of the image he uses to suggest the sweetness of what is hidden in Doctor Reefy:

> The story of Doctor Reefy and his courtship of the tall dark girl who became his wife and left her money to him is a very curious story. It is delicious, like the twisted little apples which grow in the orchards of Winesburg. In the fall one walks in the orchards and the ground is hard with frost underfoot. The apples have been taken from the trees by the pickers. They have been put in barrels and shipped to the cities . . . On the trees are only a few gnarled apples that the pickers have rejected. They look like the knuckles of Doctor Reefy's hands. One nibbles at them and they are delicious. Into a little round place at the side of the apple has been gathered all of its sweetness. One runs from tree to tree over the frosted ground picking the gnarled, twisted apples and filling his pockets with them. Only the few know the sweetness of the twisted apples.

The most remarkable of Anderson's stories of loneliness is 'Unlighted Lamps', which appeared in his second collection, *The Triumph of the Egg* (1921). It is a much longer story than any I have discussed so far— structurally more complex, and formally more satisfying. Doctor Cochran and his eighteen-year-old daughter Mary, both find it impossible to express their feelings for each other, or for anyone else. The Doctor's wife left him when Mary was an infant, believing him to be a cold, silent man incapable of love, whereas he was in fact passionately attached to her.

When the story opens, he has just told Mary that he may die of heart failure at any time. Under this threat, both are forced to reflect on their relationship and on the meaning of their lives. Mary is confused not only by the thought of how little her father has seemed to care for her, but by her own sexual maturing and awakening—a deepened longing for the love and the warm physical contact she has never known. The town she lives in is changing too, rapidly becoming an industrial centre with a cosmopolitan immigrant population. She finds the Italian families who have moved in with the new factory more congenial than the older rural Anglo-Saxon community, which had always looked askance at her because of the scandal of her mother's departure. She has divided feelings even about her father's death since, although she loves him, she knows that when he dies she will be free to go to Chicago. Doctor Cochran reflects on the past—the failure of his marriage and of his relationship with Mary. The subtle

H

alternations in point of view between these parallel trains of thought point to a technical mastery rare in Anderson's work. The story has a density of texture, too, which he does not often achieve: images, scraps of significant detail, fragments of conversation, apparently random memories, and casual encounters, are all fused into a complex poetic structure. It is striking how much his method sometimes resembles Chekhov's and, given the latter's immense superiority as an artist and all the obvious national differences, both are often concerned with remarkably similar situations: human creativity and sensitivity buried, undiscovered or paralysed, in a vast backward uncivilized land about to stumble into the twentieth century.

As in 'Paper Pills', however, it is the presence of a powerfully suggestive central image which does most for the story's success. Anderson associates moments in the Doctor's life when his feelings struggle close to the barriers of expression with transitory gleams of flickering light. One evening, as the Doctor sits in his darkened office, he imagines he hears a woman rustling in the doorway, and calls out, uncertain in his strange mood whether it is Mary or his long-departed wife. At that moment a farmer comes to fetch him, and strikes a match to see whether he is there. Startled by the Doctor's voice, he lets the match fall to the floor, where it burns feebly, throwing a grotesque light upward on his legs. Doctor Cochran is reminded of a stronger, more beautiful light, which flickered briefly into life many years earlier. His wife, who was trying to furnish their apartment, had been given a quaint old mirror at a farm they were visiting. As they drove back through the country, she told her husband that she was pregnant:

> The mirror on his knees caught the rays of the departing sun and sent a great ball of golden light dancing across the fields and among the branches of trees. Now as he stood in the presence of the farmer and as the little light from the burning match on the floor recalled that other evening of dancing lights, he thought he understood the failure of his marriage and of his life. On that evening long ago when Ellen had told him of the coming of the great adventure of their marriage, he had remained silent because he had thought no words he could utter could express what he felt. There had been a defense for himself built up. 'I told myself she should have understood without words and I've all my life been telling myself the same thing about Mary. I've been a fool and a coward. I've always been silent

because I've been afraid of expressing myself—like a blundering
fool. I've been a proud man and a coward.

'Tonight I'll do it. If it kills me I'll talk to the girl.'

But this impulse is defeated as all the others have been. Late that night
when Doctor Cochran returns exhausted from delivering a child, his
heart stops at the very moment when he is trying to collect his confused thoughts to speak to Mary. The light from a forgotten cigarette
in a bystander's hand dances up and down in the darkness over his
dead body.

III

Judge Turner, in the autobiographical volume *A Story-Teller's Story*
(1924), sums up the qualities of the people in his Ohio home-town in
terms which could well speak for Anderson himself:

> 'We are what we are, we Americans, . . . and we had better stick
> to our knitting. Anyway, . . . people are nice here as far as I have
> been able to observe and although they are filled with stupid preju-
> dices and are fools, the common people, workers and the like, such
> as the men of this town, wherever you find them, are about the nicest
> folk one ever finds.'

Anderson's feelings about the mid-West are highly ambivalent. On
the one hand it is home: it gives him a warm sense of people he knows
and understands intimately, and, at a deeper level, it is, as we saw in
the story of Enoch Robinson, the source of all his deepest insights
as an artist. On the other hand, it is a place where life is intolerably
narrow and restricted, and where the niceness praised by Judge Turner
is balanced by a strong undercurrent of cruelty. This expresses itself
through gossip, vicious practical jokes, and the systematic persecution
of those who do not belong to the herd. Anderson exposes these shortcomings unsparingly in 'Nobody Laughed' and 'Morning Roll Call'
(both from *The Sherwood Anderson Reader*), and in certain episodes
of *Poor White*. Sensitive men and women like George Willard and
Mary Cochran must leave if they can, otherwise they will be warped
and imprisoned like Wash Williams, the central character of 'Respectability', whose grotesque appearance cuts him off from other people
as completely as if he were a hideous monkey in a cage.

For Anderson, however, the mid-West is not solely a background for his characters, nor even a set of conditions which helps to shape their lives. Like so many American novelists—Cooper, Hawthorne, Hamlin Garland, Willa Cather, Edith Wharton, Faulkner, Steinbeck, Wright Morris—he has a developed historical sense, and his work often reflects the broad pattern of evolution and disintegration to be seen in American provincial life. The parts of 'Godliness' (*Winesburg, Ohio*) which deal with Jesse Bentley, and the novel *Poor White*, are outstandingly good examples of this kind of writing.

In Jesse Bentley, the fanaticism of the American protestant tradition and nineteenth-century economic individualism combine to produce a diseased restlessness of spirit:

> Jesse Bentley was a fanatic. He was a man born out of his time and place and for this he suffered and made others suffer. Never did he succeed in getting what he wanted out of life and he did not know what he wanted.

At first, in the post-Civil War years, Jesse sees himself as a primitive patriarch, an Old Testament man of God owning flocks and lands like his biblical namesake. In exalted moods he is convinced that in acquiring more land he is fulfilling God's special plan, since the other farmers of the valley are Philistines who must be driven out, as David the son of Jesse drove the Philistines of his day from the Valley of Elah. But as the pressure of industrialism comes to Ohio he gradually loses this grandiose primitive vision, and begins to dream of fortunes to be made by 'shrewd men who bought and sold':

> Faintly he realized that the atmosphere of old times and places that he had always cultivated in his own mind was strange and foreign to the thing that was growing up in the minds of others. The beginning of the most materialistic age in the history of the world, when wars would be fought without patriotism, when men would forget God and only pay attention to moral standards, when the will to power would replace the will to serve and beauty would be well-nigh forgotten in the terrible headlong rush of mankind toward the acquiring of possessions, was telling its story to Jesse the man of God as it was to the men about him.

Anderson's treatment of the development of Jesse Bentley reflects very strongly the dilemma of the American who sees his country emerging from puritanism. He feels that in many ways American puritanism is hateful, cruel, bigoted and narrowing, and that an escape from it is spiritually necessary. Nevertheless, he finds that the American road away from puritanism does not lead to liberation and a better life, but to materialism, impoverishment of spirit and a loss of human dignity. Jesse, instead of being imbued with the language of the Bible and the exalted if warped imaginings it once aroused in him, becomes obsessed merely with the vulgar commercialism of the provincial newspapers and business magazines which begin to circulate with the coming of industry.

Similarly Hawthorne had observed seventy years earlier that, while the New England of Hester Prynne's day was a cruel and detestable society, it also contained a grandeur lacking in the 'exhausted soil' of the Salem of his own day; and that the savagely heroic figure of the brutal, witch-hunting Colonel Pyncheon had been replaced by the contemptibly furtive, hypocritical and corrupt Judge Pyncheon.

Anderson explores this phase of historical development in America on a much larger scale in *Poor White* (1920). Although he attempted the full-length novel a number of times, this is the only one in which he achieved a convincing artistic success. Even so it has serious weaknesses, and any claim one makes for it must rest largely on the first seven chapters.

In part, it is the story of what might have happened to Huck Finn if he had been 'sivilized', and thrown into the ferment of the Gilded Age. Hugh McVey grows up in a squalid little Mississippi river-town, like those Huck passes through in the company of the King and the Duke. Hugh's father is a drunken loafer like Pap, though without the latter's streak of manic violence. Anderson's attitude to Hugh's poor White heritage of 'bad blood' and indolence is divided: he is clearly repelled by the filth and squalor, and the mindless ignorance it represents, and yet at the same time he is aware of a certain richness and expansiveness in Hugh's loafing, day after day, on the banks of the immense river. When the railroad reaches Hugh's home-town, he gets a job at the station, and Sarah Shepard the station-master's wife takes him in hand. She is a New England woman—the puritan tradition personified—and she makes Hugh clean, industrious, restless and ambitious. His imaginative life is eliminated along with his idling, and he moves away from the stagnating river life to the Ohio town of Bidwell. At first there appears to be some compensatory gain: it is in his new way of life, his struggle to acquire a new identity—a puritan identity—,that Hugh finds the drive which makes him an inventor, a creative mind. His invention of a machine for planting cabbages gives Bidwell its first factory and initiates a rapid industrial growth. But Hugh has to pay for this new creativity by losing all spontaneity of response. His imaginative life had been closely linked with the life of the senses—the luxurious, almost sensual, indolence of his drowsing and daydreaming on the Mississippi shore—and when he loses this, not only is his inner life impoverished, but he is cut off from other people. He is socially isolated, he has no friends, and his capacity for love or any kind of sexual relationship is atrophied. In the long run the fiasco of his marriage with Clara Butterworth can be put down to this deprivation.

The second strand in his destruction is the industrialization he himself has done so much to bring about. The greed of his rich father-in-law Tom Butterworth (a debased version of Jesse Bentley) finally destroys the very creativity—the inventiveness—liberated in Hugh by the puritan tradition. Towards the end of the novel we find that his latest invention—a hay-loader—has been forestalled by the work of another inventor in Iowa. Tom Butterworth, having found that the other man has no financial backing, sets Hugh to modify his design so that they can get round the patent. Hugh finds he is unable to work in the climate created by this swindle. His imagination partially re-awakens: he finds himself picturing the inventor he has been told to cheat, instead of setting his mind to the mechanical problem he has been told to solve. But his imagination is not awakened in a way that helps him to re-order his life: he cannot create a relationship with his wife, but can only come to her intermittently like an animal in the dark for sexual relief. At the end he seems to regress into a kind of mindless dreaminess, playing for hours with a few coloured stones. There is a dim reflection of the days of brooding by the Mississippi, but with none of the richness, the expansiveness, the sensuous ease, of that earlier time.

It is clear from the story of Hugh McVey that Anderson takes an extremely pessimistic view of what American civilization, during the phase of industrialization, has done to many individual Americans. But there are a number of places in which he takes a wider perspective, and tries to evoke the more general qualitative changes which took place in the life of the rural and small-town communities of the mid-West. In spite of their narrowness and provincial isolation, these communities, in the last years of the nineteenth century, had begun to mature into a distinct and valuable phase of American civilization:

> In all the towns of mid-western America it was a time of waiting. The country having been cleared and the Indians driven away into a vast distant place spoken of vaguely as the West, the Civil War having been fought and won, and there being no great problems that touched deeply their lives, the minds of men were turned in upon themselves. . . . For the moment mankind seemed about to take time to try to understand itself. (chapter 3)

Anderson evokes the slow settling and maturing process which had led to this moment in chapter 7, where he describes the small frame-houses built by the Ohio farmers on their land:

> After one of the poor little houses had been lived in for a long time, after children had been born and men had died, after men and women had suffered and had moments of joy together in the tiny rooms under the low roofs a subtle change took place. The houses became almost beautiful in their old humanness. Each of the houses began vaguely to shadow forth the personality of the people who lived within its walls.

The mid-West pioneer farming community was on the verge of becoming a civilization but, at that moment, instead of a slow flowering into a life of amenity which the old farming life had largely lacked, industry struck the mid-West a paralysing blow which destroyed all human values—even the little the farming and small-town communities had already achieved:

> A sense of quiet growth awoke in sleeping minds. It was the time for art and beauty to awake in the land.
> Instead, the giant, Industry, awoke. Boys, who in the schools had read of Lincoln walking for miles through the forest to borrow his first book, and of Garfield, the towpath boy who became president, began to read in the newspapers and magazines of men who by developing their faculty for getting and keeping money had become suddenly and overwhelmingly rich. Hired writers called these men great, and there was no maturity of mind in the people with which to combat the force of the statement often repeated.

Interesting as this explicit analysis is, the success of *Poor White* depends on Anderson's power to present his vision through the creation of scene and character. One of the finest of these is the scene in which Hugh McVey gets his idea for a cabbage plant-setting machine. He watches, himself unobserved, while old Ezra French and his family plant cabbages by moonlight, crawling over the ground in an extravagant demonstration of the crushing burden of physical labour. In a flash of intuition, the principle of the invention comes to him. Wildly excited, he forgets where he is, rises to his feet, and begins to follow the crawling figures down the rows, miming the action of the revolving mechanical arms which will set the plants in the soil. When the French sons and daughters turn at the ends of their rows and see Hugh advancing on them, they flee in terror. Their life is earthbound, crude, grotesque, and yet there is a strange poetry in the workings of a folk-imagination which sees in Hugh's gesticulating figure the ghost of a redskin, risen from the Indian burying-ground which lies beneath the field, to haunt the paleface intruders.

IV

It is very difficult indeed to make a fair and balanced assessment of Anderson as an artist. Generally speaking, he has been disparaged and neglected, but it is equally easy, by discussing his best stories as if they were representative of his work, to imply that his stature is greater than it really is. The bulk of his work is characterized by extremes of foolishness, sentimentality and technical incompetence, and it is as important to account for these deficiencies as to analyse his handful of masterpieces, if one is to come to any worthwhile conclusions about the kind of writer he is.

Even before one begins to look for deeper sources of weakness, one becomes aware of his extremely shaky grasp of matters of craft and fictional technique. Clumsy changes in point of view destroy the overall coherence of *Poor White*. He is consistently unable to write good dialogue. This largely explains why he so rarely succeeds in writing scenes, or developing a situation through the complex interplay of characters, but is forced to rely heavily on description and poetic evocation. It also accounts for his inability to handle vernacular first-person narration in the manner of Mark Twain. One sees this particularly in such horse-racing stories as 'I Want to Know Why' (*The Triumph of the Egg*) and 'I'm a Fool' (*Horses and Men*), where the method produces the flat stereotyped effect of Ring Lardner's weaker tales, rather than the flexibility, irony and poetic richness of Melville and Twain.

His range is narrow: all the good writing, without exception, is drawn from the rural, small-town America he grew up in. The would-be satirical-psychological stories of urban middle-class life—'The Triumph of a Modern or, Send for the Lawyer' (*Horses and Men*), or 'There She Is—She Is Taking Her Bath' (*Death in the Woods*), for instance—are as complicated and ingenious as a rat-trap, and equally far from being works of art. In other tales of the city—particularly those dealing with artists and writers—he sometimes tries to manipulate a few generalized observations on life into a story by the rather feeble device of reminiscence. The opening of 'Milk Bottles' (*Horses and Men*) is an almost perfect demonstration of how not to begin a story: 'I lived during that summer in a large room on the top floor of an old house. . . .' The materials of the story which follows remain at the level of general ruminations on life which have not attained fictional form.

The unsatisfactory nature of stories like 'Milk Bottles' points not only to a failure of artistic form but to a lack of adequate subject matter. Indeed the absence of form is often directly caused by deficiencies in situation, action, concrete detail and intelligible analysis. The transcendental element in Anderson's work is responsible for much of this bad writing. As well as showing certain strengths that suggest the influence of Whitman, he has characteristic weaknesses that come from the same source. He tends to lose himself in ecstatic tenuities, moments in life for which he claims some great spiritual, emotional, or poetic intensity, but at which nothing clearly demonstrable happens. The closing stories of *Winesburg, Ohio* —'Death', and particularly 'Sophistication' and 'Departure'—show this weakness. We are constantly told that there is something very significant and profound about the feelings of George Willard and Helen White, but we are not told what their feelings are. The worst fiction—*Dark Laughter* and such fragments of abandoned novels as *An Ohio Pagan* (*Horses and Men*)—are full of inflated pseudo-poetic nonsense which, from a literary point of view, fully deserved Hemingway's parody in *The Torrents of Spring*, whatever light it casts on his capacity for gratitude or friendship. One is reminded in such work of the spiritual intensities of the later Whitman, the slightly suspect quality of the religious poetry written after 1870—even of a poem as fine as 'Passage to India'.

Sometimes, even when Anderson has a situation with all the potentialities of fictional form latent in it, he fails by not trusting his own tale. In 'The Other Woman' (*The Triumph of the Egg*), 'Brother Death' (*Death in the Woods*), and 'Daughters' (*The Sherwood Anderson Reader*), he intrudes clumsily, editorializing each incident and each piece of description. 'Brother Death' contains a particularly good central fictional situation—the cluster of tensions in a wealthy Virginia farmer's family which are brought to a point of crisis by the father's determination to fell two splendid trees. His elder son Don walks off the farm in protest. When Don return a few days later, he has a brief conversation with his father which is completely self-explanatory. Anderson, however, seems to feel he has not made himself clear: introducing the question 'What had the father meant?', he proceeds to a clumsy paraphrase of the original brief exchange, which is not only inartistic, but adds little in the way of understanding. He does not tell the story so that it carries its meaning entirely within itself, nor does he develop any of those subtler forms of commentary and authorial intervention of which James was so great a master.

This last observation underlines the formidable difficulties Anderson faced in trying to master the problem of fictional form. Nothing in earlier American literature could help him very much in giving artistic expression to the range of feelings and the area of American life which preoccupied him most, and this had more to do with his rejection of the genteel tradition than the flamboyant streak of anti-intellectualism which he sometimes indulged. He made what use he could of certain poetic patterns in Whitman, and he learned from foreign writers—particularly from Turgenev's *A Sportsman's Diary*—but in general his work represents an astonishing effort of innovation and discovery. This is why Faulkner said:

> He was the father of my generation of American writers and the tradition of American writing which our successors will carry on. He has never received his proper evaluation.[1]

Under the circumstances it is the measure of Anderson's success, and not the fact that he often failed, which should be emphasized.

His best stories are the ones of rural American life, in which the

---

[1] *Writers at Work* edited by Malcolm Cowley (London, 1962), p. 122. (Faulkner made the statement when he was interviewed for *The Paris Review* by Jean Stein.)

main character is usually a solitary obsessed individual in a pictorial frame, and the centre of consciousness a sensitive local observer like George Willard, or the anonymous, sympathetic 'I' of 'The Egg' and 'Death in the Woods'. Alternatively, Anderson may use the mode of quiet sensitive impersonal narration we find in 'Unlighted Lamps' and *Poor White*. When he uses either of these narrative methods, he is able to draw on a number of strengths that were denied to him in other short-story forms. He can convey that sense of intimately known persons and events, the sense of a community lived through and experienced at first hand, which is essential to these poignant nostalgic tales of a vanished way of life. While possessing this advantage, he is not limited to the lack of self-knowledge and the inarticulateness which contribute so much to the loneliness and misery of his characters, but can give full play to his gifts for poetic evocation and perceptive analysis. Again, he is able to make use of his deep apprehension of history, to place his characters in a broad social and historical perspective, so that even a figure as grotesque as Jesse Bentley, has a grandeur, a force of generality, which prevents its seeming merely odd.

I have already tried to show in discussions of 'Paper Pills' and 'Unlighted Lamps' how successful Anderson can be in using a poetic image, but in two of his later stories—'The Corn Planting' (1934—*The Sherwood Anderson Reader* 1947) and 'Death in the Woods'—we find an even more sophisticated kind of poetic evocation, a patterning which reminds us strongly of how much he owed to Whitman. 'The Corn Planting' is the most lyrically beautiful story he ever wrote, and its freshness of response recalls some of Whitman's early poems—'There Was a Child Went Forth' and parts of 'Song of Myself'. The old Hutchenson couple learn in the late hours of a moonlit spring night of the death of their son—a son born to them in their old age who, up to his death, has fulfilled all their hopes for him. A friend of the dead son, and the quiet, self-effacing narrator, have walked out from town to tell the parents of their loss. The father receives the news in silence, closing the door in their faces. They wait in the road, unable to leave the spot. Presently, they see the old couple, two nightgowned figures, cross from the house to the barn, and then re-emerging into the moonlight, enter a newly ploughed and harrowed field and begin seeding it with corn. At the end of each row they kneel and pray:

> It was the first time in my life that I ever understood something, and I am far from sure now that I can put down what I understood

and felt that night—I mean something about the connection between certain people and the earth—a kind of silent cry, down into the earth. It was as though they were putting death down into the ground that life might grow again—something like that.

The pattern of the story closely resembles that of certain of Whitman's dealing with death: section six of 'Song of Myself', 'Out of the Cradle Endlessly Rocking', and 'When Lilacs Last in the Dooryard Bloom'd'. Anderson's story and Whitman's poems begin with an affirmation of the beauty of nature; then there is a recoil into despondency as the thought of death presses on the consciousness; and finally a movement of recovery—a new vision of life as a never-ending cycle which includes death and re-birth—brings the work to a close.

'Death in the Woods' (1933) includes some different but equally striking Whitmanesque elements. Unlike 'The Corn Planting', it has a very strong narrative line, but counterpointing this there is a complex structure of images, which has marked analogies with certain forms of musical composition. It is the story of a bent old woman who lives on an isolated farm outside an Ohio town. Everyone knows her by sight, because she comes into town regularly to trade a few eggs and vegetables for food for her menfolk and meat for their dogs, but no one really knows her at all. Her life is one of utter misery, and always has been:

> All her life she had given food to animals, to cows, to chickens, to pigs, to horses, to dogs, to men.

One snowy evening she is returning to the farm with a heavy bag of food on her shoulders and followed by several of the dogs, 'tall gaunt fellows'. She takes a short-cut through some woods and falls in the snow. Overcome with weakness she is unable to rise. As the dark comes on, the dogs begin to run silently in a circle before her, and when she is dead they tear the bag of food from her shoulders, ripping away most of her clothes as they do so. They eat the food, but they do not touch her dead body, and the search-party from town find her naked and frozen on the snowy ground in the moonlight:

> She did not look old, lying there in that light, frozen and still. One of the men turned her over in the snow and I saw everything. My body trembled with some strange mystical feeling and so did my brother's. It might have been the cold.
> Neither of us had ever seen a woman's body before. It may have

been the snow, clinging to the frozen flesh, that made it look so white and lovely, so like marble. No woman had come with the party from town, but one of the men, he was the town blacksmith, took off his overcoat and spread it over her. Then he gathered her into his arms and started off to town, all the others silently following. . . .

The many times repeated details of the story—the feeding of animals, the items of trade, the dogs, memories of brutal treatment the old woman had received in the past, the beauty of her naked body in the snow, the smooth circle the dogs make with their running—are woven by Anderson into a deeply moving fabric of savagery, suffering and a strange beauty. These images reverberate together like the images of lilac, star, and hermit-thrush in 'When Lilacs Last in the Dooryard Bloom'd'. The fact that Anderson has been able to create this poetic structure without impeding the narrative flow is, I feel, what makes 'Death in the Woods' his greatest story.

This highly conscious patterning of images, which suggests the poet as much as the novelist, is one of the main strands in his best work. The other is a method one associates more specifically with the writing of fiction—the remarkably sure control he sometimes gains over a set of elusive feelings. 'Unlighted Lamps' and 'The Untold Lie' have already been discussed as examples of this kind of success, but it is important to mention in addition the two stories in which Anderson tries to objectify and to analyse his contradictory feelings towards his father— 'The Egg' (*The Triumph of the Egg*) and 'The Sad Horn-Blowers' (*Horses and Men*, 1923). The latter, set alongside 'Death in the Woods', will serve admirably to conclude this attempt at a balanced view of Anderson's achievement.

Its central character, Will Appleton, is forced by his mother's death, an accident to his father, and his elder sister's impending marriage, into a recognition of his own isolation: like George Willard, he finds that growing up is a movement into loneliness. He has to leave the Ohio small town where he was born, to work in a factory at Erie, Pennsylvania. This movement from rural to industrial life is one thread in the pattern. Most important, however, and most successful, is the extraordinary sympathy with which Anderson conveys Will's ambivalent feelings towards his father. Will feels affection and a certain sense of comradeship developed in their work together on house-painting jobs. On the other hand, he has no illusions about his father's reliability as an economic provider, and is tormented by a keen sense of the latter's lack of dignity—his tendency to clown and to act 'like a kid'. These shortcomings are reflected in a number of episodes and recurring motifs. Most important from the point of view of plot is the foolish prank which leads to Tom Appleton's accident, when he stumbles and spills two great pots of scalding coffee over himself. Even when he is writhing and screaming on the ground, his neighbours imagine at first that he is playing some practical joke. His cornet-playing is the leading motif in the story, and gives it its title. He makes Will feel embarrassed and humiliated by parading foolishly down Main Street with the town band, and by playing badly—especially in the cornet solo passages.

The little old man who becomes Will's friend in Erie is another sad horn-blower. He had tried to leave his wife, who keeps the rooming-house where they both live, and become a professional cornet-player, but he was not good enough and has returned with his tail between his legs. At first he amuses and depresses Will, just as his father does, but gradually, through his own loneliness and unhappiness, Will's attitude begins to change. His own need of warmth, security and reassurance—a kind of 'childishness' which he discovers in himself— makes him realize that he was trying to measure his father by a criterion of manhood which, if not too harsh, is at any rate one he cannot live up to himself. He learns to accept the little old man and by implication his own father with new sympathy and understanding. In the last scene, in Will's bedroom at the boarding-house, the old man urges him to blow a loud defiant blast on the cornet, but Will produces only a few soft notes. He, too, is to be a sad horn-blower.

The muted atmosphere, the sad irony, the pessimistic self-knowledge, the unheroic hero uprooted and lonely—these are the qualities which account for the resurgence of interest in Anderson today. Welcome as any appreciation of his work is, it is to be hoped that he will not be taken up only in terms of the present facile cult of 'relevance'. He belongs very much to his own time and place, but he is at the farthest possible remove from being merely symptomatic even of them. He has written only a very little work of the highest quality, but what he has achieved is enough to give him a distinctive place in American literature.

Note

Life and writing

Fitzgerald was born in 1896 in St. Paul, Minnesota. The family was not wealthy—his father was a salesman for Proctor and Gamble—but a bequest enabled them to live comfortably. Fitzgerald was educated at the St. Paul Academy and subsequently the Newman School, a Catholic boarding school in New York. In 1913 he went to Princeton, his university years turning into a curious mixture of success and failure. His love affair with Ginevra King ended in crushing disappointment ('Poor boys shouldn't think of marrying rich girls,' he noted in his Ledger in 1916); his pursuit of personal popularity turned sour; his Princeton career was interrupted by poor health and worse grades, and ended when he received a commission as second lieutenant in the U.S. Army. On 20 March 1920 he married Zelda Sayre, from Montgomery, Alabama. Six days later his first book, *This Side of Paradise*, was published—an instant best-seller, selling nearly 50,000 copies by the end of the year. The popularity of its twenty-three-year-old author was enormous; he was offered an advance of $7,000 on the serial rights of a then unwritten second book, which appeared in 1922 as *The Beautiful and Damned*. Both were careless, exuberantly youthful books. But T. S. Eliot greeted his third novel, *The Great Gatsby* (1925), as 'the first step the American novel has taken since Henry James'. The ensuing years were increasingly difficult ones: his wife's mental condition deteriorated; his financial plight meant rigorous commitment to the production of profitable but artistically disappointing stories. With a drinking problem and a deepening sense of personal despair, he made repeated efforts to block out a fourth novel. Following Zelda's collapse in 1930, he helped edit her novel, *Save Me the Waltz* (New York, 1932; London 1953). He then completed his own book, *Tender Is the Night* (1934). Depressed by its reception (only 15,000 copies sold in the first year) and his own dissipation, he wrote for *Esquire* a series of confessional essays attempting to dissect his own sense of failure; these 'Crack-Up' essays he later described as a 'spiritual change of life'. Then followed an unhappy period in Hollywood, redeemed by the fact that, in 1937, he met and fell in love with Sheila Graham (see her *Beloved Infidel* and *College of One*) and that he collected material for his final novel, *The Last Tycoon*—still uncompleted at his death in December, 1940.

Four volumes of short stories appeared in his lifetime, *Flappers and Philosophers* (1920); *Tales of the Jazz Age* (1922); *All the Sad Young Men* (1926); *Taps at Reveille* (1935). In 1951 Malcolm Cowley edited *The Stories of F. Scott Fitzgerald*; Arthur Mizener published several previously uncollected stories and sketches in *Afternoon of an Author* (1957). His letters have been collected and published by Andrew Turnbull (1964).

Biography and Criticism.   Reappraisal of Fitzgerald's work began almost immediately with Edmund Wilson's introduction to *The Last Tycoon* in 1941, and Lionel Trilling's introduction to a new edition of *The Great Gatsby* (see also Trilling's *The Liberal Imagination*, New York, 1950). Arthur Mizener's biogra-

The Two Identities of F. Scott Fitzgerald

C. W. E. BIGSBY

I

IN *The Liberal Imagination* Lionel Trilling points out that 'in any culture there are likely to be certain artists who contain a large part of the dialectic within themselves . . . the very essence . . . the yes and no of their culture'.[1] This was especially true of F. Scott Fitzgerald, who confessed, in one of his *Esquire* pieces, that he could never understand why he had come to be identified with the objects of his horror. The truth was that, at least in his early years as a writer, he squandered his talent in order to finance the very excesses against which his puritanical soul rebelled. While he denounced a period which had little time for those not in a position to enjoy the joke, those who—like the three hungry men in Hart Crane's 'The Bridge'—are left behind by the glaring rush of the 'Twentieth Century', he was fatally attracted by the very thing he sought to expose. Rather like Amory Blaine, in his first novel, he felt that 'it isn't that I mind the glittering caste system . . . but

[1] Lionel Trilling, *The Liberal Imagination* (New York, 1953), p. 7.

---

phy, *The Far Side of Paradise* (1950) was reissued, expanded as *F. Scott Fitzgerald: a Biography and Critical Study* (London 1958). In 1951 Malcolm Cowley published a new text of *Tender is the Night*, making textual changes Fitzgerald had wanted.

There is a considerable body of Fitzgerald criticism, including a bound volume of the *Fitzgerald Newsletter* (Washington, 1969). There are two useful collections of essays: *F. Scott Fitzgerald* edited by Arthur Mizener (Englewood Cliffs, N.J., 1963), and *F. Scott Fitzgerald: The Man and His Work* edited by Alfred Kazin (New York, 1951). Basic works of criticism and reference are Andrew Turnbull's *Scott Fitzgerald* (London, 1962); Sergio Perosa's *The Art of F. Scott Fitzgerald* (Ann Arbor, 1965); Richard Lehan's *F. Scott Fitzgerald and the Craft of Fiction* (Carbondale, 1966); Robert Sklar's *F. Scott Fitzgerald: The Last Laocoon* (New York, 1967); Jackson Bryer's *The Critical Reputation of F. Scott Fitzgerald: a Bibliographical Study* (Hamden, Conn., 1967), and M. R. Stern, *The Golden Moment* (Urbana and London, 1971).

gosh . . . I've got to be one of them.' As he acquired greater wealth so he compensated by adopting a romantic radicalism which never got much beyond a vague conviction that wealth, like beauty, was in some way associated with evil, and which anyway never found its way into his work as a force to counter the bland materialism which he identified around him. The conversion of the protagonist of *This Side of Paradise* to a naïve socialism had had less to do with genuine political persuasion than with Fitzgerald's sense of a universe which polarized around wealth and poverty, purity and corruption, youth and age. Yet, with *The Great Gatsby* and later with *Tender Is the Night* and *The Last Tycoon*, he did begin to appreciate the creative tensions within his own work, to admire 'the ability to hold two opposed ideas in the mind at the same time, and still retain the ability to function'.[2] If he never fully understood the precise nature of this dialectic he did sense the essential dilemmas of his age in a more profound way than his early fashionable success might have suggested. He began, with *The Great Gatsby*, to retreat from the manichean sensibility of his early work, to acknowledge a crucial ambiguity at the heart of human affairs and to reject the casual moral assumptions of his first two novels. He also began to delineate with greater care and perception the line which links the individual with the body politic, to see on a more fundamental level the connection between personal and public history.

II

While dismissing *The Great Gatsby* as a glorified anecdote H. L. Mencken went out of his way to comment on Fitzgerald's craftsmanship, remarking that 'I make much of this improvement because it is of an order not often witnessed in American writers, and seldom indeed in those who start off with a popular success.'[3] Fitzgerald himself, with characteristic lack of humility, recognized a similar advance in his work. In suggesting a comment for the dust-jacket of *All The Sad Young Men* he pointed out his own transition from the 'early exuberant stories of youth' to the later 'more serious mood which produced *The Great Gatsby* and marked him as one of the half-dozen masters of English prose now writing in America. . . . 'What other writer', he asked, 'had

[2] F. Scott Fitzgerald, *The Crack-Up and Other Pieces and Stories* (Harmondsworth, 1965), p. 39.
[3] *F. Scott Fitzgerald: The Man and His Work*, p. 91.

shown such unexpected developments?'[4] Determined to keep all his 'harsh smartness' ruthlessly out of the book, he created characters who were no longer merely the embodiment of his own youthful romanticism and cynicism. He achieves a detachment—symbolized by his use of a surrogate first person narrator—which seems to add a further dimension to his work, and which depends on a vastly greater recognition of the social and metaphysical implications of his characters' lives. It is, perhaps, worth recalling in this context that Zelda's infidelity with the young French flyer, René Silvé, took place just as he had started work on *The Great Gatsby* for the second time. His later comment on Zelda that 'never in her whole life did she have a sense of guilt, even when she put other lives in danger'[5] enforces the obvious parallels between his wife and Daisy Buchanan. But, whereas in his earlier novels he had been content simply to transfer such personal incidents into the body of his work virtually unchanged, here at last he integrated his sense of the amoral individual into a carefully controlled moral context.

The Great Gatsby came at a time when Fitzgerald's popularity was on the wane. His role as the main spokesman for his generation had been taken over by John Dos Passos and Sinclair Lewis, while his own early success was proving a two-edged weapon; he was increasingly associated with an era which was already considered passé. Allied with this was Fitzgerald's sense of his own deterioration since his completion of *The Beautiful and Damned*. *The Great Gatsby*, therefore, was to be not merely an attempt to re-establish his ascendancy, with the critics as well as with a fickle public, but also an assertion of his own confidence and integrity. It was to be a victory of the will as much as an artistic achievement.

Henry Dan Piper and others have traced the changing literary influences at work on Fitzgerald at this time, especially the significance of James and Conrad. Whatever the effect of these influences, it is certainly true that Fitzgerald approached this work with a care which had scarcely marked his earlier novels. As the author remarked, 'Never before did one try to keep his conscience as pure.'[6] To John Aldridge, writing in 1951, the achievement of *Gatsby* derived from the fact that it was written 'during that fragile moment when the drive of youth

---

[4] *Letters*, pp. 189–90.
[5] *F. Scott Fitzgerald: a biography and critical study*, p. 163.
[6] Henry Dan Piper, *F. Scott Fitzgerald* (London, 1968), p. 125.

meets with the intuitive wisdom of first maturity, and before either the diseases of youth or the waverings of age begin to show through'.[7] While this somewhat naïve concept of balance has its attractions, as a general principle it would seem to have rather limited application. However, Fitzgerald's age was certainly important in one respect at least. Although we are told that he kept Ginevra King's letters, even having them bound into a book, he was now able to regard his own youth with a degree of detachment not evidenced before. Hence, that uncritical attitude towards nostalgia and poignancy which had dominated *This Side of Paradise* and *The Beautiful and Damned* is abandoned in favour of a more complex and ambiguous response. He now succeeds in detailing emotional response without succumbing to it. He recognizes the limitations of sentiment, and sees his personal dreams as part of a larger illusion. Thus his obsession with lost youth becomes a national concern with squandered innocence and unfulfilled aspirations. Whether this was a result of 'the intuitive wisdom of first maturity' rather than a hard-earned insight derived from his own bitter experience it is impossible to say, but nevertheless it was the combination of this new vision and his own dedication to craft which resulted in the subtle nuances of *The Great Gatsby*.

The full extent of Fitzgerald's acknowledgment of ambiguity has never really been appreciated. Critics, swayed perhaps by the moral absolutes of his earlier work, have constantly been tempted to impose on this novel precisely that manichean tendency which he was attacking and from which he was struggling to escape. The contrast between city and country is apparently so deeply engrained in American sensibility that Fitzgerald's ambivalent attitude passes largely unremarked.

For Arthur Mizener, '*The Great Gatsby* becomes a kind of tragic pastoral, with the East the exemplar of urban sophistication and culture and corruption, and the West, "the bored, sprawling, swollen towns beyond the Ohio", the exemplar of simple virtue.'[8] To Sergio Perosa, similarly, the novel is concerned with 'the typical American myth of the geographic and moral juxtaposition between the two poles of the nation to which a symbolic meaning is attached: the innocence of the flowering fields of wheat, the corruption and sterility of the city.'[9]

[7] 'Fitzgerald: The Horror and Vision of Paradise', in *F. Scott Fitzgerald* edited by Arthur Mizener, p. 37.
[8] 'The Poet of Borrowed Time', in *The Man and his Work*, p. 36.
[9] *The Art of F. Scott Fitzgerald*, p. 73.

But the West has long since been corrupted by the forebears of Buchanan, Gatsby and even Carraway. Nick comes not from some agrarian hinterland but from a town in which his family had won ascendancy as the result of a great uncle who had sent a substitute to the Civil War (Grover Cleveland's particular sin) and himself founded a hardware business. Buchanan's careless wealth derives direct from the Mid-West as does Gatsby's amorality. Indeed, it is perhaps significant that the latter's childhood Horatio Alger principles for attaining wealth and personal success had been inscribed in a copy of *Hopalong Cassidy*. The American dream flourished in the West and the prime representative of this code, appropriately enough, is Dan Cody, 'the pioneer debauchee, who during one phase of American life brought back to the Eastern seaboard the savage violence of the frontier brothel and saloon'. It is worth remembering, after all, that the action of Fitzgerald's bitter attack on ruthless capitalism, 'The Diamond as Big as the Ritz', takes place in the West and not amid the supposed corruptions of New York.

Tom Buchanan, living in his mock-colonial mansion, seems in many ways to be a figure derived directly from the frontier. We are told, for example, that not even 'the effeminate swank of his riding clothes could hide the enormous power of that body—he seemed to fill those glistening boots until he strained the top lacing, and you could see a great pack of muscle shifting when his shoulder moved under his thin coat'. Buchanan is an exploiter. Like the villains of Cooper's novels he is a careless man who 'smashed up things and creatures'. He is close kin to Devereux Warren in *Tender Is the Night* who, with his 'fine shoulders shaking with awful sobs inside his easy-fitting coat', sees innocence as a provocation. Fitzgerald explodes the old mythology and in *Tender Is the Night* denounces 'the illusions of eternal strength and health, and of the eternal goodness of people: illusions of a nation, the lies of generations of frontier mothers who had to croon falsely, that there were no wolves outside the cabin door.' The exchange of the old world for the new can no longer be looked on as the exchange of innocence for corruption or the substitution of the dream for a sordid reality. This was an ambivalance which had previously escaped him. Gatsby, the sun-burned attractive young man who had discovered that 'people liked him when he smiled', is thus an inheritor of an already tarnished dream. Having naturalized his alien-sounding name he pursues a romantic vision but does so in a country whose primal innocence has long since been destroyed. Gatsby's experience is in many ways a simple re-enactment of the American experience. He has lost 'the old warm world' and in return has inherited 'an unfamiliar sky through frightening leaves. . . . A new world, material without being real, where poor ghosts', like himself 'breathing dreams like air, drifted fortuitously about'.

Yet, while Fitzgerald is at pains to avoid the simple polarity which Mizener identifies he does draw heavily on the usual images of east and west. East and West Egg in some ways present a microcosm of this situation. Yet, once again, despite Nick's remark that there is a 'bizarre and not a little sinister contrast' between the two communities, their differences are more apparent than real. They are both composed of essentially the same forces, as Fitzgerald makes plain in his Whitman-esque list of their inhabitants. West Egg may demonstrate a 'raw vigour' that chafes 'under the old euphemisms' but it is distinguished from East Egg only in the degree of its soulless wealth. While the East has the 'quality of distortion' and occupies the physical centre of the novel, this, as Nick finally realizes, had been 'a story of the West, after all'. The reductive irony of Nick's retreat to the corrupt Mid-West at the end of the novel depends, of course, precisely on our acceptance of the integrity of America's central myth.

But if the West provides evidence of Fitzgerald's new sense of ambiguity, the city too is in many ways the image of his double vision. He is at once attracted and repelled by what he sees. It represents corruption and graft but, with its towering white buildings, it seems to contain the essence of that pure dream of national and self-fulfilment. As he wrote in 'My Lost City', 'New York had all the irridescence of the beginning of the world', yet whole sections 'had grown rather poisonous'. Thus he must eventually leave the city which 'no longer whispers of fantastic success and eternal youth', only lamenting that 'I have lost my splendid mirage' and calling out with mock romantic intonation, 'Come back, come back, O glittering and white.' Daisy Buchanan, similarly associated throughout with white, contains the same ambivalence and as we penetrate the disguises of the one so we do those of the other. Nothing is what it seems; innocence is merely an invitation to corruption, the historical process is irrevocable, program-matic categories are an illusion to be destroyed.

Within the novel it is Nick Carraway who insists on identifying moral polarities. It is with 'a sort of heady excitement' that he imposes a radical simplicity on the people who surround him. 'There are', he feels, 'only the pursued, the pursuing, the busy and the tired.' The real progress of the book is thus Carraway's growing perception of the inadequacy of such an attitude. His early conviction that 'Life is much more successfully looked at from a single window' has to bow before Gatsby's demonstration of the fallibility of such a stance. In fact the reader's acknowledgment of the immorality of Nick's values and his unreliability as a neutral observer is as crucial to an understanding of *The Great Gatsby* as a similar appreciation is to an understanding of *The Turn of The Screw*.

Most of the contrasts in the book are more apparent than real and Fitzgerald is at pains to link the experiences of Nick, Gatsby, Tom, Daisy and the Wilsons until it is obvious that they are all aspects of the same malaise. As Nick remarks, 'perhaps we possessed some deficiency in common'. In fact in many ways the parallels between Gatsby and Tom Buchanan, for example, are more important than the obvious divergences. Like Tom, Gatsby 'took what he could get, ravenously and unscrupulously'. Despite the romantic facade with which he cloaks his relationship with Daisy it is no different in kind to Tom's tawdry relationship with Myrtle Wilson.

This is a society lacking in moral responsibility and having no ethical basis for action. The chain of motor accidents which occur throughout the book merely provides evidence of the carelessness with which the characters conduct their lives. Nor is it the Buchanans alone who show evidence of this irresponsibility. Jordan Baker, who lacks any kind of moral code, retreats into amused neutrality in the face of the crisis in her friends' lives. Fitzgerald's description of her as 'balancing something . . . which was quite likely to fall' is not merely an arbitrary device of characterization but an accurate image of her moral neutrality. The same is essentially true of Nick who, our sympathies notwithstanding, plays a morally ambiguous role in cooperating with Gatsby's adulterous schemes. As he plays pander to Gatsby's somewhat ponderous attempts at adultery he shares both the excitement and the tawdriness of his amoral pursuit of the ideal. He is by no means the innocent from the Mid-West to be contrasted with the corruption of the city dweller. A man determined to 'reserve all judgment' he attracts confidences and trust and yet responds to 'the secret griefs of wild, unknown men' with 'feigned sleep, preoccupation, or a hostile levity'. When at the height of the showdown at the hotel he suddenly remarks,

'I just remembered that today's my birthday' his comment is an indication of his own self-absorption. In pursuit of their own fantasies individuals abandon moral considerations. As Fitzgerald himself wrote, 'That's the whole burden of this novel . . . the loss of those illusions that give such colour to the world that you don't care whether things are true or false so long as they partake of the magical glory.'[10] On a more personal level this leads to the menacing disinterest of Jordan Baker and Nick Carraway, to the destructiveness of Daisy and Tom Buchanan, and to the sad corruption of Jay Gatsby. The point is not so much that the dream has been corrupted but rather that it always carried within it the seeds of its own corruption. As he wrote later in 'My Lost City' 'innocence is no end in itself'. In order to preserve his youthful vision of himself and of Daisy, Gatsby sells out to Wolfsheim and sees his adulterous advances as an attempt to rescue Daisy from a loveless marriage. He reshapes reality to fit his own delusions. But as a consequence he bears a direct responsibility both for his own death and for the death of Myrtle Wilson. In a sense, therefore, the deranged Mr. Wilson is right in singling out Gatsby for his revenge for, as one of Arthur Miller's characters remarks in 'After the Fall', to maintain our innocence we 'kill most easily'.[11]

Yet, despite his stringent analysis of the failure of the American dream, in a novel which was to have borne the significant title, *Under the Red White and Blue*, Fitzgerald cannot bring himself to denounce the embodiment of that vision. Even in the face of corruption and defeat there is an attraction in that man who can preserve his illusions intact. Like Willy Loman, Gatsby has all the wrong dreams but the single-mindedness, the spiritual integrity with which he pursues them, commands respect. It is perhaps to be expected that Fitzgerald, who wrote in a letter that 'like Gatsby I have only hope',[12] would react ambiguously to Gatsby's vulgar yet curiously glorious quest. Gatsby simplifies his life by mortgaging himself to a single dominating obsession and though the novel demonstrates the danger of doing so Fitzgerald, who was tempted by the same strategy, could not condemn him. Like Nick Carraway, who was 'within and without, simultaneously enchanted and repelled by the inexhaustible variety of life'; he and his hero contain the 'yes and the no' of their culture without fully

[10] Henry Dan Piper, *op. cit.*, p. 106.
[11] *Saturday Evening Post*, 1 February 1964, p. 58.
[12] *The Letters of F. Scott Fitzgerald*, p. 485.

appreciating the conflict between historical process and animating myth.

Gatsby does become a kind of hero. His wealth, though ill-gotten and squandered to little real purpose, nonetheless gives him a spurious stature, even in Fitzgerald's eyes. But surely the defeat of Gatsby finally signifies little but the demise of a kind of futile romanticism which had little to recommend itself anyway. If he represents anything beyond himself it is the impossibility of pursuing romantic dreams in an unromantic world and the emptiness of Horatio Alger promises. Carraway's action in rubbing out the obscenity scrawled on the steps of Gatsby's mansion is his attempt to preserve what he sees as the essential purity and innocence of the dead man, but not only is this innocence naïve and nonfunctional, it is also, as we have seen, dangerous. Fitzgerald never really confronts the paradox which he has constructed for himself, nor has he fully worked out his attitude towards the rich. Gatsby, after all, is corrupted not simply by money but by his naïve faith in the integrity and permanence of innocence, while the vulgarity of the rich Buchanans is matched by the crassness of the poor Myrtle Wilson and her friends. The symbols of wealth, the motor car and the swimming pool, are certainly associated with death but so is the ash-landscape which surrounds the Wilson garage. Gatsby is betrayed not by wealth or the assumption that money can buy anything but by his belief that anything of value can survive the standards of the market place. In so far as his quest for a lost past is linked to the national mythology of New World innocence he has a symbolic dimension, but Fitzgerald's ambiguous response leaves the reader uncertain of the writer's view of the future.

III

The nine years between *The Great Gatsby* and *Tender Is the Night* were years of continued frustration and despair for Fitzgerald. Zelda suffered a major breakdown, his literary reputation continued to plummet and he was forced to fall back on short-story writing to remain solvent. After a period of literary inactivity he started to write stories at the rate of one every five weeks for five years, alternating a degree of dissipation with attempts at writing a fourth novel. Although his work still rated extremely satisfactory fees—$4,000 a story at one time—he was profoundly dissatisfied with the standard of the material which he was producing. It is scarcely surprising, therefore, that the mood and tone of his work should have altered. Faced with Zelda's breakdown and his own deterioration, he became more and more convinced that 'all life is a process of breaking down', while the Crash of 1929 established a persuasive parallel between individual deterioration and social disintegration. As he suggested in 'The Crack-Up' 'my recent experience parallels the wave of despair that swept the nation when the Boom was over'. In his reading of Henry Adams and Oswald Spengler he found justification for his sense of national decay, while in Freud he discovered confirmation of his belief in the individual's movement towards anomie. Thus, his early pose of melancholic regret at the passing of time gives way now to a profound sense of precariousness. In 'The Crack-Up' he uses the image of a cracked plate as William James had used that of a cracked bell and cracking ice.

All his stories, as he admitted, were touched with disaster, but until *Tender Is the Night* this disaster was limited in scope and application. Anthony Patch's madness in *The Beautiful and Damned* was a kind of poetic justice while even Gatsby's death is not without some consolation since he manages to maintain his sense of integrity to the last. Dick Diver's retreat into obscurity and Monroe Stahr's intended death, however, spell out all too clearly the demise of a kind of idealism which, if itself touched with corruption from its too-close association with money, nonetheless represents the tenuous survival of values which society can ill afford to lose.

Fitzgerald's stay in Europe, from 1924 to 1926 and again in 1928, certainly seems to have given him a sense of objectivity, and hence of irony and ambiguity, lacking in his early work. But while this discovery of functional ambiguity, as opposed to the confusions and contradictions of his earlier work, was of crucial importance to his development as a writer, it was his final period abroad, from 1929 to 1931, that precipitated the change in tone between *The Great Gatsby* and *Tender Is the Night* and which provided the perfect imagery and setting for his analysis of a culture in decline. Zelda broke down in April 1930 and two months later began a fifteen-month stay in a Swiss sanatorium. Not only did the hospital provide him with an ideal background, but his increasing interest in psychology provided him with a potent new imagery. The anarchic state of society is embodied in the perverse sexual pairings of *Tender Is the Night*, much as Poe's sense of disorder had been encapsulated in the sexual threat contained in the crumbling walls of the house of Usher. But where for many nineteenth-century American writers sexuality had been a rebellious gesture, in the context of *Tender Is the Night* and *The Last Tycoon* it constitutes a submission to the forces of dissolution and power. If this assumption is coloured by his own bitter experience, it also becomes a highly effective image of the move away from an almost ascetic integrity. As in Hemingway's *To Have and Have Not* the rich are almost invariably associated with perversion: Devereaux Warren with incest, the son of Sēnor Poro y Cuidad Real with homosexuality, and Mary North and the aristocratic Lady Caroline Sibley-Biers with lesbianism. If there is something a little too casual about such imagery, it is clear that Fitzgerald felt it particularly appropriate to a study of the decline of modern civilization. The deterioration of the rich provided a particularly appropriate symbol of social dislocation. As he remarks, 'The suite in which Devereaux Warren was gracefully weakening and sinking was of the same size as that of the Sēnor Pardo y Cuidad Real— throughout this hotel there were many chambers wherein rich ruins, fugitives from justice, claimants to the thrones of mediatized princi-palities, lived on the derivatives of opium or barbitol listening eternally as to an inescapable radio, to the coarse memories of old sins.'

There is something of the atmosphere of Chekhov's *Three Sisters* about *Tender Is the Night*. It is set in a period which Fitzgerald describes in 'Echoes of the Jazz Age' as enervated and static: 'by 1929, at the most gorgeous paradise for swimmers on the Mediterranean no one swam any more, save for a short hang-over dip at noon. There was a pictur-esque graduation of steep rocks over the sea and somebody's valet and an occasional English girl used to dive from them, but the Americans were content to discuss each other in the bar. This was indicative of something that was taking place in the homeland—Americans were getting soft'. Americans going to Europe were no longer repositories of the simple virtues, which by now were dead or dying, but 'fantastic neanderthals', the distorted money-mad caricatures of the newspaper cartoon which appears at the beginning and end of *Tender Is the Night*, both as a frame and a bitter comment. With wealth, it seemed to Fitzgerald, came inertia, hysteria, perversion and insanity. Simultane-ously there came the extinction of all genuine values, which in turn brought a whole society to the verge of apocalypse.

Fitzgerald had not shared the war experiences of many of his con-temporaries and felt little inclination to identify with the profound pessimism of the expatriate writers, despite his own largely unspoken and unacknowledged sense of despair. He did adopt a fashionable show of cynicism; but his sense of the sterility of American life, its distorted values and perverted ethics, was rooted, it seemed, in a satirist's conviction that true values did exist. There is nothing here of Dos Passos's violent rejection of capitalism (except in his early story, 'The Diamond as Big as the Ritz'). In a short story, published four years after the appearance of *The Great Gatsby*, his expatriate protagonist

> had a sense of overwhelming gratitude and gladness that America was there, that under the ugly debris of industry, the rich land still pushed up, incorrigibly lavish and fertile, and that in the heart of the leaderless people the old generosities and devotions fought on, breaking out sometimes in fanaticism and excess, but indomitable and undefeated. There was a lost generation in the saddle at the moment, but it seemed to him that the men coming on, the men of the war, were better; and all his old feeling that America was a bizarre accident, a sort of historical sport, was gone forever. The best of America was the best of the world. . . .[13]

Fitzgerald can scarcely have missed the irony whereby this declaration of faith came to be published in the *Saturday Evening Post* only four days after the Crash. Nevertheless, as Robert Sklaar has pointed out, this story is the first to show the impact of Fitzgerald's interest in the work of Oswald Spengler. For if he sees some residual value in the traditional standards he does identify the poison in the national bloodstream as money. 'Money is power,'[14] as one of the characters reminds us. In the context of this story, however, wealth has to bow to the intuitive wisdom and integrity of an honest and mature individual. He has not, in other words, embraced the full Spenglerian thesis. But the impact of the Depression, a further period of expatriation and more personal indignities, led him to draw the full apocalyptic implications from his analysis of contemporary life. The trauma of the Crash and the threatened break-up of his own life did for him what the war had done for others. It convinced him of the precarious nature of existence, of individual helplessness, of the chaotic nature of reality and of the momentum of history which could no longer be read simply in terms of man's inevitable progress. It is entirely appropriate, therefore, that his characters should visit the trenches in *Tender Is the Night*

[13] Quoted in *F. Scott Fitzgerald: The Last Laocoon*, p. 239.
[14] *Ibid.*, p. 238.

because he, like them, is suddenly aware that 'All my beautiful lovely safe world blew itself up here.' *Tender Is the Night* is essentially Fitzgerald's war novel. It is his version of *The Sun Also Rises*.

In *The Crack-Up* essays he explains that he had lived 'distrusting the rich, yet working for money with which to share their mobility and the grace that some of them brought into their lives'. This ambivalence derived in part from a private line of imagery dating back to his experience with Ginevra King and Zelda and to a haunting sense of evil which seemed to lurk at the core of American experience, and in part to the ambiguity which he found in such writers as Henry James. But while recognizing a certain grandeur and freedom in the lives of the rich which he was tempted to imitate, his attitude towards wealth, by the time of *Tender Is the Night*, had been tempered by his reading of Spengler's *The Decline of the West*. As Robert Sklaar has pointed out, Fitzgerald discovered Spengler's book in 1927 and was profoundly influenced by it. Here he found a rationale for his suspicion of money power and a historical dimension to his sense of personal degeneration and decay. In *The Great Gatsby* he had sensed the failure of the dream but he had not confronted the implicit pessimism of the book's conclusion. The ambiguity of tone seemed to grant at least a provisional vitality to the survivors of Gatsby's futile but apparently heroic sacrifice. But now, writing after the 1929 Crash and with the authority of Spengler's analysis behind him, he was ready to draw the inevitable conclusions from what he saw to be a disintegration of social values and the integrity of the personality. By the time he came to write 'The Crack-Up' he was able to point the real moral of Gatsby's death— an apocalyptic implication which had seemed curiously inappropriate to a novel in which total commitment is not without its attractions. Now, however, it seemed to contain the very essence of his dialectic. The tendency, he insisted in that essay, 'is to refuse to face things as long as possible by retiring into an infantile dream . . . hoping that things will adjust themselves by some great material or spiritual bonanza. But as the withdrawal persists there is less and less chance of the bonanza—one is not waiting for the fade-out of a single sorrow, but rather being an unwilling witness of an execution, the disintegration of one's own personality.' The truth of this on a personal and social level seemed to be confirmed by the Crash and by the cataclysmic prophecies of Spengler's account. It also received confirmation from the work of another author whose work affected

Fitzgerald. In *Civilization and its Discontents* Freud had pointed out that 'each one of us behaves in some respect like the paranoiac, substituting a wish-fulfilment for some aspect of the world which is unbearable to him, and carrying this delusion through into reality'.[15] Hence Fitzgerald's decision to write 'a novel of our time' inevitably meant a decision to show 'the break-up of a fine personality'[16] and to use insanity as an appropriate image of modern life. Gatsby had survived the onslaught of reality spiritually intact; Fitzgerald determined now to show a man 'who is a natural idealist, a spoiled priest, giving in for various causes to the ideas of the haute Burgeoise [sic], and in his rise to the top of the social world losing his idealism, his talent and turning to drink and dissipation.'[17] It was a 'novel of our time' because in his hero he saw the pressures and 'tragic forces' of his age. The decline of Dick Diver is the decline of society seen in directly Spenglerian terms.

But if in *Tender Is the Night* Fitzgerald was drawing on his reading of Spengler, he also owes something to his knowledge of Henry Adams, another apocalyptic historian. Adams, obsessed with the 'total, irremediable radical rottenness of our whole social, industrial, financial and political system',[18] continually prophesied the decline of the West. In his massive *History* he saw the replacement of idealism by nationalism as signifying the end of an apparently glorious dream, tarnished by a ruthless materialism and the reckless pursuit of money. Like the later Fitzgerald, however, he was also alive to the fact that the dream itself was a dangerous illusion. Both felt that failure was almost inevitable given the nature of society and the drift of history. Hence Diver, whom Fitzgerald associates with General Grant, and, later and more especially, Monroe Stahr, whom he likens to Lincoln, were bound to succumb because the dictates of art and integrity must be destroyed by the power of wealth and the momentum of a system beyond human control. To some extent, of course, this analysis provided a convenient excuse for Fitzgerald's own sense of failure, but more fundamentally it offered a rationalization for his increasing belief in the anarchy which lay at the root of things.

[15] Sigmund Freud, *Civilization and its Discontents* translated by Joan Riviere (London, 1930), p. 36.
[16] *The Art of F. Scott Fitzgerald*, p. 109.
[17] Henry Dan Piper, *op. cit.*, p. 211.
[18] Quoted in George Hockfield, *Henry Adams* (New York, 1962), p. 97.

In the light of his interest in Adams, whom he knew personally and included in one of his novels, it is intriguing that Fitzgerald should present Dick Diver as a modern General Grant, for Grant had been Adams's idea of the final hope for idealism in America. Upon his success or failure would turn his own faith in the possibility of defeating the wealthy and corrupt, whom he saw as dedicated to destroying the promise of his country. Grant was elected, according to Adams, because he 'represented order'.[19] He was the man to counterpose to moral and political anarchy. The General's surrender to the corrupt and powerful thus destroyed all hope of a justifiable optimism: 'To the end of his life, he [Adams] wondered at the suddenness of the revolution which actually, within five minutes, changed his intended future into an absurdity so laughable as to make him ashamed of it.'[20] Almost at once a general 'dissolution of ties in every direction'[21] commenced. So, too, the defeat of Dick Diver, his surrender to the wealthy and privileged, marks, not merely the abandonment of an idealized though constructive approach to life, but also confirmation of the anarchic nature of human existence.

Dick Diver represents the effort of will whereby the genteel middle class tries to oppose the movement of history. As he himself recognizes he is 'the last hope of a decaying clan', a vestigial man, the remnant of a type exposed and destroyed by the war and by the Crash which followed some ten years later. If he represents 'the exact furthermost evolution of a class', he also signifies the futility of imagining that the course of history can be altered by fiat. He is a dreamer who sets his illusions up against the power of reality and thus, in Spenglerian terms, is doomed to failure. For, as Spengler suggested, 'the forces of actuality ... rally and thrust the dreamers aside ... reminding men of the fact that one can make use of constitutional rights only when one has money.'[22] Since, as Fitzgerald himself noted later, the sensitive can hardly make themselves overnight into specimens of the tough-minded, Diver cannot succeed. He becomes merely an instrument, even ceasing to function as a doctor. We are told that in watching 'his father's struggles in poor parishes' he 'had wedded a desire for money to an essentially unacquisitive nature. ... Yet he had been swallowed up like a gigolo, and somehow, permitted his arsenal to be locked up

[19] *Ibid.*, p. 126.   [20] *Ibid.*, p. 127.   [21] *Ibid.*, p. 128.
[22] Oswald Spengler, *The Decline of the West* translated by Charles Francis Atkinson (London, 1934), p. 456.

in the Warren safety-deposit vaults.' As he becomes richer 'teaching the rich the ABC's of human decency', so his self-sufficiency is deflected into a specious egotism—that 'onanism' which Fitzgerald identifies with wealth. As Spengler insisted, 'If in the world of truths it is *proof* that decides all, in that of facts it is *success*. Success means that one triumphs over others. Life has won through and the dreams of the world-improvers have turned out to be but the tools of *master-natures*.'[23]

Nevertheless, Diver does attempt to establish order. When Rosemary is in his presence she 'had a conviction of homecoming, of a return from the derisive and salacious improvisations of the frontier'. So too with Nicole, who had been raped by her father. To Freud, incest had signified man's urge towards anarchy and Dick's attempt to help his wife depends on his ability to build a new structure for her to have faith in. When she finally deserts him it is to welcome 'the anarchy of her lover'. Dick's faith in form and order is an inheritance from another age and makes little sense of the disintegration of self and society which seem to Fitzgerald to be the prime fact of twentieth-century life. His power, therefore, is provisional, dependent on the willingness of others to play the roles which he hands them: 'So long as they subscribed to it completely, their happiness was his preoccupation, but at the first flicker of doubt as to its all-inclusiveness he evaporated before their eyes.'

In *The Last Tycoon*, Monroe Stahr is compared to Lincoln rather than Grant, but the point is the same. In his own field Stahr too represents an ordering process, imposing his own ideas of craft and values on the movie industry: 'Stahr like Lincoln was a leader carrying on a long war on many fronts; almost single-handed he had moved pictures sharply forward through a decade, to a point where the content of the "A productions" was wider and richer than that of the stage.' But like Lincoln his idealism was to lead him directly to his death. His power derived from the need for some sense of authority and direction, but in conflict with 'the money-man . . . the rulers' he was fated. The materialistic and anarchic powers would inevitably dominate and, indeed, according to the notes which Fitzgerald left behind, corrupt him. Lest the reader should miss the logic of this process Fitzgerald actually introduces a reference to Spengler into the text. Stahr's new mistress, Kathleen, tells him of her former lover who 'wanted me to

[23] Oswald Spengler, *The Decline of the West*, p. 463.

read Spengler—everything was for that. All the history and philosophy and harmony was all so I could read Spengler.'

The other historical referent in *The Last Tycoon*, Andrew Jackson, is equally meaningful. Jackson is popularly thought of as the man who had overthrown the money forces in America—even taking on and defeating the Bank of America. In terms of the novel, therefore, he is vitally important, for Stahr is in many ways attempting to emulate him. But when various characters visit Jackson's home they find it closed. Presumably, therefore, his values are simply not available to the modern world and Stahr's attempt is blighted from the start. It is conceivable, too, that Fitzgerald intended to make use of the irony implicit in Jackson's responsibility for the Crash of 1837, for Stahr himself is not without blame as he assumes the possibility of exerting control and establishing his own reality.

For Fitzgerald, then, as later for Tennessee Williams, the essential conflict in America was that between the romantic and the materialist, the visionary and the realist. It was a battle in which, like Williams, he naturally tended to identify with the corrupted romantic. But, also like Williams, and despite the new insights of his later years, he evidenced a covert admiration for the uncultured, physically direct and powerful individual. For if such writers believe that the Stanley Kowalskys and Tom Buchanans of this world are bound to triumph, their ostensible contempt for such creatures is always tempered by a regard for their power and cunning: the 'yes and no' of the culture. Like Freud, Fitzgerald was attracted to 'men of action, unshakable in their convictions, impervious to doubt, and insensitive to the sufferings of anyone who stands between them and their goal'.[24] In common with the naturalists, whom he admired, he was tempted by an historical perspective which declared with Spengler that

> World history is the world court, and it has ever decided in favour of the stronger, fuller and more self-assured life, decreed to it, namely, the right to exist, regardless of whether its right would hold before a tribunal of waking consciousness. Always it has sacrificed truth and justice to might and race and passed doom of death upon men and peoples in whom truth was more than deeds and justice than power.[25]

[24] Quoted in Philip Rieff, *Freud: the Mind of the Moralist* (London, 1965), p. 246.
[25] Oswald Spengler, *op. cit.*, p. 507.

Thus, though half of him follows the broken Dick Diver into exile and extinction the other half is drawn to the powerful figures who, for a brief while at least, are able to dominate their surroundings. If the Crash is a reminder that their power is finite this scarcely marks the resurgence of the weak and defeated.

At the very centre of all this is Nicole Diver. She, with her wealth and her sickness, is the epitome of the system of power, containing within herself the animating principle of her society and the seeds of its destruction. Constructing delicate iron bars for the patients of the sanatorium she is herself trapped by the power which she wields. 'For her sake ... dreamers were muscled out of patent rights ... these were some of the people who gave a tithe to Nicole and, as the whole system swayed and thundered onward it lent a feverish bloom to such processes of hers as wholesale buying. . . . She illustrated very simple principles, containing in herself her own doom.'

Freud assumes that the interests of the individual and his society are n opposition. Although Fitzgerald sensed something of the kind he never entirely lost his admiration for the style of his social environment or for those at whose hands he fancied himself to suffer. That alone could have given him the perspective to accept this Freudian assumption. He was profoundly distrustful of the rich and their historical role but he lacked the security which could transmute this perception into genuine social criticism. Thus, while denouncing the crassness of the Warren family and the degenerate rich who inhabit Dick Diver's sanatorium he recognizes naked power and is inexorably drawn to it as he had been in his youth to the very excesses which were the object of his scorn. He could see that his was an age of crisis, but could offer no way of avoiding the collapse. He had a sense of an America which was not merely transitional but on the verge of apocalypse. Following the war 'the silver cord is cut and the golden bowl is broken'. This was a time in which the 'strong are too strong for us and the weak too weak'.[26] When Diver finds that he simply lacks the strength and will to impose his sense of order on the flux of existence, this is Fitzgerald's own admission as a creative artist of his own failure to exert his will on the brutal dictatorship of American reality. As he acknowledges in 'The Crack-Up' the destruction of values spawns a 'passionate belief in order, a disregard of motives or consequences'. From Nick Carraway, desperate for a world at moral attention, and Gatsby, seeking to dis-

[26] *Letters*, p. 154.

cover 'some idea of himself' with which to counter a life which had become 'confused and disordered', through to Dick Diver, finally losing control over his creation, Fitzgerald has written of his own experience as a writer in a world which steadfastly refuses to comply with his urgent need for purpose. Like Gatsby and Diver he is attracted by the elaborate structures of capitalist society but like them he also has a disturbing sense of insufficiency which can never leave him content with wealth and power as goals in themselves. Denied, like his heroes, a lasting sexual relationship he tended to see the anarchic powers of sexuality as an appropriate metaphor of universal determinism. Like Spengler, he believed that the historical process is inexorable, the urge towards entropy inevitable. Yet, in common with writers like Cooper and Melville he could never quite reconcile himself to a process that must condemn the artist as it destroys all sensitive individuals who hold up the romantic banner in the face of advancing Caesarism. While he had few illusions about the desirability of a pre-lapsarian sensibility, Fitzgerald could still not accept with any degree of equanimity a world swayed by the autocratic whim of birth and money. Diver attempts to compromise in order to live out his messianic impulses and is corrupted as much by his own failure of nerve as by the destructive power of the social system. If Diver at first appears as something of a superman, creating a fictive world of his own, he lacks the sheer drive and power of the Warrens and Barbans. He substitutes taste for vitality; is a kind of compassionate Gilbert Osmond, lacking his callous disregard for others but sharing his substitution of sensibility for active involvement. His attempt to redeem Nicole is not without overtones of paternalism. He trifles with her affections and delights in the achievements of his own creation, but his power is contingent and provisional.

But for all this, Fitzgerald lacks that faith in the historical process that Cooper, Hawthorne and Melville had shown. This is a world without the civilized integrity of Judge Temple, the constructive insight of Holgrave or the stunning courage of Captain Vere. The passing of Deerslayer and the sacrifice of Billy Budd had made sense in terms of nineteenth-century optimism over the inevitable progress of man. By contrast, Gatsby floating dead in his swimming pool and Dick Diver drifting into oblivion stand as ironical comments on a future represented by the Buchanans, Tommy Barban and the rich but empty Nicole Diver. Because he cannot believe in that concept of order which was an article of faith to an earlier period he can see no redemption in human or spiritual terms. Speaking of Gibbon's *Decline and Fall of the Roman Empire* he felt it necessary to point out that it was written '*before* the French Revolution and the Industrial Revolution—when man believed that "The Age of Reason" had indeed arrived' but delighted in what he took to be Gibbon's irony in comparing 'the rich men of antiquity to those of his own time—to the *pretended* advantage of the latter'.[27] The frustrations of his own life seemed merely to confirm an analysis which identified the determinism of individual psychology and national history alike. Spengler's prognostications had seemed proved by the First World War. Fitzgerald felt that his own awareness of a disordered universe and fragmenting personality were proved not only by the war but by the empty frenzy of the twenties and the economic apocalypse of the Depression. The rich could buy a limited immunity ('the snow of twenty-nine wasn't real snow. If you didn't want it to be snow, you just paid some money'[28]) but even their immunity was temporary. The fact of the Crash hangs over the whole action of *Tender is the Night* as Stahr's death hangs over *The Last Tycoon*.

IV

In 1919 Fitzgerald sent a telegram to Zelda Sayre:

DARLING HEART ENTHUSIASM AND CONFIDENCE I DECLARE EVERYTHING GLORIOUS. THIS WORLD IS A GAME AND WHILE I FEEL SURE OF YOU[R] LOVE EVERYTHING IS POSSIBLE IN THE LAND OF AMBITION AND SUCCESS.[29]

The sentiment matched the mood of his early work exactly and established the connection which he later felt between his personal circumstances and his faith in the American system. In a decade which eagerly succumbed to its own image of itself he was a poseur who found himself acting out the roles which he had created. Yet by 1934 he was prophesying the decline of civilization and the threatened extinction of art and integrity. The facile reporter of America's gaudy spree had moved from the naïvety and prolixity of his early novels, one of which Edmund Wilson justly described as 'always just

[27] Sheilah Graham, *College of One* (London, 1967), p. 130.
[28] 'Babylon Revisited', in *The Crack-Up and Other Pieces and Stories*, p. 133.
[29] *F. Scott Fitzgerald: a biography and critical study*, p. 79.

verging on the ludicrous',[30] to the controlled brilliance of *The Great Gatsby*, and from there into the carefully formulated apocalyptic vision of *Tender Is the Night* and *The Last Tycoon*.

The paradox of the early Fitzgerald was that he could never quite bring himself to face his essential pessimism. He had too little faith in personal relationships even then to feel that they could radically effect the physical and mental regression which he was coming to suspect formed the basis of human life. Despite his catholicism and his naïve conception of socialism he could find no faith to redeem the emptiness of society as he saw it. Yet he consistently refused to draw the obvious conclusions of his insights into the social charade, resting content, instead, with confusions and contradictions. Thus he condemned himself to seeking affirmations which always rang hollow, from Amory's proud but empty boast at the end of *This Side of Paradise* that 'I know myself' to the unwarranted claims for Gatsby which open his third novel. Despite the ostensible cynicism of *The Beautiful and Damned*, by implication even this book seems simply to endorse the puritan virtues of thrift and godliness. It was only with *Tender Is the Night* that Fitzgerald finally brought himself to face the full implications of his vision and to establish the irrevocable connection between personal tragedy and cultural decline which formed the basis of his dialectic.

[30] Edmund Wilson, 'Fitzgerald before *The Great Gatsby*', in *F. Scott Fitzgerald: The Man and his Work*, p. 79.

Note

Life and Writing

Hemingway was born in 1899 at Oak Park, Illinois, where his father practised medicine. His mother taught music and painted. The family spent summers in the Michigan woods, where Hemingway's lifelong interest in fishing and other outdoor physical activities developed. He had begun writing poetry, stories and journalistic features while in high school and served briefly as a reporter for the Kansas City *Star*. Severely wounded in 1918 while a Red Cross ambulance driver in Italy, he returned and became a feature writer for the Toronto *Star*. For some months, he lived in Chicago, where he married the first of four wives and met Sherwood Anderson. The latter urged him to go to Paris, for which Hemingway departed as freelance feature correspondent of the Toronto *Star*. Hemingway soon became an associate of such literary expatriates as Gertrude Stein, Ezra Pound, Ford Madox Ford, and F. Scott Fitzgerald. He travelled widely in Europe and the Near East, enjoying sports and participating in amateur bullfights, his legend as a bon vivant and tough guy-athlete being established. Believing that journalism was hampering his literary progress, he devoted himself wholly to fiction and poetry in 1924, though in the nineteen thirties he returned to journalism as a magazine and newspaper correspondent who reported wars, commented an international politics and the literary life, and recounted personal exploits as hunter, fisherman and sailor. His journalistic writing is available in *The Wild Years* edited by Gene Hanrahan (New York, 1962) and *By-Line: Ernest Hemingway* edited by William White (New York, 1967), but most of it—like his poetry—is still uncollected. Hemingway's poetry and early journalism, like his short novel *The Torrents of Spring* (1926), reveal strains of comedy, satire and the macabre that were relatively subdued in the books that established his fame: two novels, *The Sun Also Rises* (1926; *Fiesta* in England) and *A Farewell to Arms* (1929), and two short-story collections, *In Our Time* (1925) and *Men Without Women* (1927).

Hemingway settled in Key West, Florida, in the late nineteen twenties, subsequently residing in Cuba and Ketchum, Idaho. The impulse to write fiction, as well as his famous stylistic objectivity and tautness, slackened during the nineteen thirties. During that decade and subsequently, he wrote three autobiographically orientated works of non-fiction (*Death in the Afternoon*, 1932; *Green Hills of Africa*, 1935; *A Moveable Feast*, 1964), a third short-story collection (*Winner Take Nothing*, 1933), and five novels (*To Have and Have Not*, 1937; *For Whom the Bell Tolls*, 1940; *Across the River and Into the Trees*, 1950; *The Old Man and the Sea*, 1952; and *Islands in the Stream*, 1970). He continued to travel and live vigorously, receiving the Nobel Prize in 1954. His death by suicide occurred in 1961. Carlos Baker's *Ernest Hemingway: A Life Story* (1969) is the authorized biography.

Criticism.   Audre Hanneman's *Ernest Hemingway: A Comprehensive Bibliography* (Princeton, 1967) lists over 466 books and over 1,612 newspaper and magazine pieces dealing in part or in whole with Hemingway. Helpful introductory collections of criticism include: *Ernest Hemingway: Critiques of Four Major Novels* edited by Carlos Baker (New York, 1962); *Hemingway and His Critics*

VII

Ernest Hemingway's Genteel Bullfight

BROM WEBER

ONE WONDERS why *The Sun Also Rises* (1926) and *A Farewell to Arms* (1929) now seem unable to evoke the same awesome sense of a tottering world, captured poignantly and precisely in language, which in the nineteen twenties established Ernest Hemingway's reputation. These novels should be speaking to us. Our social structure is as shaken, our philosophical despair as great, our everyday experience as unsatisfying. We have had more war than Hemingway ever saw or dreamed of. Our violence—physical, emotional and intellectual—is not inferior to that of the nineteen twenties. Yet, though Hemingway's books still offer great moments, they no longer seem to penetrate too deeply and steadily below the surface of existence; one begins to doubt that they ever did so significantly in the nineteen twenties.

It is not merely that our times are worse, which they are. Life in the nineteen twenties, after all, tended on the whole to be more excruciating than life in the two previous decades. In retrospect, however, Hemingway's novels cajoled the dominant genteel tradition in American culture while seeming to repudiate it. They yielded to the functionalist, technological aesthetic of the culture instead of resisting in the manner of Frank Lloyd Wright. Hemingway, in effect, became a dupe of his culture rather than its moral-aesthetic conscience. As a consequence, the import of his work has diminished.

There is some evidence from his stylistic evolution that Hemingway himself must have felt as much, for Hemingway's famous stylistic economy frequently seems to conceal another kind of writer, with much richer rhetorical resources to hand. So *Death in the Afternoon* (1932),

edited by Carlos Baker (New York, 1961); *Hemingway: A Collection of Critical Essays* edited by Robert P. Weeks (Englewood Cliffs, N.J., 1962). Useful full-length, introductory studies include: Sheridan Baker, *Ernest Hemingway* (New York, 1967), Earl Rovit, *Ernest Hemingway* (New York, 1963) and Charles A. Fenton's *The Apprenticeship of Ernest Hemingway* (New York, 1954).

Hemingway's bullfighting opus and his first book after *A Farewell to Arms*, reveals great uneasiness over his earlier accomplishment. One of the more important of the aggressive defences of his literary method that appear in the work incorporates a doctrine of ambiguity which justifies confusion and encourages ambivalence:

> If a writer of prose knows enough about what he is writing about he may omit things that he knows and the reader, if the writer is writing truly enough, will have a feeling of those things as strongly as though the writer had stated them. The dignity of an ice-berg is due to only one-eighth of it being above water.

Regarded as a loose explanation of irony in general, the statement raises no quarrel. But when we consider that 'feeling' denotes a response of vague nature and low psychological intensity, it becomes apparent that a physical object or action embodied in words by Hemingway must lose its particular objective characteristics while being transformed into a feeling by the reader. Not only will Hemingway's objective details be blurred during the transfer process, but the psychological state of his reader is likely to become lethargic rather than emotionally highly charged. The 'ice-berg' process is dangerous, furthermore, because an author, consciously or unconsciously, may conceal or misrepresent his materials and his attitudes towards them, damaging the truth and artistry of his work.

Implicit in the 'ice-berg' theory is the bourgeois economic principle that the greatest amount of output should be derived from the smallest amount of input, as well as the bourgeois 'plain style' principle that economy and precision of language and syntax are essential for a scientific prose whose descriptive accuracy may be harmed by the inclusion of humanistically orientated emotion and verbal richness. It is no accident that the conduct of Jake Barnes in *The Sun Also Rises* is distinguished by his devotion to 'work' whereas his friends idly carouse and play. It is as a fellow-technician of industrial simplicity that Barnes admires the matador Romero, who 'never made any contortions, always it was straight and pure and natural in line.'

Hemingway made much the same theoretical point in another way in *Death in the Afternoon* ('prose is architecture, not interior decoration, and the Baroque is over'), apparently believing that a formal reduction of aesthetic complexity, such as that typified by the machine-dominated architecture of the Bauhaus group in the nineteen twenties, was the only kind of design that had value. Ironically, in rejecting architectural 'Baroque', Hemingway symbolically emulated his middle-class, WASP parents of Oak Park, Illinois, whose values and mode of life he so frequently condemned in his fiction. It had apparently never occurred to the elder Hemingways that the house they built in 1905 should have been designed by their neighbour Frank Lloyd Wright, whose freely emotional, baroque handling of space, colour, and texture violated the strait-laced code governing Hemingway's parents.

But in fact Hemingway's famous economy of prose was by no means as omnipresent as he himself suggests; he had his own baroque inclinations. His work is really a mixture of stylistic forces. Thus a still greater irony of *Death in the Afternoon* was its unmistakably baroque prose, which he at one point embarrassedly admitted was 'flowery'. Reviewers, unable to challenge Hemingway's expertise in the art of bullfighting and confused by the eccentricities of the book, noted that its style was 'awkward, tortuous, belligerently clumsy', 'laboured', as 'highly involved and intricate [as] the later stages of Henry James'. Much of this stylistic bravura, coupled with technical exposition, had appeared in somewhat less exuberant form in the bull-fighting sections of *The Sun Also Rises*, but the reviewers had forgotten.

The fact that *Death in the Afternoon* also violated its postulated 'ice-berg' theory is another of the major ironies that dot Hemingway's career. Essentially, the theory rationalized *The Sun Also Rises*, *A Farewell to Arms*, and many of the short stories and sketches collected in *In Our Time* (1925) and *Men Without Women* (1927), the body of work on which Hemingway's repute rested. The theory was not applicable on the whole to the great amount of journalism, much of it comic, macabre and satiric, which he had written from 1920 through 1923, nor to his burlesque novel *The Torrents of Spring* (1926) and the comic-satiric (often scatological) poetry that kept appearing during the nineteen twenties. That Hemingway's journalism was significant in his development did not become evident until Charles Fenton's study of it appeared in 1954; none of the articles was reprinted until after Hemingway's death in 1961. *The Torrents of Spring* (1926) amused only a few critics and was forgotten by most since it seemed like an anomalous, atypical hybrid. As for the poems, some of which had appeared in his first book (*Three Stories and Ten Poems*, 1923) and the rest in small-circulation 'little' magazines in Europe, Edmund Wilson's judgment in his review of the 1923 volume probably was typical of the general reaction: 'Mr. Hemingway's poems are not particularly important. . . .'

Accordingly, when *Death in the Afternoon* appeared, ostensibly a 'technical' study of bullfighting, almost every reviewer was startled and puzzled. Little wonder, for the book was visibly as different from *The Sun Also Rises* and *A Farewell to Arms* as Rabelais' *Gargantua and Pantagruel*, Melville's *Moby-Dick*, and Sterne's *Tristram Shandy*. Hemingway had written an extraordinarily personal, self-indulgent, garrulous, capricious, playful, bellicose and satiric book, even more unruly and clownish than *The Torrents of Spring*. He had obviously aimed to provoke, instruct and entertain readers in pell-mell fashion. There is no need here for a schema of the book, beyond noting that it contains scrambled chronology and thematic arrangement, wilful digressions, mock-scholarly apparatus (for example, a 'bibliographical note' refers readers to a Spanish bibliography—undated—for the '2077 books and pamphlets in Spanish dealing with or touching on tauromaquia' which he mock-modestly claimed to have read), fictional interludes, scathing allusions and references to contemporary writers and critics, self-derision ('the fellow is no philosopher, no savant, an incompetent zoologist, he drinks too much and cannot punctuate readily and now he has stopped writing dialogue'), sporadic statements of his literary aesthetics and method, and descriptions and analyses of bullfighting technique and background.

One of his most amusing inventions is a racy, intermittent dialogue with an 'Old Lady', perhaps modelled after the *New Yorker's* 'old lady in Dubuque' who symbolized provincial gentility in the late nineteen twenties. Hemingway's old lady initially earns his admiration because she finds the goring of horses 'homey'. His boisterous rudeness, scatology and violence fail to shock her—she can even chastise him upon occasion—but when she shows signs of being technically old-fashioned, demanding that he end a story with a 'wow', the kind of classical summary conclusion against which Sherwood Anderson and Hemingway both rebelled, he peremptorily throws her out of the book and continues without her.

Death in the Afternoon has all the earmarks of a volcanic psychological explosion. The roster of likely causes is long: his departure from Europe in 1928, after many years there, in order to resume residence in the United States, where he wrote *A Farewell to Arms*; the strains of his second marriage; his father's suicide in the fall of 1928; critics' jibes at his fiction's failure to reveal much psychological and social depth; the physical effects of much outdoor activity and drinking, as well as of an automobile accident suffered in 1930. Carlos Baker's biography does not integrate the experiences of these years into any meaningful pattern for us. But it is clear enough that Hemingway endured great stress. One clue to what occurred appears in *Death in the Afternoon*. Hemingway's statement that 'a serious writer is not to be confounded with a solemn writer' appears never to have been taken with the seriousness it deserves.

What it signalizes, I think, is Hemingway's awareness that in *A Farewell to Arms* the relatively rich comic thrust of his earlier writing is absent. The interchanges between the Italian Major Rinaldi and Lieutenant Frederic Henry are undoubtedly comic, as is the baiting to which the hapless young Catholic chaplain is subjected by his fellow-officers. Henry's retreat from the front, accompanied by three bumbling Italian soldiers, is vivified by light, incongruous misadventure. There are other comic elements to be sure, including witty word-play. Nevertheless, the comedy is drastically muted, so much so that a special analytic effort must be made to discern what lies subdued in the laconic prose. It is no accident that *A Farewell to Arms* became a best-seller despite the stock-market crash of October 1929 and was sold to the films for a substantial sum. The 'old lady in Dubuque' found little that disturbed her sense of proper comedy.

Hemingway's awareness of the withering away of his comedy was probably sharpened by the reviews of *A Farewell to Arms*. Though he affected to despise reviewers, and perhaps did, he was unusually sensitive to their judgments from the outset of his career. Echoes of their remarks, for example, keep popping up in *Death in the Afternoon*; he had satirized them recently in a poem, 'Valentine' (*Little Review*, May 1929). Few reviewers of the novel mentioned its 'humour'. Those who did were vague, noting without elaboration that the novel revealed a 'mordant humour' or that the humour possessed a 'grim dryness' or a 'peculiar hopelessness'. At least two critics were more specific. Lewis Galantière (*Hound & Horn*, January–March 1930) and Henry Hazlitt (New York *Sun*, 28 September 1929) explicitly stressed the limitations of the comedy, pointing out that it arose only when minor characters moved into the foreground.

The critical response had changed greatly from that evoked by *The Sun Also Rises*, which contained a visibly more powerful comic component. An anonymous reviewer (*Time*, 1 November 1926), for example, had characterized that novel as a 'semi-humorous love tragedy'; Ernest Boyd (*Independent*, 20 November 1926) had labelled the characters 'tragic comedians' and observed that humour was pervasive throughout; Percy Hutchinson (New York *Times*, 16 October 1927), in the course of reviewing *Men Without Women*, had reminded readers that *The Sun Also Rises* offered a 'mingling of tears and smiles .... spiritual pathos and human comedy'.

The extravagant discordance of *Death in the Afternoon* represents Hemingway's self-liberating, recuperative effort to revive a tragicomic mode of vision that had been dimmed. The book had had a lengthy gestation, Hemingway first having expressed his enthusiastic intention of writing it during 1925. Its subject—bullfighting—provides the metaphoric core as well as the dominant action of *The Sun Also Rises*, which Hemingway began writing in 1925. Some of the novel's pages, as suggested earlier, have a close, stylistic resemblance to parts of *Death in the Afternoon*.

Under the influence of Gertrude Stein and others, he earlier had written a vignette of a matador in action, based on a friend's anecdote, before ever seeing his first bullfights in the summer of 1923. That experience was almost immediately reflected in two ecstatic articles for the Toronto *Star Weekly* (20 and 27 October 1923). Not long thereafter, Hemingway composed five more bullfighting vignettes. These, together with the first one, appeared in the *Little Review* (Spring 1923), then were assembled as six of the seventeen 'chapters' of *In Our Time* (1924). The ferment of bullfighting led in the fall of 1924 to one of Hemingway's most famous stories, 'The Undefeated', (*This Quarter*, Autumn–Winter 1925-6), which received wide acclaim when published later in *Men Without Women*. Hemingway's final word on the subject prior to *Death in the Afternoon* was 'Bullfighting, Sport and Industry' (*Fortune*, March 1930), an article lavishly illustrated with works by Goya and others. From 1923 through 1931, Hemingway nurtured his avocation with regular attendance at bullfights in Europe.

Despite the extensiveness of Hemingway's involvement with bullfighting, however, it was not until he wrote *Death in the Afternoon* that he was able, for the first time, to project the idea that comedy and tragedy were both integral to the action. Indeed, it is only with the perspective afforded by his apologia in the opening chapter of the book —a placement that suggests the idea's importance to him—that we can gauge the extent to which his rigorously applied 'ice-berg' theory had prevented him from 'writing truly' earlier, not only about the bullfight, but about other experience as well.

Even in *Death in the Afternoon*, as it happens, the concept of tragicomedy as the key to bullfighting is articulated with difficulty. One must supplement Hemingway's rather incoherent discussion in the first chapter with scattered statements in other parts of the book. He muddied his exposition because of his felt need to repudiate forcefully the 'modern moral point of view', the 'Christian point of view' which had repressed his self-realization. The undertaking was essential, but it made his prose circuitously defensive and aggressive. He raged against the sentimental humanitarianism of those more concerned with animals in the ring than with the men also present, against the middle-class American tourist, embodiment of 'Christian' gentility: 'the citizens who knew they were morally bound to leave the bull ring after the first bull [and] stand up to make their well-fed, skull and bones-ed, porcellian-ed, beach-tanned, flannelled, Panama-hatted, sport-shod exits.' In these lines and others like them, Hemingway again sported the satiric verve which had enlivened the ridicule of 'romantic gentility' in his journalism of the early nineteen twenties.

Incoherently formulated though it may be, the interpretation of bullfighting as tragicomedy nevertheless emerges. Hemingway, it must be granted, persists in terming the bullfight a 'tragedy'. But that classification, the result of his limited terminology, is contradicted by the archetypal pattern of rebirth he presents, which takes precedence. The pattern is one encompassing tragedy and going beyond it, as Wylie Sypher has succinctly put it:

> From the anthropologist's point of view the tragic action, however inspiring and however perfect in artistic form, runs through only one arc of the full cycle of drama; for the entire ceremonial cycle is birth: struggle: death: resurrection. The tragic arc is only birth: struggle: death. Consequently the range of comedy is wider than the tragic range—perhaps more fearless—and comic action can risk a different sort of purgation and triumph.[1]

Man, 'in rebellion against death', assumes the 'Godlike' privilege of meting it out. Thus he achieves a pagan 'ecstasy of ordered, formal, passionate, increasing disregard for death' that transforms him, leaving him with a 'feeling of life and death and mortality and immortality'.

[1] *Comedy* edited by Willie Sypher (New York, 1956), p. 220.

The bullfight is a ritually disciplined, religious drama through whose fixed succession of acts man transcends death, either as participant or as observer, risking his life in combat with a sacrificial animal doomed to die in the arena. Should man die by accident, having performed as bravely and artfully as the ritual requires, he also gains the 'ecstasy' and the 'feeling'.

The comedy in all this was provided by the emaciated, worn-out horses who performed in act one of the complex drama, serving as picadors' mounts. Gored, lifted into the air on a bull's horn, the horse was a grotesquely 'comic character'. His 'disembowellings' were often 'funny', especially when after the goring he galloped 'in a stiff old-maidish fashion around a ring trailing the opposite of clouds of glory'. These 'visceral accidents' were as comic as those in the burlesque bullfights staged in Paris by the Fratellini clowns, for the mishaps turned act one into a 'complete burlesque' that travestied, and by contrast emphasized, the profound death-drama of which it was the introduction. No one responsive to the tragic quality of the whole could 'separate the minor comic-tragedy of the horse so as to feel it emotionally'.

It had taken Hemingway a long time to define the quintessential character of the bullfight. Oddly, Waldo Frank, whose *Virgin Spain* (1926) Hemingway caustically condemned as a mystical 'fake' in *Death in the Afternoon*, had not hesitated in his book to deal forthrightly with the horse as 'comedian'. Frank's details anticipate Hemingway's. The bullfight is a 'gross comedy of blood . . . dionysian and sadistic'. The gored horse is a comic 'presentiment of death':

> whipped to its feet by grooms. . . . The old nag's entrails hang in a coiled horror within a foot of the ground. The horse is comedian of the drama. . . . He lies on his back and his four anguished legs beat like drumsticks on the barrier. Or, losing his saddle, he plunges mad and blind around the ring, kicking his own intestines, until death takes him. Or the bull mangles him at once, and he disappears in a swirl of flesh. This is farce. . . . (p. 232)

During the nineteen twenties, obviously and ironically, the baroque Jewish outsider enjoyed a perceptual and expressive advantage over the WASP insider insofar as the bullfight was concerned.

Hemingway's bullfight prose of 1923 (the *Little Review* vignette and the 27 October newspaper article) either ignored the horse or else (the 20 October article) merely treated him as a ludicrous, insignificant element of the proceedings. The 20 October article likened the horse to

'Spark Plug', the grotesquely awkward racehorse in the newspaper comic strip 'Barney Google'. Stressing that the fight was a 'tragedy' rather than a 'sport', Hemingway reported the entrance of 'decrepit', picador-mounted horses into the arena, where they were protected from the bull's charges by the picadors. However, Hemingway probably knew already that picadors really encouraged bulls to gore and lift horses. This weakened the bull's neck muscles and made him lower his head, over which the matador then could easily place banderillas and the final, killing sword-thrust into the proper position between the bull's shoulders.

Only one of the five new bullfight vignettes published in *In Our Time* (1924)—the first ('chapter 12')—dealt with the horse. Here, as he would not again until eight years later in *Death in the Afternoon*, Hemingway looked directly and unabashedly at the horse as a tragic—though not comic—participant in the drama of death. The piece is crucial for our discussion and short enough to quote in its entirety:

> They whacked the white horse on the legs and he knee-ed himself up. The picador twisted the stirrups straight and pulled and hauled up into the saddle. The horse's entrails hung down in a blue bunch and swung backward and forward as he began to canter, the *monos* whacking him on the back of his legs with the rods. He cantered jerkily along the barrera. He stopped stiff and one of the *monos* held his bridle and walked him forward. The picador kicked in his spurs, leaned forward and shook his lance at the bull. Blood pumped regularly from between the horse's front legs. He was nervously wobbly. The bull could not make up his mind to charge.

This exercise in literary objectivity has all the passionless, scientific clarity of a police reporter relating neutral, existential facts. The 'iceberg' technique effectively conceals the intellectual and/or emotional meaning the facts possess for the reporter. No selective clues to any meaning are provided for the reader's benefit. He is free, dependent upon his make-up, to impose meaning, to laugh at the frivolity or to shudder at the horror, or to do neither. If a tragicomic effect is to be obtained, however, the reader must laugh and shudder, must yoke experiences and responses conventionally thought incompatible. The necessary fusion cannot be left to chance as it is in the vignette. Hemingway's literary nihilism derives not from any philosophical conviction, but from methodological constriction that enabled him to rationalize his repression of the comedic aspect of the horror, an aspect unpalatable to genteel American culture. The result is that the vignette does not project the specific ritual role assigned the horse in *Death in the Afternoon*, a role Hemingway surely was cognizant of, along with Waldo Frank, in the early nineteen twenties.

The 1924 vignette was reprinted in *In Our Time* (1925) with none of the potentially tragicomic details omitted. But a dilution of the sanguinary occurred in a version of the vignette written into 'The Undefeated':

> 'I got to go over there,' Manuel said and started on a run for the other side of the ring where the *monos* were leading a horse out by the bridle toward the bull, whacking him on the legs with rods and all in a procession trying to get him toward the bull who stood dropping his head, pawing, unable to make up his mind to charge. (*This Quarter* I [Autumn–Winter 1925–6], p. 219)

In immediately succeeding passages, the horse is gored by the bull and lifted into the air, but there are no details to indicate any consequent wounding, disembowelling or bloodying. The goring of another horse, whom a bull continues to savage after he has knocked him to the ground, is viewed with detachment by the matador-hero of the story. We observe objects and events through his eyes and, like him, see nothing sanguinary or comic. Before the bullfights begin, some of the picadors ironically term the otherwise undescribed horses 'beautiful' and deride them as 'skins'. Their conversation concludes as follows:

> 'This thing I'm on barely keeps me off the ground,' the first picador said.
> 'Sardines for the canning factory.'
> They laughed, sitting their gaunt horses in the dark.   (*Ibid.*, p. 213)

These lines were altered, eliminating most of the callous jocularity of the men, when 'The Undefeated' was published in *Men Without Women* (1927):

> 'This thing I'm on barely keeps me off the ground,' the first picador said.
> 'Well, they're horses.'
> 'Sure, they're horses.'
> They talked, sitting their gaunt horses in the dark.

Surprisingly, bullfighting as tragicomedy becomes least visible in *The Sun Also Rises*. Jake Barnes, the American newspaperman-narrator, has a deep sense of guilt about 'the spilling open of the horses in bull-fighting'. It is something too 'shameful' for him to talk about. He is obsessively worried that Lady Brett Ashley, whom he loves, will be disappointed in bullfighting when she sees picadors in action on their horses. 'Don't look,' he advises earlier, as they watch a bull gore a steer. Though he notices that she has been 'fascinated' by the occurrence, has remained so well balanced that she has caught the bull's 'shift from his left to his right horn' during the onslaught, Jake persists in believing that her sensibilities require his protection. On the first of several days of bullfighting, Jake advises Brett in advance not to 'look at the horses, after the bull hits them'. Predictably, she does not find it necessary to avert her gaze, even though she discovers that 'some rather awful things happen' to the horses. Her reaction does not keep him, on the second day, from repeating the identical words of caution, though he now explains the ritual to her 'so that it became more something that was going on with a definite end, and less of a spectacle with unexplained horrors'. There is no indication here or elsewhere that Jake has men-tioned or alluded to the horse as tragic comedian.

Jake Barnes generalizes about the horses and watches them in action. With one exception—in chapter XVIII—he does not describe them concretely. The other characters, whose conversations Jake recounts, also speak generally. The single exception conceals the awful things that happen to horses in the ring. A 'white horse'—nothing more specific is cited—is charged by a bull. The latter is diverted by the picador from goring the horse and the confrontation concludes thus: 'He [the bull] did not really want to get at the horse.'

Hemingway's evasive failure to grapple even slightly with the bloody 'comic-tragedy' of bullfighting in *The Sun Also Rises* weakens his novel considerably. It is inconceivable, first of all, why Jake Barnes should be such a reluctant narrator. One may argue that Jake's irrevers-ible wound—apparently his phallus had been damaged—has over-sensitized him to wounds in others. But this argument is not convinc-ing. Although Jake may weep in bed at night, he is essentially as 'hard-boiled' as he fancies himself. He can absorb physical punishment, social humiliation and verbal baiting without losing his tough equilibrium. As a working newspaperman, he is not averse to filling his dispatches with 'dirt'. Observing a man gored in the streets of Pamplona during the running of the bulls, Jake is unmoved; soon thereafter, he recites a comprehensive newspaper report of the funeral. The pic-ing of bulls does not upset him; he is stirred and vitalized by their slaughter. By virtue of his temperament and narrative role, Jake is in a position to fulfil the catalytic, interpretive assignment which Hemingway withheld from him.

Equally pertinent when considering Jake's qualifications for weaving together the ritual structure and thematic progression of the novel is his possession of 'aficion', that 'passion' for and of bullfighting which only masters of its rites may claim, their title of 'aficionado' acknowledged mutely by the laying on of hands. Jake is not a bullfighter, of course; not all bullfighters, however, possess aficion. The perfect young bullfighter Romero, for example, loses his aficion when he succumbs to the Circe-like wiles of the lustful Brett. None of Jake's friends is sufficiently purified by experience and knowledge to share his rare and religious passion. As early as Chapter II, Jake tells Robert Cohn of his regular attendance at the summer bullfights in Spain. Only a bullfighter, Jake says then, lives life to its utmost, 'all the way up'. The vernacular sexual allusion points up the symbolic importance of bullfighting in the novel, its literal importance for Jake. Still potent despite his phallic injury, Jake remains capable of sexual desire which the bullfight can render orgasmic.

The first third of the novel is a preparation for Jake's departure with Bill Gorton for Spain, marked by the preliminary cleansing in water made possible by their trout-fishing expedition. The remaining two thirds is dominated by the Dionysian fiesta in Pamplona which is both secular and religious, followed by Jake's post-fiesta rebirth in the ocean waters off San Sebastian. The completion of the tragicomic cycle begun in Paris, which will be repeated again by Jake in succeeding years, is marked by the symbolic baton held aloft at the novel's close . . . Jake's injured phallus returned intact.

Central to the structure of the novel is the archetypal rebirth pattern embodied in the ritual drama of the bullfight, whose full cycle was not—but should have been—developed in *The Sun Also Rises*. The novel is replete with many compatible though unlinked tragic and comic elements that beg for the powerful unifying fusion and focus which the true bullfight would have provided. For example, the parallel plot involving Cohn's comic love for Brett and Jake's tragic love for Brett would have been strengthened in tragicomic force. Jake's literal and symbolic distance from his psychologically and socially disordered associates would have been more firmly delineated from the outset.

Romero would not have remained the artist-technician he now is, but would have become the archetypal surrogate for Jake that he was intended to be. The satire, wit and clowning that enliven the novel would not have been susceptible to the charge of being mere entertainment, but would have been recognized as the essential surface complement of the tragicomic strain residing at all levels of the novel. To sum up, it would not have been necessary for Hemingway to have written *Death in the Afternoon* as he did, and for us to read it in order to understand *The Sun Also Rises*, if he had not distorted his understanding of the bullfight and so, in effect, throttled the imaginative reach that from the outset was necessary to produce a long-enduring book.

Note

Life and Writing

Faulkner was born in 1897 at New Albany, Mississippi. In 1902, his family moved 30 miles to Oxford, Mississippi, where he lived most of his life. During the First World War, rejected by the American army, Faulkner joined the RAF but did not see service abroad. Afterwards he spent a short time at the University of Mississippi, worked in New York and at home in Oxford, then lived in New Orleans. Here his determination to become a writer took final shape, and friendship with Sherwood Anderson helped him find a publisher for his first novel, *Soldiers' Pay* (1926). *Mosquitoes*, about a group of New Orleans artists and their hangers-on, was published in 1927. Subsequently Faulkner 'discovered that my own little postage stamp of native soil was worth writing about . . . and that by sublimating the actual into the apocryphal I would have complete liberty to use whatever talent I might have to its absolute top.' *Sartoris* (1929), *The Sound and the Fury* (1929), *As I Lay Dying* (1930), *Sanctuary* (1930), *Light in August* (1932), *Absalom, Absalom!* (1936), *The Unvanquished* (1938), *The Hamlet* (1940) and *Go Down, Moses* (1942), among other novels and story-collections, were the products of this creative explosion—all set in an imaginary Mississippi county he named after an actual river, the Yoknapatawpha. Though he spent a little time in Hollywood, Faulkner held himself aloof from literary and cultural *milieux* and cultivated a reputation for solitariness, calling himself primarily a farmer. Important novels in his later writing include *Intruder in the Dust* (1948), *A Fable* (1954), *The Town* (1957) and *The Mansion* (1959)—volumes II and III of a trilogy begun with *The Hamlet*—and *The Reivers* (1962). After receiving the Nobel Prize in 1950, he consented to become something more of a public figure, going on speaking tours and opening himself to question from interviewers and students: see *Faulkner in the University* edited by F. L. Gwynn and J. L. Blotner (New York, 1965) and *Lion in the Garden* edited by J. B. Meriwether and M. Millgate (New York, 1968). He died in 1962.

Criticism. Two essay-collections provide a useful conspectus of criticism: they are *William Faulkner: Three Decades of Criticism* edited by Frederick J. Hoffman and Olga W. Vickery (East Lansing, Mich., 1960; Harbinger paperback, 1963) and *Faulkner: A Collection of Critical Essays* edited by Robert Penn Warren (Englewood Cliffs, N.J., 1966). The essays by George Marion O'Donnell, Malcolm Cowley, Robert Penn Warren, Conrad Aiken and Jean-Paul Sartre (most in both volumes) are of particular historical importance; each collection reprints chapters from major books on Faulkner, including Olga W. Vickery, *The Novels of William Faulkner: A Critical Interpretation* (Baton Rouge, 1959), Walter J. Slatoff, *Quest for Failure: A Study of William Faulkner* (Ithaca, 1963), Michael Millgate, *The Achievement of William Faulkner* (New York/London, 1965) and Cleanth Brooks, *William Faulkner: The Yoknapatawpha Country* (New Haven/London, 1963). F. W. Volpe, *A Reader's Guide to William Faulkner* (New York/London, 1964) and Dorothy Tuck, *A Handbook of Faulkner* (New York, 1964) are useful guides to difficulties. A recent study which qualifies the 'historical myth' first posited in O'Donnell and Cowley and questioned in this essay is Melvin Backman, *Faulkner: The Major Years* (Bloomington/London, 1966). (See also footnote 5 below.)

VIII

Faulkner and the Revision of Yoknapatawpha History

ARNOLD GOLDMAN

I

MY CONCERN in this essay is with the sources of Faulkner's energy and complexity, and with the relation of these to the character of his fiction as a historical report. As I understand the former, they require a strenuous critique of the view that the Yoknapatawpha novels and stories constitute a coherent sequence, a legendary history. Over a dozen years ago it was already possible for scholars, like Florence Leaver, to assert with confidence that 'few readers doubt that the Yoknapatawpha novels constitute a myth.' At that time, as *inter alia* now, the major articles of critical faith were to be found in George Marion O'Donnell's essay 'Faulkner's Mythology', which appeared in the *Kenyon Review* in 1939, and in Malcolm Cowley's 'Introduction' to *The Portable Faulkner*, which was published in 1946. Florence Leaver herself drew attention to these two critics, noting that they 'based their analysis upon the narrative element, upon the dovetailing of the pieces of the total story, not always precisely, from novel to novel.'[1]

In view of the importance this emphasis on Faulkner's work has had, and the stress that has been given to the idea of the existence of a total story or a legend that lies behind his work, it is worth recalling the terms of reference those early essays set. This is Cowley's view:

> Faulkner might divide his work into a number of cycles: one about the planters and their descendants, one about the townspeople of Jefferson, one about the poor whites, one about the Indians . . . and one about the Negroes. Or again, if he adopted a division by families, there would be the Compson–Sartoris saga, the still unfinished

[1] Florence Leaver, 'Faulkner: the Word as Principle and Power', *South Atlantic Quarterly* (Autumn, 1958), p. 464; reprinted in *William Faulkner: Three Decades of Criticism*, p. 199.

Snopes saga, the McCaslin saga . . . and the Ratliff–Bundren saga, devoted to the backwoods farmers of Frenchman's Bend. All the cycles or sagas are closely interconnected; it is as if each new book was a chord or segment of a total situation always existing in the author's mind. . . .

All his books in the Yoknapatawpha saga are part of the same living pattern. It is this pattern, and not the printed volumes in which part of it is recorded, that is Faulkner's real achievement. . . .

Briefly stated, the legend might run something like this: The Deep South was settled partly by aristocrats like the Sartoris clan and partly by new men like Colonel Sutpen. Both types of planters were determined to establish a lasting social order on the land they had seized from the Indians (that is, to leave sons behind them). They had the virtue of living single-mindedly by a fixed code; but there was also an inherent guilt in their 'design', their way of life; it was slavery that put a curse on the land and brought about the Civil War. After the War was lost, partly as a result of their own mad heroism (for who but men as brave as Jackson and Stuart could have frightened the Yankees into standing together and fighting back?) they tried to restore 'the design' by other methods. But they no longer had the strength to achieve more than a partial success, even after they had freed their land from the carpetbaggers who had followed the Northern Armies. As time passed, moreover, the men of the old order found that they had Southern enemies too; they had to fight against a new exploiting class descended from the landless whites of slavery days. In this struggle between the clan of Sartoris and the unscrupulous tribe of Snopes, the Sartorises were defeated in advance by a traditional code that kept them from using the weapons of the enemy. As a price of victory, however, the Snopeses had to serve the mechanized civilization of the North, which was morally impotent in itself, but which with the aid of its Southern retainers, ended by corrupting the Southern nation.[2]

Though the term 'legend' is ambiguous, leaving us suspended between the idea of Faulkner's fiction as a narrative history and as a myth, Cowley's emphasis is quite clear. There is, so to speak, a 'total situation' in terms of imagined history behind Faulkner's individual fictions and having a prior existence to any given occasion of writing, and only a portion of it is present in any one Yoknapatawpha novel or collection. The whole becomes acknowledgedly greater than the sum of the

[2] Cowley, quoted from *William Faulkner: Three Decades of Criticism*, pp. 98, 99, 102–3.

parts and the critic's task the reconstitution of the presumed whole by fitting the pieces together.

Robert Penn Warren, reviewing Cowley's *The Portable Faulkner* in the *New Republic* in 1946, pointed out that 'The emphasis on the unity of Faulkner's work may, however, lead to an underrating of the degree of organization within individual works.'[3] Moreover, the tendency of Cowley's approach is to call attention away from any sense that Faulkner, even when he uses the same characters and places from novel to novel, may have been attempting less to fill in the whole history of Yoknapatawpha than to re-envisage and reinterpret his themes and subjects, to reinvent his South. Cowley's assumption of a linear unity to Yoknapatawpha history still persists—a significant recent instance is Cleanth Brooks's study *Faulkner: The Yoknapatawpha Country*. My argument in this essay is that the holistic view of the fiction can and should be questioned, that Faulkner viewed Yoknapatawpha 'history' less as a matter for report than a basis for reinvention and scepticism.[4] Criticism which qualifies a holistic view can discover significant alteration, development, progression and dialectic in Faulkner's *œuvre*, and, in the end, give a truer account of its sophisticated and 'modernistic' nature.[5]

II

In *The Faulkner–Cowley File* we can watch Malcolm Cowley discovering inconsistencies that follow hard on the heels of his vision of the integrity of Faulkner's 'myth of the South'. He comes to see that

[3] Quoted from *William Faulkner: Three Decades of Criticism*, p. 123.

[4] In answer to a student's question about widely divergent appearances by one of his characters, Faulkner said, 'These people I figure belong to me and I have the right to move them about in time when I need them.' (*Faulkner in the University*, p. 79).

[5] When this essay was going to press, the author was privileged to hear Professor James B. Meriwether give a lecture titled 'Is There a Yoknapatawpha Saga?' It is his thesis that Faulkner had no intention to write a continuous or connectable saga and, further, that there is no O'Donnell–Cowley 'Myth of the South' which can be stretched over the length and breadth of Faulkner's fiction. Professor Meriwether believes that primary attention should now be given to the principle of organization in particular works, and that it is still premature, twenty five years after Warren's warning, to hazard any 'unity' to replace the one he demolishes. Professor Meriwether's lecture is shortly to appear in the *Nouvelle revue française*. For some earlier remarks by Professor

mere carelessness and forgetfulness on Faulkner's part is not the full explanation—and that the effect of certain discrepancies makes it difficult to retain the idea of a unitary Yoknapatawpha. Faulkner had written to Cowley that he 'realized some time ago you would get into this inconsistency and pitied you'.[6] But he in fact compounded Cowley's difficulty by writing '1699–1945 Appendix: The Compsons' in answer to Cowley's request for something with which to round off *The Portable Faulkner*. Cowley, though pleased with what he had fathered, then noted further inconsistencies—now between the 'Appendix' and *The Sound and the Fury*. Faulkner then wrote to him:

> Would rather let the appendix stand with the inconsistencies, perhaps make a statement (quotable) at the end of the introduction, viz.: The inconsistencies in the appendix prove to me the book is still alive after 15 years, and being still alive is growing, changing. . . I was even wrong now and then (in 1929) in the very conclusions I drew from watching them (the Compsons), and the information in which I once believed.[7]

Cowley's own comment, as he surveys his 'file', puts a brave face on the matter:

> The true Compson story was the one that lived and grew in his imagination. The published book contained only what he had known about the story in 1929, in other words, only part of the truth.[8]

But neither Faulkner's 'statement' (which Cowley did not include in *The Portable Faulkner*)[9] nor Cowley's gloss answer some very real questions. What did Faulkner mean by saying 'the book is still alive . . .

Meriwether about Cowley's *Portable Faulkner*, see 'The Textual History of *The Sound and the Fury*', in *Studies in The Sound and the Fury* compiled by James B. Meriwether (Columbus, Ohio, 1970), pp. 25–9.

[6] Malcolm Cowley, *The Faulkner–Cowley File* (New York, 1966), p. 54.

[7] *Ibid.*, p. 90.

[8] *Ibid.*, p. 47.

[9] He merely noted that there were 'inconsistencies of detail', 'errors . . . comparatively few and inconsequential . . . . most of them . . . afterthoughts rather than oversights' (Cowley, in *William Faulkner: Three Decades of Criticism*, pp. 98–9). Faulkner remembered his disclaimer, however, and in 1959 prefaced *The Mansion* with a version of it, to account for the differences between that novel and the two earlier volumes of the 'Snopes trilogy'.

and . . . is growing, changing'? Why did he introduce the notion of 'information . . . once believed', in doing which he 'was even wrong now and then'?

Most of the items at issue between Faulkner and Cowley seemed small enough at first—which tree did Quentin's (Caddy's daughter) climb down, how much did Jason steal from his mother. But Faulkner widened the issue. Are the explanations only concerned with additions and further developments in the Compson 'saga', with perhaps the qualifications amounting to an additional point-of-view? Or could it be a matter of an even more radical process of recomposition in which neither character nor event, neither attitude nor time is sacrosanct? Is Faulkner's 'Appendix' in fact a different story? The matter is worth pursuing as an index to Faulkner's method from work to work, and even from part to part in a single fiction.

The Modern Library edition of *The Sound and the Fury* (first published in 1929) long wrongly printed Faulkner's 'Appendix' to *The Portable Faulkner* as a preface. Faulkner later spoke of it as his fifth try 'to get the story told' and of chapters I–IV as four similar attempts:

> I wrote it five separate times, trying to tell the story. . . .
>
> I had already begun to tell the story through the eyes of the idiot child, since I felt that it would be more effective as told by someone capable only of knowing what happened, but not why. I saw that I had not told the story that time. I tried to tell it again, the same story through the eyes of another brother. That was still not it. I told it for the third time through the eyes of the third brother. That was still not it. I tried to gather the pieces together and fill the gaps by making myself the spokesman. It was still not complete, not until fifteen years after the book was published, when I wrote as an appendix to another book the final effort to get the story told and off my mind. . . .[10]

Four versions did not exhaust the ways in which it might be told, and neither did the fifth. Faulkner was soon speaking of his 'Appendix' as a more limited production, as embodying a quite special viewpoint, the angle, he wrote to Cowley, of 'a Garter King-at-Arms, heartless, not very moved, cleaning up "Compson" before going on to the next "C-o" or "C-r".'[11] To see the Appendix as embodying a particular

---

[10] From *The Paris Review* interview with Jean Stein. As reprinted in *William Faulkner: Three Decades of Criticism*, the quotation is on pp. 73–4.

[11] *Faulkner–Cowley File*, p. 44.

point of view—perhaps not quite so 'heartless' as Faulkner says—
suggests that there can be no final version, no completion to his story.

Benjy's Saturday is the point of maximum suspension of the story's
elements: Caddy is present in a world without 'was' and her daughter
not yet fled with the money Jason has been filching from her. Richard
Chase commented that 'what happens' in Benjy's chapter 'epitomizes
and forecasts the rest of the novel'.[12] His particular examples, however,
only show that the characters of Jason and Quentin are recognizable
even in childhood. The first chapter is more truly a kind of 'primal soup'
of Compson-matter, a teeming, disorderly whole from which all things
will stem and to which they return. (Similarly O'Donnell and others
have seen *Sartoris* as the matrix of the entire Yoknapatawpha saga.)

With Quentin's day in 1910, we turn not just to a point in the past
but to one which, by being *about* the past, stands for the whole relation
of the Compson story in 1928 to its past. There is a truth to the idea
that *The Sound and the Fury* moves from a Sartoris-world to a Snopes-
world: by claiming an incestuous relation with Caddy, Quentin has,
as his father puts it, attempted to keep his family free of 'the loud
world'. His failure to invest her with a suitable 'doom' opens the way
to Jason's Friday chapter, so very much set in the new and unromantic
time—'Once a bitch always a bitch, what I say.' (There is a pointed
dating to Jason's chapter, with its stock market reports and reflections
on Babe Ruth and the New York Yankees.) But just as Quentin could
not 'isolate' Caddy, Jason cannot contain young Quentin: the victim-
izer becomes the victim he has always seen himself as. Again the story
washes on past effort to terminate it.

With Faulkner himself taking on the narrative in the final section,
our expectation of a more comprehensive point of view and a completion of the action increases. We get them only ironically. Dilsey, for all
that she is an antithetical model to Jason or Mrs Compson's methods of
promoting family solidarity, is equally ineffective. With Caroline
Compson crying 'Find the note. . . . Quentin left a note when he did
it', and Jason off after the 'red tie', Dilsey takes refuge in the sermon of
Rev. Shegog, conflating his 'ricklickshun' with the history of the
Compsons, 'de first en de last'. She is more successful than Quentin was
in putting a fate on the family. But for the fourth time a chapter washes
on past the ending it would have had if its focal character could provide

[12] Richard Chase, *The American Novel and Its Tradition* (New York, 1957),
p. 227.

a resolution. Faulkner takes us with Jason to Mottson and failure, and then to the town square of Jefferson where a bellowing Benjy threatens to reintroduce the chaos of the novel's beginning. Jason is left to restore the merely trivial orderliness now ironically possible.

Malcolm Cowley noted not only factual discrepancies. He saw a more sympathetic treatment of Jason in the 'Appendix'. Faulkner agreed:

> Jason is the new South too. I mean he is the one Compson and Sartoris who met Snopes on his own ground and in a fashion held his own.[13]

The 'Appendix' contains a 'new view' of Jason not really to be got out of the novel proper, a reconception of not only 'the very conclusions I drew from watching them' but also 'the information in which I once believed'.

The individual sections of The Sound and the Fury do not conflict with one another as they do with the 'Appendix'. Different first-person narratives restrain overt conflicts, making them largely *personal* differences of view. Each major character resists change and is either incapable of or actively seeking *not* to have to reinterpret himself, his family and their history. Quentin's resistance, like young Bayard's in *Sartoris*, requires suicide to prevent the necessity of reinterpretation. (In *Absalom, Absalom!*, Quentin, at one remove from his own family situation, becomes an arch-promoter of the reconceptualization of Thomas Sutpen and his family.) Thus, in The Sound and the Fury, Faulkner is able to create a margin of room for the reconception of the Compson story against the very grain of his characters, who cannot, will not and do not.

Sartoris (1929) contains a similar past/present scheme to The Sound and the Fury. Events in the Civil War, particularly the madcap raid across Federal Lines, lie behind the contemporary situation. Jenny (Sartoris) Dupré endows the Sartorises, extrapolating from the Civil War exploits, with an aura of fatality. More recent events are interpreted by her only in this light, and her interpretation comprises a kind of choric temptation for young Bayard to believe it made him get his brother killed in the recently ended World War. One centre of the contemporary story is Bayard's resistance to and flight from that interpretation, one which permits no reinterpretation of his action in other terms. In the end he succumbs: surrounded by the altogether admirable

13 *The Faulkner–Cowley File*, p. 25.

MacCallum hill-folk (surely a poignant symbol of an unavailable alternative mode of life to the doom-haunted Sartorises), Bayard accuses himself of killing both his grandfather, who has died of a heart attack, and his brother:

> [He] stared into the fire for a time, rubbing his hands slowly on his knees, and for an instant he saw the recent months of his life coldly in all their headlong and heedless wastefulness; saw its entirety like the swift unrolling of a film, culminating in that which he had been warned against and that any fool might have foreseen. Well, damn it, suppose it had: was he to blame? Had he insisted that his grandfather ride with him? Had he given the old fellow a bum heart? and then coldly: *You were afraid to go home. You made a nigger sneak your horse out to you. You, who deliberately do things your judgment tells you may not be successful, even possible, are afraid to face the consequences of your own acts.* Then again something bitter and deep and sleepless in him blazed out in vindication and justification and accusation; what he knew not, blazing out at what, Whom, he did not know: *You did it! You caused it all; you killed Johnny.*

From this point Bayard sleep-walks his life, like Quentin on the day of his suicide, no longer resisting the 'doom' of the Sartorises. Again, as in *The Sound and the Fury*, Faulkner has created a little space for himself, though the margin of freedom, after this second excursion, is less. It is only that the author does not himself wholly need to subscribe to the 'myth' of fatality, though he shows its dreadful victory within and over his characters.

Already the main historical aspect of Faulkner's need to recreate his world within the framework of 'the Yoknapatawpha country' is becoming clear. Is there a way for a man to face the present, without succumbing to the pattern of the past, freely and with honour? And, as a corollary, by what means does the author himself refrain from accepting as a premise an interpretation which his primary characters, however unwillingly, come to accept and to live within?

III

We have so far traced a relation from certain discrepancies to a technique of re-envisioning a fiction as it proceeds to the theme of interpretation and reinterpretation in two early novels. Each of these aspects can be followed throughout Faulkner's work. At this point we will look at the growth of certain techniques which are variants of the first two, after which we will return to the question of reinterpretation as Faulkner's way of dealing with 'the burden of Southern history'. Faulkner's strategies for variegating his fictional surface suggest a certain attempt at detachment from the 'reality' of a unitary Yoknapatawpha history and his more direct dealings with the successive interpretations of Southern history represent increasingly bolder, and possibly more desperate attempts to discover both an explanation of its condition and a saving grace of freedom of action.

A certain heterogeneity of styles and themes characterizes Faulkner's first two novels, *Soldiers' Pay* and *Mosquitoes*, as well as *The Sound and the Fury*. The dramatization of Sartoris 'fatality' brought a new uniformity of style to Faulkner, but as young Bayard's actions begin to commit Faulkner to the reality of that fatality, a certain fragmentation of styles re-enters his prose (as in the serenading of Narcissa Benbow).[14] *As I Lay Dying*, carrying further the method of the first three chapters of *The Sound and the Fury*, formalized the heterogeneity of styles by giving the novel to a dozen or more characters to comment on the death and funeral journey of Addie Bundren. Though the interpretations each character puts upon events conflict radically—and their conflicting interpretations have led to even more polarization of opinion among the commentators—having characters to lodge these interpretations within considerably domesticates the heterogeneity. The author does not seem to be contradicting himself.

There are signs, however, that the restraints of a point of view treatment are not wholly observed. Addie speaks out of a timeless grave, and some of the 'inventions' of Darl are so circumstantial that Faulkner's later defence of them as likely in a madman falters:

> Anyway, nobody can dispute it and that was a very good way, I thought, a very effective way to tell what was happening back there at home—well, call it a change of pace. A trick, but since the whole book was a *tour de force*, I think that this is a permissible trick.[15]

'Trick' is a word Faulkner often used when asked to comment upon his juxtapositions, changes of focus and other alogical techniques,

[14] We will know more about this aspect of Faulkner's technique and more about how he developed his Yoknapatawpha people when the earlier draft of *Sartoris*, titled *Flags in the Dust*, is eventually published.

[15] *Faulkner in the University*, p. 113.

although he could get unhappy with its derogatory connotations. He implies that what there was to be seen in individual portions of an action had to be said, regardless of whether, from a realistic point of view, there was anyone *there* likely to say them. The fabric of the novel is thereby striated, with no simple unity of narrative structure along a horizontal plane.

Though 'nobody can dispute it', for much of what we think *happened* in *As I Lay Dying*, and out of which we build our interpretations, our only authority is a Darl Bundren who was not present at (nor could even in many cases have heard of) the events recorded. The only wholly satisfactory aesthetic hypothesis is not that the novel records a number of different points of view located in particular characters, but that the whole takes place in the mind of its creator, Faulkner, and is a kind of dream or surrealistic drama.[16]

In Faulkner's subsequent longer fiction, the point-of-view section moves specifically outward from the character to the writer himself. The sections begin to fall more and more into short-story-like units and the fictions as a whole conflate the genres of the novel and the short-story collection. A comparable effect of stratification follows: the parts begin to compete with one another as interpretations of the action. Even before this conflation of forms is total (in *The Unvanquished* and *Go Down, Moses*), something of the same result begins to appear.

The chapter which seems almost to be a new beginning to the novel is a case in point. The description of Red's funeral in *Sanctuary* (1931) and the Percy Grimm chapter of *Light in August* (1934) have this effect.[17] Grimm's 'story' comes between two panels concerning Joe Christmas's paradoxical abandonment of the flight which has characterized him from the beginning and creates a denser texture, a new interpretation of the context in which the equivocal gesture occurs.

The Jefferson through which the killer Grimm moves is, however, only the most nightmarish of the communities through which Christmas has fled in the novel, places where every man's hand has been turned against him. On the other side we have the responses to Lena Grove, opposite

---

[16] I have interpreted the brothel chapter of Joyce's *Ulysses* along similar lines in *The Joyce Paradox* (London and Evanston, Ill., 1966), pp. 96–100.

[17] Interestingly, Cowley used both of these in *The Portable Faulkner*, in the 'Modern Times' section of his chronological presentation.

in character, even in that same Jefferson. Everyone bends to sympathize, to care. The difference is so great as to strain one's credence, viewed realistically. But as these two 'stories' which thread through the novel proceed without really touching, a less *realistic* impression begins to impose itself. It is as though Jefferson is a different town in each case, one dark, one light—one a nightmare world of hostility, the other a fantasy-world of gratification. It is interesting to speculate that just as Faulkner had turned aside from his Jefferson families in *As I Lay Dying* to the hill folk—'simpler in mind and liv[ing] more remotely from the Snopes world than the younger Sartorises and Compsons'[18]—so in returning to Jefferson in *Light in August* (though still avoiding the main families) he gives us less of the mixed world of *The Sound and the Fury* than one polarized into a positive and a negative dream.[19]

Where *Light in August* counterpoints its characters' resolutions in one place and time, *The Unvanquished* (1938) requires a longer period to expose the range of fates for those involved in its central action, the Civil War. It is interesting that O'Donnell made *The Unvanquished* the centrepiece of his exposition of the 'series of related myths (or aspects of a single myth)' he found in the Yoknapatawpha novels:

> In a rearrangement of the novels, say for a collected edition, *The Unvanquished* might well stand first; for the action occurs earlier, historically, than in any other of the books, and it objectifies, in the essential terms of Mr. Faulkner's mythology, the central dramatic tension of his work. On one side of the conflict there are the Sartorises, recognizable human beings who act traditionally. Against them the invading Northern armies, and their diversified allies in the reconstruction era, wage open war, aiming to make the traditional actions of the Sartorises impossible.
>
> The invaders are unable to cope with the Sartorises; but their invasion provides another antagonist with an occasion within which his special anti-Sartoris talent makes him singularly powerful. This antagonist is the landless poor-white horse trader, Ab Snopes; his special talent is his low cunning as an entrepreneur. He acts without regard for the legitimacy of his means; he has no ethical code. In the crisis brought about by the war, he is enabled to use a member of the Sartoris family for his own advantage because, for the first time, he can be useful to the Sartorises. Moreover, he is enabled to make this Sartoris (Mrs Rosa Millard) betray herself

[18] O'Donnell, in *William Faulkner: Three Decades of Criticism*, p. 87.
[19] Hence the crucial role of Byron Bunch, who moves in both.

into an act of self-interest such as his, and to cause her death while using her as his tool.

The characters and the conflict are particular and credible. But they are also mytholgical. In Mr. Faulkner's mythology there are two kinds of characters: they are Sartorises or Snopeses, whatever the family names may be. And in the spiritual geography of Mr. Faulkner's work there are two worlds: the Sartoris world and the Snopes world. In all of his successful books, he is exploring the two worlds in detail, dramatizing the inevitable conflict between them.[20]

One might point to the extent which this interpretation, compelling though its boldness may be, is ultimately reductionist in import. Where Ab Snopes's victory over Rosa Millard in the eighteen sixties can be seen as an epitome of a cycle which stretches from 1810 to 1950 (in round figures),[21] an assumption of a static, repetitive whole is apparent.

That Faulkner was interested, here and elsewhere, in the moment in time when a pattern is set, a point from which one may see subsequent history as explained if not determined, is indubitable. That he, or the characters whom he involves in such a search, fear as much as they long to find such a moment is equally true. It is important also to note how much he invested in finding a counter-moment in history, one which would not close off hope but open it up. The defeat of Rosa Millard—and even that is not as unambiguous as O'Donnell seems to think—is balanced in *The Unvanquished* by thrusts in another direction.

Subsequent to the publication of the magazine version of 'Retreat' (in October, 1934), Faulkner added a section on Buck and Buddy McCaslin's ideas about farming and the land:

> Father said they were ahead of their time; he said they not only possessed, but put into practice, ideas about social relationship that maybe fifty years after they were both dead people would have a name for. These ideas were about land. They believed that land did not belong to people but that people belonged to land and that the earth would permit them to live on and out of it and use it only so long as they behaved and that if they did not behave right, it would

[20] O'Donnell, *op. cit.*, p. 83.
[21] O'Donnell had forgotten that *Absalom, Absalom!* has some events set as far back as 1807, and an important section in 1833, when Sutpen comes to Yoknapatawpha. Writing in 1939, he could not of course have known that Faulkner in subsequent novels was to bring his Yoknapatawpha characters past 1929.

shake them off just like a dog getting rid of fleas. They had some kind of a system of book-keeping which must have been even more involved than their betting score against one another, by which all their niggers were to be freed, not given freedom, but earning it, buying it not in money from Uncle Buck and Buddy, but in work from the plantation. Only there were others besides niggers, and this was the reason why Uncle Buck came hobbling across the square, shaking his stick at me and hollering, or at least why it was Uncle Buck who was hobbling and hollering and shaking the stick. One day Father said how they suddenly realized that if the county ever split up into private feuds either with votes or weapons, no family could contend with the McCaslins because all the other families would have only their cousins and kin to recruit from, while Uncle Buck and Buddy would already have an army. These were the dirt farmers, the people whom the niggers called 'white trash'—men who had owned no slaves and some of whom even lived worse than slaves on big plantations. It was another side of Uncle Buck's and Buddy's ideas about men and land, which Father said people didn't have a name for yet, by which Uncle Buck and Buddy had persuaded the white men to pool their little patches of poor hill land along with the niggers and the McCaslin plantation, promising them in return nobody knew exactly what, except that their women and children did have shoes, which not all of them had had before, and a lot of them even went to school.

It was not, however, in *The Unvanquished* but in *Go Down, Moses* (1942), that a full exposition of the McCaslin fortunes was given, and there, significantly, no trace of this 'system' appears.

Indeed, the whole question of their being or having been a moment of *social* solution, a moment to look back to as part of an ameliorative tradition, is an issue of hot debate in the final story in *The Unvanquished*, 'An Odour of Verbena'. In the section beginning 'Drusilla said he had a dream', young Bayard Sartoris argues out with his stepmother the social significance of his father's actions during Reconstruction, introducing the figure of Thomas Sutpen as a kind of antithesis:

'But nobody could have more of a dream than Colonel Sutpen,' I said. He had been Father's second-in-command in the first regiment and had been elected colonel when the regiment deposed Father after Second Manassas, and it was Sutpen and not the regiment whom father never forgave. He was underbred, a cold ruthless man who had come into the country about thirty years before the War, nobody knew from where except Father said you could look at him

M

and know he would not dare to tell. He had got some land and nobody knew how he did that either, and he got money from somewhere—Father said they all believed he robbed steam-boats, either
as a card sharper or as an out-and-out highwayman—and built a
big house and married and set up as a gentleman. Then he lost
everything in the War like everybody else, all hope of descendants
too (his son killed his daughter's fiancé on the eve of the wedding
and vanished) yet he came back home and set out single-handed to
rebuild his plantation. He had no friends to borrow from and he had
nobody to leave it to and he was past sixty years old, yet he set out
to rebuild his place like it used to be; they told how he was too busy
to bother with politics or anything; how when Father and the other
men organized the nightriders to keep the carpet baggers from
organizing the Negroes into an insurrection, he refused to have
anything to do with it. Father stopped hating him long enough to
ride out to see Sutpen himself and he (Sutpen) came to the door with
a lamp and did not even invite them to come in and discuss it;
Father said, 'Are you with us or against us?' and he said, 'I'm for my
land. If every man of you would rehabilitate his own land, the
country will take care of itself' and Father challenged him to bring
the lamp out and set it on a stump where they could both see to
shoot and Sutpen would not. 'Nobody could have more of a dream
than that.'

'Yes. But his dream is just Sutpen. John's is not. He is thinking of
this whole country which he is trying to raise by its bootstraps, so
that all the people in it, not just his kind nor his old regiment, but all
the people, black and white, the women and children back in the
hills who don't even own shoes—Don't you see?'

'But how can they get any good from what he wants to do for
them if they are—after he has—'

'Killed some of them? I suppose you include those two carpet
baggers he had to kill to hold that first election, don't you?'

'They were men. Human beings.'

'They were Northerners, foreigners who had no business here.
They were pirates.' We walked on, her weight hardly discernible
on my arm, her head just reaching my shoulder. I had always been a
little taller than she, even on that night at Hawkhurst while we listed
to the niggers passing in the road, and she had changed but little
since—the same boy-hard body, the close implacable head with its
savagely cropped hair which I had watched from the wagon above
the tide of crazed singing niggers as we went down into the river—
the body not slender as women are but as boys are slender. 'A dream

is not a very safe thing to be near, Bayard. I know; I had one once. It's like a loaded pistol with a hair trigger: if it stays alive long enough somebody is going to be hurt. But if it's a good dream, it's worth it. There are not many dreams in the world, but there are a lot of human lives. And one human life or two dozen—'

'Are not worth anything?'

'No. Not anything. . . .'

Thomas Sutpen appears to exist for Bayard as an alternative to his father's course of action. Drusilla's disparagement of Sutpen carries some weight, but is partly rendered suspect by her own obsessed vision. She comes more and more to embody a sterile code of 'honour' which Bayard attempts to repudiate by facing his father's killer unarmed. Though the end of *The Unvanquished* is not without its own ambiguity —was Bayard's attempt to put an end to a chain of violence merely foolhardy or even a disguised death-wish?—it is not possible to remove wholly the idea that Faulkner has pressed forward beyond a Snopes defeat of Sartoris tradition to discover a point when an individual might have acted with dignity and freedom. In this sense Bayard's act of bravery is a counter-movement to the mad Sartoris pursuit of honour which is indistinguishable from its lapse into 'fatality'.

Here is a case where a felt need to iron flat the history of Yoknapatawpha has produced difficulties which the partial abandonment of an unbroken saga can overcome. Old Bayard in *Sartoris* seems not to have any trace in him of the young man who stood up to his father's murderer in *The Unvanquished*. The explanation comes too patly: Faulkner had not yet thought of Bayard's deed. But when he did, he appears to have felt no necessity to preserve a continuous character for Bayard— unless he had 'forgotten' *Sartoris*. The integrity of 'An Odour of Verbena' puts to shame any small-minded thesis. Resifting the history of his South through his 'first family', Faulkner can be thought of as searching for a moment in time when something counter to his earlier picture of Sartoris 'fatality' might be discovered. That Faulkner still leaves Bayard's intent and motives surrounded by doubt shows how cautious he was in rewriting Yoknapatawpha history, for while rewriting was a necessity if human values were to find a positive lodging-place, the triumph of man's spirit was not yet assured.

The dramatic complexity of the story's ending is suggested in further ways. There seems to be a difference of vision even from story to story in a collection which is both a grouping of short stories and a novel.

For one thing, Faulkner's moral vision seems to gain in intensity as the collection proceeds. It is a long distance from Bayard and Ringo, as children, hiding from the Yankees under Granny's skirts to Bayard's gunless duel with Redmond. Faulkner's vision of the 'code of honour' grows progressively darker in each story. As the writer's imagination ponders, we see each time a slightly altered War, a newly envisaged South.[22]

This progressive darkening of vision is also present in Faulkner's even greater conflation of the short story and novel forms, Go Down, Moses, and I would like to compare Bayard in 'An Odour of Verbena' to Ike McCaslin, whom Faulkner also pictured as repudiating a heritage, by applying to Bayard what R. W. B. Lewis has said of Ike as he appears in the fourth section of 'The Bear':

> What we are given in the fourth section is essentially not a narrative of past events, but a vision of the future. We can justify its appearance between the third and fifth sections—between, that is, episodes of Ike's sixteenth and his eighteenth years—by thinking of it as a dream; perhaps, though this is not necessary, a dream in the year between. It is a true dream to be sure, issuing securely from the gate of horn, but passing before our eyes events which, at this moment of perception, exist only in a state of possibility. A condition of potentiality, as of something not yet fully realized, is carried in the prose itself.[23]

It is a question, says Lewis, of 'the mode of existence of this moment in the experience', and it is clear that Lewis believes 'The Bear' accommodates more than one mode.[24] 'An Odour of Verbena' seems to share something of this altered mode of existence in respect of The Unvanquished, to be something of a 'condition of potentiality', a dream-

---

[22] ' "An Odour of Verbena" . . . inverts or revalues so many of the previous stories that it seems scarcely to belong within the covers of the same book.' Michael Millgate, Faulkner (Edinburgh and London, 1961), p. 68.

[23] R. W. B. Lewis, 'The Hero in the New World: William Faulkner's The Bear', Interpretations of American Literature edited by Charles Feidelson, Jr., and Paul Brodtkorb, Jr. (New York, 1959), p. 341. Reprinted from The Kenyon Review XIII (1951), pp. 641–60. Another version of the essay is in The Picaresque Saint (New York, 1959).

[24] In retaining the figure of the 'dream', Lewis is underplaying the significance of his idea. If there is a 'dream', it is Faulkner's, not Ike McCaslin's. The suggestion is really that in different parts of 'The Bear' Faulkner has re-conceived his characters.

possibility of a maturing Bayard Sartoris requiring not merely his growing up but a reconceived sense of the War, of the South and of the possibility of action which is not merely a reflex of 'history'. In sum a reconception so qualitatively different from the earlier chapters that we can almost speak of another War, another South.

Absalom, Absalom!, written almost concurrently with the stories in *The Unvanquished*, demonstrates how much Faulkner could make the matter of the reconception of 'Southern' history his very subject. The novel displays in the highest degree of tension the impulses towards the 'linear' elaboration of Yoknapatawpha history and a thrust of intense revision barely contained within a fabric of formal realism by supposing differences attributable to the 'characters' of the several narrators— Rosa Coldfield, Mr. Compson, Quentin and Shreve MacCannon. Quentin, for example, can be thought only with difficulty to have had access to the information which permits his ultimate reconception of the murder of Charles Bon.[25] Yet if he does not have that access, the status of Bon as Sutpen's son and part-negro—and not merely Henry's friend and Judith's lover—shrinks only to a notion (perhaps a necessity) of Quentin's. But if Faulkner was satisfied with this, why did he append a 'Chronology' and 'Genealogy' certifying that Charles Bon was indeed Thomas Sutpen's son by a woman he abandoned because he suspected her to have black blood? The notion of miscegenation, which even supersedes incest as the final attempt to pluck out the heart of Sutpen's mystery, must finally be left in uneasy suspension between 'historical' truth and Quentin's hypothesis.

The narrative method of *Absalom, Absalom!* made it the prime example for Conrad Aiken's famous description of Faulkner's style as

> the whole elaborate method of *deliberately withheld meaning*, of progressive and partial and delayed disclosure, which so often gives the characteristic shape to the novels themselves.[26]

But Aiken has a note of cadence, as though when the novel ended everything would fall into place. This is not true, and especially not true of *Absalom, Absalom!*, where the conflicts of view and vision—and of modes of existence—continue on to its last page. Having Quentin

---

[25] See Brooks, *op. cit.*, pp. 429–41, for a summary. Brooks concludes that 'Quentin probably had ten minutes to talk with Henry' (p. 441). (See *Note* at beginning of chapter.)

[26] Quoted from *William Faulkner: Three Decades of Criticism*, p. 138.

and Shreve as narrative filters for Rosa Coldfield, Quentin's grandfather and father and for the progressive disclosures of September 1909 to January 1910, helps to give an appearance of a single 'mode of existence' for the novel, but the very circumstantiality of each version (among much else) suggests a countervailing notion that there is no integrated vision of Thomas Sutpen in the novel.

In pulling back from the cooperative recreation of the Sutpen story he has engaged in with Quentin, Shreve MacCannon appears merely to be reacting with adolescent cynicism against its 'romantic' aspect ('So it takes two niggers to get rid of one Sutpen, don't it?'). The simplicity of Shreve's self-encouragement to curtail the discussion is not available to Quentin, for whom the situation at the novel's end is pointedly un-resolved: if the explanation he has at length arrived at is true, has he only discovered the South's eternal fixity and his own impotence? Richard Poirier notes that at the end of telling 'the whole story of Sutpen', Shreve implies that 'man and his history are mutually hostile and alien; that he is merely the reflex of some impersonal and abstract historical process', but that

> The form of the novel itself insists that the act of placing Sutpen in the understandable context of human society and history is a con-tinually necessary act, a never-ending responsibility and an act of humanistic faith.[27]

The novel may suggest that the 'act' is 'necessary' and a matter or 'responsibility' and 'faith', but that it has resulted, for Quentin or the reader, in success is open to question. There is indeed some indication that if the act is not itself doomed to failure, in this case at least Quentin has failed, or given up, as much in the romanticization of the incest and miscegenation theorizing as in any subsequent exhaustion of mind. If *Absalom, Absalom!* can sometimes seem another 'sound and fury' novel —'signifying nothing'—the thought should be seen less as criticism of the author for a mere *tour de force* of alternative visions as a haunted search ending in awful failure. The novel takes on a wider historical panorama than was hitherto attempted, probing more deeply back into Southern history to establish the career and motives of that 'second wave' of planters, non-aristocrats, of whom it is said they battened

[27] William R(ichard) Poirier, ' "Strange Gods" in Jefferson, Mississippi', in *William Faulkner: Two Decades of Criticism* edited by Frederick J. Hoffman and Olga W. Vickery (East Lansing, Michigan, 1951), p. 243.

slavery upon the South.[28] The search through history has not resulted in either a clear moment of freedom or of fatality, but rather a dark emblem behind both in the murder of Charles Bon by Henry Sutpen.

IV

Faulkner published *The Hamlet* in 1940. Parts of it may have been written as early as 1925, and sections had been published from 1931. Though published piecemeal, the novel does not present that tension of fragmentation we have seen elsewhere, and does not appear to involve any major historical reconsideration. The story of the origins of the Snopes family and the gradual takeover of Frenchman's Bend by Flem Snopes is subject generally to a single 'interpretation', that of the itinerant sewing-machine salesman V. K. Ratliff, who brings to Faulkner's narrators or *raisonneurs* a new voice of easy reasonability. *The Hamlet* thus appears more devoted to the linear filling-out of Yoknapatawpha history than to a tense re-evaluation or a layered, jostling series of reinterpretations.

It is easy, perhaps too easy, to see Faulkner taking time off from more intense exploration to pad out, as 'Sole Owner & Proprietor' the history of his 'little postage stamp of native soil'.[29] It is better to watch the slow dawning realization that Flem's horse-trading is a serious matter after all. By the end of the novel, as Flem moves on to Jefferson, we have moved back into the world of consequences we merely thought we had set aside.

The novel is, of course, saturated with the imagery of gambling and betting of all sorts—horse-trading, card-playing, all forms of the battle of wits. Flem always wins, and it is both consistent and a horrendous augury that at the novel's half-way mark we have Ratliff's comic but nightmare vision of Flem in Hell, beating the Devil out of his own Domain:

So they brought him in and went away and closed the door. His clothes was still smoking a little, though soon he had brushed most

---

[28] See Ward L. Miner, *The World of William Faulkner* (New York, 1959), pp. 27–9, 48, for a description of the 'new settlers . . . not people already either wealthy or well educated' (like the Sartorises and the Compsons) (p. 29).

[29] The two phrases are Faulkner's, from the map of Yoknapatawpha he drew for *Absalom, Absalom!* and from *The Paris Review* interview, *op. cit.*, p. 82.

of it off. He come up to the Throne, chewing, toting the straw suitcase.

'Well?' the Prince says.

He turned his head and spit, the spit frying off the floor quick in a little blue ball of smoke. 'I come about that soul,' he says.

'So they tell me,' the Prince says. 'But you have no soul.'

'Is that my fault?' he says.

'Is it mine?' the Prince says. 'Do you think I created you?'

'Then who did?' he says. And he had the Prince there and the Prince knowed it. So the Prince set out to bribe him his self. He named over all the temptations, the gratifications, the satieties; it sounded sweeter than music the way the Prince fetched them up in detail. But he didn't even stop chewing, standing there holding the straw suitcase. Then the Prince said, 'Look yonder,' pointing at the wall, and there they was, in order and rite for him to watch, watching his self performing them all, even the ones he hadn't even thought about inventing to his self yet, until they was done, the last unimaginable one. And he just turned his head and spit another scorch of tobacco onto the floor and the Prince flung back on the throne in very exasperation and baffled rage.

'Then what do you want?' the Prince says. 'What do you want? Paradise?'

'I hadn't figured on it,' he says. 'Is it yours to offer?'

'Then whose is it?' the Prince says. And the Prince knowed he had him there. In fact, the Prince knowed he had him all the time, ever since they had told him how he had walked in the door with his mouth already full of law; he even leaned over and rung the fire-bell so the old one could be there to see and hear how it was done, then he leaned back on the Throne and looked down at him standing there with his straw suitcase, and says, 'You have admitted and even argued that I created you. Therefore your soul was mine all the time. And therefore when you offered it as security for this note, you offered that which you did not possess and so laid yourself liable to . . .'

'I have never disputed that,' he says.

'—criminal actions. So take your bag and—' the Prince says.

'Eh?' the Prince says, 'What did you say?'

'I have never disputed that,' he says.

'What?' the Prince says. 'Disputed what?' Except that it don't make any noise, and now the Prince is leaning forward, and now he feels that ere hot floor under his knees and he can feel his self grabbing and hauling at his throat to get the words out like he was digging potatoes outen hard ground. 'Who are you?' he says, choking and gasping and his eyes a-popping up at him setting there with that straw suitcase on the Throne among the bright, crown-shaped flames. 'Take Paradise!' the Prince screams. 'Take it! Take it!' And the wind roars up and the dark roars down and the Prince scrabbling across the floor, clawing and scrabbling at that locked door, screaming. . . . [*All italicized in original.*]

Given this much respect for Flem Snopes, Ratliff ought to avoid to the death any situation which might involve him in 'bargaining' with Flem. Yet he does get involved, and in the novel's final section, 'The Peasants', he succumbs to the notion that the Old Frenchman's Place contains buried treasure and buys the land from Flem. Flem has out-witted even this reasonable man by 'salting' the ground with a little money, and Ratliff, along with more obviously gullible folk, falls for it.

Ratliff's defeat is ominous and not without analogy to Rosa Millard's being outwitted by Ab Snopes or even to young Bayard Sartoris's suc-cumbing to Sartoris 'fatality'. For one thing, the image of a buried Con-federate treasure is significant: in order to believe that there was one to bury you subscribe to the existence of the glories of a pre-Civil War planter class 'civilization', in a myth of Southern grandeur. Ratliff mostly thinks about mere financial gain, but Flem Snopes is playing on his background susceptibility to be swayed by the myth of the glorious past. It is notable that this myth, like everything else for him, is some-thing which Flem will *use* to his advantage, without any question of belief entering into the calculation. The defeat of the 'reasonable' Ratliff thus forms part of a dialectical series of 'observers' who struggle to retain an area of freedom from historical reflex. When even the most detached of these figures must confess his moral helplessness—Ratliff puts an end to the 'stock-diddling' of the idiot Ike Snopes 'simply be-cause I am strong enough to keep him from it'—when his deepest imagination sees Flem Snopes as able to beat the Devil, and when he succumbs to greed over a suppositious buried treasure, the newest last, best hope in Faulkner for a position of independent balance has been lost. (In later work, Ratliff, along with Gavin Stevens, will purchase the appearance of freedom and detachment by a narrative stance of wilful uninvolvement with the action before them.)

In *Go Down, Moses*, the movement towards the short-story novel reaches its apex and converges with Faulkner's most literal reinterpreta-tion of history. His comment that the fourth section of 'The Bear' belongs more to the novel than to the story indicates the tension present in the hybrid form. As in *The Unvanquished*, the shadow lengthens as we move through *Go Down, Moses* and even 'Uncle' Ike moves in the generally darker vision at the end. As a younger man, however, Isaac McCaslin has undergone an agonizing process of dual initiation. In 'The Old People' and 'The Bear' Sam Fathers, part Indian, part Negro, has inducted Ike into a participation with nature older than history itself. However, even as the process 'valorizes' Ike (to use the anthropologists' term), the lumber company's axe is heard on the wilderness which had preserved the link, and in subsequent stories we travel further, and further, faster and faster, to seek out 'the big woods'. The other part of his initiation is into the role of his own family within a specific historical time, and it likewise has negative and positive poles. For what he discovers first is a kind of primal curse on the land and its people.

Isaac McCaslin's interpretation of his family history, based on his search through the family ledgers, both symbolizes and leads him to an apocalyptic version of Southern history itself. The imposition of a curse upon the land through the institution of chattel slavery is paralleled in the familial plot by the iniquity of his grandfather, L. Q. C. McCaslin, in fathering a child upon his own Negro daughter. This violation of the father–daughter incest taboo is an ultimate outrage to the humanity of both blacks and whites. He has treated his own bastard child as an object, a thing, not a person. Ike (and Faulkner) think of him as

> that evil and unregenerate old man who could summon, because she was his property, a human being because she was old enough and female, to his widower's house and get a child on her and then dismiss her because she was of an inferior race, and then bequeath a thousand dollars to the infant.

As a form of non-recognition, this exceeds even Thomas Sutpen's treatment of his (presumably) mixed-blood son, Charles Bon. It violates the essential bond of humanity and provides a convincing emblem for the 'meaning' of slavery.

The years 1832–3 are a fitting time for the symbolic outrage to occur, when slavery itself, in one interpretation, was fastened for good upon the Deep South—remember Thomas Sutpen came to Jefferson at this time. The events, familial and sectional, usher in an apocalyptic period of chaos, an interval between epochs perhaps heralding the end of time itself. Eunice, the mother of McCaslin's Negro daughter

Thomasina ('Tomy'), drowns herself when she realizes whom her child is pregnant by. It is a thing unheard of, beyond belief—'*23 June 1833 Who in hell ever heard of a niger drownding him self.*' But it has happened: '*Drownd herself.*' Other portents of chaos follow: '*Thomasina called Tomy Daughter of Thucydus @ Eunice Born 1810 dide in Child bed June 1833 and Burd. Yr stars fell.*' The ominous last phrase is repeated in the ledger-entry for the child of the incestuous union: '*Turl Son of Thucydus @ Eunice Tomy born Jun 1833 yr stars fell Fathers will.*'[30]

'The year stars fell' has always had an eerie significance for Southerners, and its apocalyptic import can be heard clearly in Carl Carmer's explanation in his preface to *Stars Fell on Alabama*:

Alabama felt a magic descending, spreading, long ago. Since then it has been a land with a spell on it—not a good spell, always. Moons, red with the dust of barren hills, their pine trunks barring horizons, festering swamps, restless yellow rivers, all are part of a feeling—a strange certainty that above and around them hovers enchantment —and emanation of malevolence that threatens to destroy men through dark ways of its own. . . .

What the strange influence is or when it began is a matter for debate. . . .

But those who really know, the black conjure women in their weathered cabins along the Tombigbee, . . . say that on the memories of the oldest slaves their fathers knew there was one indelible imprint of an awful event—a shower of stars over Alabama. Many an Alabamian to this day reckons dates from 'the year the stars fell'— though he and his neighbour frequently disagree as to what year of our Lord may be so designated. All are sure, however, that once upon a time stars fell on Alabama, changing the land's destiny. What had been written in eternal symbols was thus erased—and the region has existed ever since, unreal and fated, bound by a horoscope such as controls no other country.[31]

It was common, in fact, to date the 'coming' of the Civil War from the star shower of 1833. The holocaust of the War itself looks like being the end of all time, and from the other side of time, Ike McCaslin scrutinizes the War to see if life subsequently is merely post-mortem existence in Hell, or whether somewhere, somehow, something might

[30] L. Q. C. McCaslin is of course the real father both of Tomy and (incestuously) of Tomy's son, Turl.

[31] Carl Carmer, *Stars Fell on Alabama* (London, 1935), pp. xiii–xiv.

have been done to expiate and overturn the primal family and general curse, and so redeem time and begin a new era.

In the event Ike does discover the twin events, one 'national' and the other familial, by which he decides time has been renovated and the land saved from destruction. In a long parable, Ike describes God's loss of faith in his South and the paradoxical moment of His regaining it, resulting in the new Covenant:

> one day He said . . . : *This will do. This is enough:* . . . and looked about for one last time . . . upon this land this South for which He had done so much . . . and saw no hope anywhere and looked beyond it where hope should have been, where to East North and West lay illimitable that whole hopeful continent dedicated as a refuge and sanctuary of liberty and freedom . . . and saw . . . the thundering cannonade of politicians earning votes . . . to whom the outrage and the injustice were as much abstractions as Tariff or Silver or Immortality . . . and He could have repudiated them . . . until not only that old world from which He had rescued them but this new one too which He had revealed and led them to as a sanctuary and refuge were become the same worthless tideless rock cooling in the last crimson evening except that . . . one silence, among that loud and moiling all of them just one simple enough to believe that horror and outrage were first and last simply horror and outrage and was crude enough to act upon that. . . .

The 'one' whose 'act' stays God's hand is, astonishingly, the Abolitionist John Brown. God tests Brown:

> a lesser than He might have even missed the simple act of lifting the long ancestral musket down from the deerhorns above the door, whereupon He said *My name is Brown too* and the other *So is mine* and He *Then mine or yours cant be because I am against it* and the other *So am I* and He triumphantly *Then where are you going with that gun?* and the other told him in one sentence one word and He: amazed: Who knew neither hope nor pride nor grief *But your Association, your Committee* . . . and the other *I aint against them. They are all right I reckon for them that have the time. I am just against the weak because they are niggers being held in bondage by the strong just because they are white.*

'So,' Ike concludes to a scarce comprehending cousin Cass Edmonds, 'He turned once more to this land which He still intended to save.'[32]

[32] Ike's God, despite his irritated questioning of 'Brown', seems to turn back to the land in pride at Brown's initiative and decisiveness. Gavin Stevens'

Despite the fact that the actual War followed, the world has been already saved from apocalypse. Ike's cousin McCaslin ('Cass') Edmonds takes him to task on this score, seeing the War as only a further extension of the chaos, rubbing Ike's nose in its horrors. 'Turned back to us? His face to us?' Cass demands. Ike now has faith. 'How else have made them fight,' he answers, reinterpreting the Northern war effort as proof of God's presence in the land.

For Ike, this restoration of God's grace to His South is a vision of historical renovation. It will be his Covenant and guarantee, and in accordance with it he will himself act. In working out his ideas with Cass, Ike is trying to

> explain to the head of my family something which I have got to do which I don't quite understand myself, not in justification of it but to explain it if I can.

What he had decided he has 'got to do' is to repudiate his McCaslin inheritance, the land bought from the Indians by his grandfather and soiled by slavery and old McCaslin's hideous action. This personal action has been suggested to him by his interpretation of sectional history, and functions for Ike as a parallel to it.

Ironically, Ike is surer of his historical interpretation, paradoxical though it is, than of his personal/familial one, and the novel carries the question forward: does Ike's repudiation have the effect and the meaning he had hoped to endow it with? In 'Delta Autumn', a descendant of the incestuous union of L. Q. C. McCaslin and Thomasina, herself the mother of a child by the grandson of Ike's cousin Cass (who inherited the land Ike repudiated), is once again turned away—and by Isaac McCaslin himself, now an old man:

> *Maybe in a thousand or two thousand years in America*, he thought. *But not now! Not now!* He cried, not loud, in a voice of amazement, pity, outrage: 'You're a nigger!'
>
> Then he cried again in that thin not loud and grieving voice: 'Get out of here! I can do nothing for you! Can't nobody do nothing for you!'

Like his grandfather before him, Ike will not recognize the black man. He helps Cass's grandson Roth to evade paternity by offering the girl

---

disparaging reference to the abolitionist as having delayed the Negroes' true freedom (*Intruder in the Dust*, chapter 10) should be compared with the passage in 'The Bear'. Even if God returns to His South in defiance of the Northerner Brown, Ike's renovatory pattern holds.

money, which she rejects: ' "Old man," she said, "have you lived so long and forgotten so much that you dont remember anything you ever knew or felt or even heard about love?" ' It is a terrible reversal, calling into question Ike's ability to live out his own insight and decision of some sixty years before and, indeed, questions the very nature of the interpretation on which that insight and decision were based.[33] Through Ike McCaslin Faulkner has traced just how far you have to go to redeem history and what the process can do to you, in hope and in glory, and in shame and in defeat.

V

Subsequent to *Go Down, Moses*, Faulkner's fiction shows a certain formalization of the techniques of fragmentation. The original publication of *The Wild Palms* (1939) had already presented the novella 'The Old Man' in alternating chapters with the story of Charlotte and Henry. Faulkner noted that he wrote one story until some 'problem' arose, then deserted it for a time to work on the other. Then he presumably printed them in the order of writing.[34] Thematic contrasts can be made between the two stories, but Faulkner has not even gone to the length of any nominal interconnection. The process is one step removed from *Light in August*.

In Faulkner's next two novels, a similar formalization overtakes the relation between the substance of the plots and the historical interpretation. The latter remains at the high level of generalization present in *Go Down, Moses* but its connection with the narrative appears more merely wilful and less naturally symbolic or dramatic. In *Intruder in the Dust* (1948), the Jefferson lawyer Gavin Stevens has numerous passages of reflection on the status of the Negro in the modern South, 'the people named Sambo'. He consciously attempts to use the plot's Negro protagonist Lucas Beauchamp—a black descendant of L. Q. C. McCas-

---

[33] For an interpretation of D. H. Lawrence and George Eliot based on the 'complementary types of decadence and renovation', also showing the writers' 'clerkly scepticism' exercised upon the apocalyptic patterns they have themselves created, see Frank Kermode, 'D. H. Lawrence and the Apocalyptic Types', *Continuities* (London, 1968), pp. 122–51; and more generally on apocalyptic figures in fiction, his *The Sense of an Ending* (London/New York, 1967).

[34] I am unclear as to on whose authority the stories were later printed sequentially, removing the chapter interleaving. Michael Millgate tells me that it was not Faulkner's decision. It appears to have been done for the 1954 Signet edition.

lin— as a figure for that condition. Lucas has been imprisoned, awaiting trial or lynching, for a murder he did not commit. Gavin, thinking more generally about civil rights, says: 'That's why we must resist the North . . . That's what we are really defending: the privilege of setting him free ourselves.' He also claims the privilege of protecting 'Lucas Beauchamp, Sambo' from

> that part of him which is trying to escape not even into the best of the white race but into the second best—the cheap shoddy dishonest music, the cheap flash baseless overvalued money, the glittering edifice of publicity foundationed on nothing like a cardhouse over an abyss and all of the noisy muddle of political activity which used to be our minor national industry and is now our national amateur pastime—all the spurious uproar produced by men deliberately fostering and then getting rich on our national passion for the mediocre . . . [etc., etc.]

It is not really possible to see around Stevens in the novel, to have a firm sense of Faulkner's dramatic 'placing' of him. (This is why *Intruder in the Dust* attracted such attention as Faulkner's 'answer to the civil rights programme'.) Are we to understand Faulkner here to be pointing to Stevens's frustrated projection of his dislike of the 'flash' modern onto the Negro? Or is that unintended, because Faulkner shares Stevens' view? Stevens himself does almost nothing for Lucas. Proof of his innocence is established by the derring-do of two young boys in rather a hocus-pocus of midnight graveyard visits. Nor does their action symbolize in any but the most arbitrary way the larger issues ('setting him free') Stevens had raised.

Faulkner acknowledged that he began the novel in response to the kind of children's detective stories he was always finding around the house. Perhaps this accounts for the thinness of *Intruder in the Dust*'s bonds to Yoknapatawpha, despite the invitations to relate it to Gavin Stevens and the Mallisons and Lucas Beauchamp as they appear elsewhere. The connections are only nominal and contain no real resonance.[35]

Similar disjunctions are present in *Requiem for a Nun* (1951). Prose sections, historical and epical, describing the founding of Jefferson and its courthouse, the state capital at Jackson, Mississippi and the Jefferson

[35] Faulkner himself retained a fairly unsure sense of the novel's place in time. While it contains clear references to the era of The Bomb and The Cold War, he once dated its action in 'about 1935-40' (*Faulkner in the University*, p. 141).

jail, alternate with a three-act play in which the Negro servant Nancy Mannigoe foils Temple Drake Stevens's elopement by the bizarre expedient of murdering Temple's child. Courthouse and jail have obvious relevance, but to give the 'statehouse' a place, Gavin Stevens takes Temple before the governor of Mississippi. As she complains at the time, however, there is nothing the governor can do, and he remains a curiously etiolated figure. Similarly with the 'historical' state capital: the novel singularly fails to link the fictionally-historical world of Yoknapatawpha with the actually-historical one of Mississippi. Matters of individual guilt and responsibility remain unrelated to the social issues of the institution of city and county. The confessional drama and the public historical guide combine uneasily and point in differing directions.

While he was working on *The Town*, Faulkner told Jean Stein that his 'Last book will be the Doomsday Book, the Golden Book of Yoknapatawpha County.'[36] (A dozen years before he had agreed to cooperate with Cowley under a similar aegis: 'By all means let us' make the *Portable* 'a Golden Book of my apocryphal county':

> I have thought of spending my old age doing something of that nature: an alphabetical, rambling genealogy of the people, father to sons to son.[37]

In the event, that time, he wrote the Compson 'Appendix'.) *The Town* (1957) more than any novel including the actual 'last book', *The Reivers*, does satisfy 'Doomsday' conditions.

Foremost perhaps, is that recurrent retelling and incapsulation of earlier work, that revisitation which Steven Marcus allies to the creation of the post-Homeric fragments: 'he takes a past which he has created himself and deals with it as received reality. It is "out there", independent of his ministration.'[38] This sense of 'the historicity of his imagination' (in Marcus's words) stands at one pole of Faulkner's creativity. In a way, of course, it is a new 'voice' (the Garter King-at-Arms?) which does this summarizing, so that the effort to write a novel which would in a manner incorporate all his other novels requires even at the last

---

[36] *The Paris Review* Interview, quoted from Hoffman and Vickery, *Three Decades*, p. 82.

[37] *The Faulkner–Cowley File*, p. 25.

[38] Steven Marcus, 'Snopes Revisited', *Partisan Review* (Summer 1957), quoted from *William Faulkner: Three Decades of Criticism*, p. 388.

a point of view not to be identified as the novelist's own say on the matter. Marcus's 'post-Homeric' voice is a country voice and it is gently, but noticeably, guyed throughout the novel, particularly in the extent to which Gavin Stevens is actually mocked for attempting to make Flem Snopes and 'Snopsism' a *key* to the history of Yoknapatawpha and Jefferson. Almost two decades after George Marion O'Donnell adumbrated the history of Yoknapatawpha as a declension from Sartorises to Snopeses, Faulkner was parodying the thesis.

The Town is, moreover, highly selective in respect of the Faulkner canon. Sartoris-matter is the most usual subject of Faulkner's post-creation, McCaslin-matter a poor second. Faulkner preserved even unto 'Doomsday' the territorial integrity of certain crucial supposed Yoknapatawpha events and interpretations. Charles Bon, Quentin Compson, Joe Christmas and Gail Hightower make no appearance here. (Jason gets only a bare mention.) Having narrators (Gavin Stevens, V. K. Ratliff, Charles Mallison) offers opportunities of instant retreat into merely public knowledge: *What the town knew* is the basis of their speculations. But the narrators seem hardly keen to deploy specialized knowledge even where—if we recall what they should know from other novels—they might be thought to have it. To encapsulate *Sartoris*, Gavin Stevens drops into an uncharacteristic cynicism over the romantic-mysterious:

> the racing car which Bayard Sartoris drove too fast for our country roads (the Jefferson ladies said because he was grieving so over the death in battle of his twin brother that he too was seeking death though in my opinion Bayard liked war and now that there was no more war to go to, he was faced with the horrid prospect of having to go to work).

In effect, even the most nearly summatory ('Doomsday') version of Yoknapatawpha, the one which should make the greatest presumption of the wholeness and integrity of its life, does not presume too far. The diversity of Yoknapatawphas was not compromised, even at the last.

VI

As new interpretations accumulated, even requiring new and different 'facts', the linear historical surface of the cycle was considerably, though not entirely, undercut. To think of it in terms of the psychology of creation, it may well be that the 'real' Yoknapatawpha is a fiction *behind* the fictions Faulkner wrote and published. This 'real' Yoknapatawpha lived and lived only in Faulkner's head and was something he set up as a buffer between himself and his experience of actual Mississippi life. Upon that fiction he drew for the books he created, treating it as we ordinarily assume artists deal with their real life, giving himself the freedom to manipulate, alter and recreate it. For if the creation of a mythical county and its history (in his head) kept contemporary Mississippi at an aesthetic distance, only its continual recomposition could satisfy the demands of art.

In a few cases, particularly in collections of short stories not so far dealt with, we can see Faulkner beginning to deal with Yoknapatawpha events whose final form lodges in novels in a way in which makes it extremely difficult to imagine *both* versions as having happened in a historical continuum.

The stories 'Hair' and 'Dry September' (both published in 1931) have as their main character Hawkshaw, a Jefferson barber. In 'Hair' his history filters through a present involvement with one of the town girls, Susan Reed, whom he fussily watches grow to womanhood. All the while he vanishes periodically, and only the narrator knows of his devoted, quixotic fathfulness to his late fiancée's dying request (Take care of Maw. The mortgage'). The task requires holy foolishness of Hawkshaw, for as soon as the mortgage is paid off, the relatives will swoop and repossess the house. 'Hair' has multiple connections with Faulkner's novels. Hawkshaw is a kind of Anse Bundren in his determination. His relation to Susan Reed is worked over more fully when Gavin Stevens meets Linda Snopes. Susan herself is a nexus for the characters of Caddy and her daughter, Temple Drake and Eula and Linda Snopes.

'Dry September' chronicles a lynching and Hawkshaw's anguished inability to prevent it. Here the barber has distinct connections with Horace Benbow in *Sanctuary* and not a few with Gail Hightower in *Light in August.* It is difficult, however, to think of Hawkshaw as having lived in the *same* Jefferson as they: not, in this case, because Faulkner's conception of Jefferson is so different when he appears, but because he is so *like* other characters. Thus the linear history of Yoknapatawpha, minor discrepancies aside, breaks down not only in the matter of altered 'modes of existence' but in overlapping similarities.

Faulkner's dual dedication to a single history of his chosen county and to successive reconstitutions of that history is analogous to the paradox of the Southern condition as he presents it. Its history was the burden of the South and its temptation. Twice, in Quentin Compson and Isaac McCaslin, Faulkner embodied literal searchers of the Southern past for an explanation which might free them of that past: yet the search, though itself a revision of history, might turn tragically into that selfsame past. Faulkner permitted neither any character nor himself anything but the minimal foothold on the impossible, necessary freedom.

Faulkner spoke consistently of his own Yoknapatawpha fictions as neither a history nor a testament but as *apocrypha*, uncanonical:

By all means let us make a Golden Book of my apocryphal county. . . .[39]

by sublimating the actual into the apocryphal, I would have complete liberty to use whatever talent I might have to its absolute top. . . .[40]

[there was] probably no tribe of Snopses in Mississippi or anywhere else outside of my own apocrypha. . . .[41]

The term is a proper compromise: a *history* of Yoknapatawpha County had both to be and not to be. The paradox generated the major tensions, in terms of art and of history, in his fiction. In the end, he wrote not the history of his imaginary county but its literature.

[39] *The Faulkner–Cowley File*, p. 25.
[40] *Paris Review* Interview, *op. cit.*, p. 82.
[41] *Faulkner in the University*, p. 282.

Note

Life and Writing

John Dos Passos was born in 1896, in Chicago, the son of a successful corporation and criminal lawyer descended from Portuguese and American Quaker stock. Dos Passos went to Harvard, where he contributed to several magazines, some of his college verse being later published in *Eight Harvard Poets* (1917). His father, who had fought in the Civil War, prevented him from joining an American Ambulance Unit in 1916 by financing a year of architectural study in Spain; when his father died, however, Dos Passos enlisted in the Norton-Harjes unit, and served in Italy and France. These experiences provided the background for his first novels, *One Man's Initiation: 1917* (1920), and *Three Soldiers* (1921). Throughout the twenties he travelled extensively, and wrote about Europe, the Near East and Russia. He found time to produce two novels, *Streets of Night* (1923) and *Manhattan Transfer* (1925); two plays, *The Garbage Man* (1926) and *Airways Inc.* (1928); and a defence of Sacco and Vanzetti, *Facing the Chair* (1927). He also helped found and worked for both *The New Masses* magazine and The New Playwrights Theatre.

Throughout the thirties Dos Passos continued his career as playwright, novelist and political reporter, though his major literary effort went into the writing of the three volumes of *U.S.A.*—*The 42nd Parallel* (1930), *1919* (1932), and *The Big Money* (1936). During and after the Second World War, Dos Passos became increasingly interested in the roots of American culture and produced a number of historical studies relating to the problems of American democracy. At the same time he was at work on his second trilogy of novels, *Adventures of a Young Man* (1939), *Number One* (1943), and *The Grand Design* (1949)— brought together as *District of Columbia* in 1952. By now he had severed all connections with left-wing political movements, becoming at one period a Goldwater Republican; and though he continued to publish novels like *Midcentury* (1961), loosely patterned on *U.S.A.*, much of his work was autobiographical or semi-autobiographical, such as *Chosen Country* (1951) and *The Great Days* (1958).

Criticism. Only two full length studies of Dos Passos have been published in English: John D. Brantley's *The Fiction of John Dos Passos* (The Hague, 1968), and John H. Wrenn's *John Dos Passos* (New York, 1961). More important than these are the handful of essays and chapters in books which have helped to reinterpret his best fiction. Jean-Paul Sartre's essay on 'John Dos Passos and *1919*' in *Literary and Philosophical Essays* (London, 1955) contains the most intelligent and perceptive criticism; Marshall McLuhan also isolates the central critical problems in his essay, 'John Dos Passos: Technique versus Sensibility' in *Fifty Years of the American Novel: A Christian Appraisal*, edited by Harold C. Gardiner, S.J. (New York, 1968); and so does Alfred Kazin in *On Native Grounds* (New York, 1942).

IX

History and John Dos Passos

BRIAN LEE

I

DOS PASSOS's best fiction has a pessimism different in kind and more profound than that found in the works of any of his American contemporaries. His attitudes to life in general and to American society in particular derive from the Naturalists, of course, and his novels have many superficial features in common with those of Crane, Norris and Dreiser. In this passage, taken from the Introduction to the one-volume edition of *U.S.A.*, some of the characteristic techniques are easily recognizable as he paints a rapid picture of a society dehumanized by the mechanical pressures of an indifferent, material environment:

> The streets are empty. People have packed into subways, climbed into streetcars and buses; in the stations they've scampered for suburban trains; they've filtered into lodgings and tenements, gone up in elevators into apartmenthouses. In a showwindow two sallow windowdressers in their shirtsleeves are bringing out a dummy girl in a red evening dress, at a corner welders in masks lean into sheets of blue flame repairing a cartrack, a few drunk bums shamble along, a sad streetwalker fidgets under an arclight. From the river comes the deep rumbling whistle of a steamboat leaving dock. A tug hoots far away.

People in the mass are seen packing, climbing, scampering or filtering away from the city, and what remain behind—store window dummies, masked welders, drunken bums and prostitutes—typify the isolated, sub-human or broken detritus of industrial civilization.

In the next paragraph, though, the focus of our attention is shifted as we are brought gradually into the consciousness of a young man, aware of his necessary exclusion and pathetically anxious to embrace and affirm experience in its varied particulars:

> The young man walks by himself, fast but not fast enough, far but not far enough (faces slide out of sight, talk trails into scattered

scraps, footsteps tap fainter in alleys); he must catch the last subway, the streetcar, the bus, run up the gangplanks of all the steamboats, register at all the hotels, work in the cities, answer the wantads, learn the trades, take up the jobs, live in all the boardinghouses, sleep in all the beds. One bed is not enough, one job is not enough, one life is not enough. At night, head swimming with wants, he walks by himself alone.

No job, no woman, no house, no city,

This young man is a recurrent type in Dos Passos's fiction. He appears as Jimmy Herf in *Manhattan Transfer*, Vag in *U.S.A.*, and in slightly different postures as John Andrews in *Three Soldiers* and Martin Howe in Dos Passos's first novel, *One Man's Initiation: 1917*. Into these various characters Dos Passos pours all his democratic, Whitmanesque passion for total immersion. Typically these heroes spend their lives struggling against the crushing power of machines, variously depicted as the Army, the Law, the Corporation, the Party or the City. Occasionally small victories are achieved, if only temporary ones; and the hero is able, like Andrews when he breaks free from the routine of his army life, to sink himself into 'the misty, sparkling life of the streets'. In the earlier fiction, escape is into a world whose allure is primarily aesthetic:

> Andrews darted down a side street. He could hardly keep from shouting aloud when he found himself alone, free, with days and days ahead of him to work and think, gradually to rid his limbs of the stiff attitudes of the automaton. . . . He was walking very fast, stopping suddenly now and then to look at the greens and oranges and crimsons of vegetables in a push cart, to catch a vista down intricate streets, to look into the rich brown obscurity of a small wine shop where workmen stood at a counter sipping white wine. Oval, delicate faces, bearded faces of men, slightly gaunt faces of young women, red cheeks of boys, wrinkled faces of old women, whose ugliness seemed to have hidden in it, stirringly, all the beauty of youth and the tragedy of lives that had been lived; the faces of the people he passed moved him like the rhythms of an orchestra. After much walking, turning always down the street which looked pleasantest, he came to an oval with a statue of a pompous personage on a ramping horse. 'Place des Victoires,' he read the name, which gave him a faint tinge of amusement.

These minor triumphs of individual freedom are always quickly squashed, and only serve in the plots of the novels to underscore the inevitable defeat of the anarchic individual. More importantly, they introduce into Naturalistic fiction a more subtle technique for representing life in its subjective/objective states. Sartre, who comes closer than anyone to understanding the significance of Dos Passos's major novels, maintains that 'Dos Passos' man is a hybrid creature, an interior-exterior being. We go on living with and within him, with his vacillating, individual consciousness, when suddenly it wavers, weakens, and is diluted in the collective consciousness.'[1] A growing awareness of the failure of the individual consciousness to resist usurpation by the machine led him to say in 1936—the year of the Spanish Civil War—that the world had arrived at 'one of the damnedest tragic moments of history'. If the twenties were years which, for Dos Passos, stripped the bunting off the great illusions of our time and laid bare 'the raw structure of history' beneath, they were also the years in which he learned to create a fiction of impassioned objectivity with some of the quality he so admired in *The Last Tycoon*—the 'quality of detaching itself from its period while embodying its period.'[2]

The quality of this detachment underwent a radical change at the end of the twenties, brought about undoubtedly by Dos Passos's political experiences in general, and as Alfred Kazin argues, more particularly as the result of his bitter involvement in the Sacco and Vanzetti affair. Whatever the cause, it made possible the writing of his masterpiece, *U.S.A.*, in which the ineffectual struggles against the world of his earlier aesthete-romantic heroes is superseded by a more complex and subtle dialectic. The phenomenology of *U.S.A.* is unique; not only in Dos Passos's *œuvre*, but in twentieth-century fiction as a whole. To argue, as many critics have, that Dos Passos mechanically applies the superficial tricks of neo-modernist technique to a Naturalist novel, is to miss completely the point of his structural and stylistic innovations. The relationship between individual characters (there are, of course, no heroes in *U.S.A.*) and the historical and environmental forces they shape and are shaped by, does not admit of any but an artificial separation. In contrast, the prose poems of *District of Columbia*, preceding each chapter, are not only crudely written themselves, but are also related to the book's fictional and historical structure, in the crudest possible way.

The poise and balance of *U.S.A.* had not been easily achieved, nor

---

[1] *Literary and Philosophical Essays*, p. 96.

[2] F. Scott Fitzgerald, *The Crack-Up* edited by Edmund Wilson (New York, 1945), p. 343.

was it to be maintained in the novels following *U.S.A.* Dos Passos's gradual loss of passion as he abandoned the romantic radicalism of his earlier years has been documented and lamented by Irving Howe[3] and Granville Hicks[4] among others. What is of more interest to anyone concerned with Dos Passos's major achievements is the way in which he takes the fictional techniques of Naturalism—particularly those used by Crane and Dreiser—and out of them develops a mode uniquely successful in its ability to relate character to environment and to subsume both to the large shifts and pressures of history.

II

The first major traumatic experience of Dos Passos's life, and the most enduring in his memory, was that of the First World War. His service with the Norton-Harjes Ambulance Unit and the Medical Corps in France provided the material for two novels, *One Man's Initiation: 1917* and *Three Soldiers.* The first of these, written on the ship returning to America, and published in 1920, is manifestly the work of a young Harvard aesthete, tricked out with what Dos Passos was later to call 'twenty-one-year-old rhetoric'. His descriptions of the battles and his attempts to order his hero's experiences symbolically are not much of an advance on the *fin-de-siècle* verse he had contributed to an earlier anthology of *Eight Harvard Poets*. In reading it one gets the sense of a mind beginning to grapple with the larger problems of war and social disintegration, but not coming very close to any understanding of them, and ultimately falling back on the inadequate devices of ironic contrast and the juxtaposition of vivid impressions. He was to admit later with disarming simplicity that 'the high point for me of the Avocourt offensive was the day I caught myself quietly opening a can of sardines for my lunch in the rear of a dressing station while some poor devil of a poilu was having his leg sawed off on the operating table up front.'[5] Even when he does try to embody larger ideas in his writing, they are rather laboriously contrived out of a literary or aesthetic background:

[3] Irving Howe, 'John Dos Passos: the Loss of Passion', *Tomorrow* VII (1949), pp. 54–7.
[4] Granville Hicks, 'The Politics of John Dos Passos', *Antioch Review* X (1950), pp. 85–98.
[5] *The Best Times: An Informal Memoir* (New York, 1968), p. 55.

It was the fifth time that day that Martin's car had passed the cross-roads where the cavalry was. Someone had propped up the fallen crucifix so that it tilted dark despairing arms against the sunset sky where the sun gleamed like a huge copper kettle lost in its own steam. The rain made bright yellowish stripes across the sky and dripped from the feet of the old wooden Christ, whose gaunt, scarred figure hung out from the tilted cross, swaying a little in the beating of the rain. . . . He stared curiously at the fallen jowl and the cavernous eyes that had meant for some country sculptor ages ago the utterest agony of pain. Suddenly he noticed that where the crown of thorns had been about the forehead of the Christ someone had wound barbed wire. He smiled, and asked the swaying figure in his mind. 'And you, what do you think of it?'

For an instant he could feel wire barbs ripping through his own flesh.[6]

The political and social significance of the events he witnessed did not escape Dos Passos entirely. He could hardly have failed to see the growing signs of mutiny among the front line soldiers, and he became convinced that the real aim of American intervention was to put down the European revolution. In the novel he includes a chapter of dis-cussion between various French radicals in which the hero, Martin Howe, is given a speech about the 'dark forces' which are at work enslaving the minds of Americans. He makes a feeble effort to locate the evil spirits—'America, as you know is ruled by the press. And the press is ruled by whom? Who shall ever know what dark forces bought and bought until we should be ready to go blinded and gagged into war?' Later he was to see that the malevolence cannot be isolated like this and that its effects have to be studied in the impersonal operation of man-made institutions.

Given the conventional form of his novel, it is not easy to see how the experiences of the hero could have been meaningfully related to the patterns of history of which he was a part, even had Dos Passos been able to perceive such a relation. His failure to find a form which would allow him to express the war's general significance can be seen in the fact that, while he was still engaged in writing the novel, his mind was busy with schemes for writing a series of 'Junius' letters as propaganda for peace. Nothing came of this, however, and after his discharge from the army he made his way to Spain and started work on his second novel.

[6] *One Man's Initiation: 1917* (1920), p. 72.

III

Three Soldiers is not entirely successful, whether judged as a war novel or as a novel of social protest. It is possible to believe that Dos Passos was attempting to do for the First World War what Stephen Crane had done for the Civil War, but it makes more sense to restrict the comparison to that section of the later book which deals with Chrisfield, the Indiana farm boy turned soldier who, in his actions and responses, certainly does suggest a critique of Henry Fleming. Viewed as a whole, and more especially in the perspective of the later work, one can see Dos Passos in this novel working towards the complexity of structure that gives *U.S.A.* its great density. He obviously wanted to show the crushing effect of the army upon those who are made to serve it, at every possible level of their lives. Rather than follow the fortunes of one chosen 'hero' though, who would have had to be the articulate and highly sophisticated autobiographical figure, John Andrews, he shows in the first two sections, 'Making the Mould' and 'The Metal Cools', how a rather malleable and ingratiating second generation San Franciscan is inducted into the organization and quickly cowed by it. Chrisfield's section, 'Machines', which is written in a more opaque style and therefore more like *The Red Badge of Courage*, deals with actual warfare in France; and the three sections in which Andrews figures most prominently, 'Rust', 'The World Outside' and 'Under the Wheels', allow us to penetrate more fully the consciousness of the individual rebelling against the system.

In its conception this is an interesting structure, and Dos Passos had by this time developed enough basic skill to manipulate his characters and their actions within it. The novel fails, though, because Dos Passos while still passionately believing in the 'dark forces' behind the war, fails utterly in his attempts to locate them and so takes refuge in one or other aspect of what Edmund Wilson calls his 'stubborn sentimentalism'.[7] That is to say he falsifies his picture of life either by introducing melodramatic values into it or by introducing values into it in a melodramatic way. This results in the creation of three characters who relate to each other and to their common environment only disjunctively, and who come to life only insofar as they are made

[7] Edmund Wilson, 'Dos Passos and the Social Revolution', in *The Shores of Light: A Literary Chronicle of the Twenties and Thirties* (New York, 1952), p. 433.

to serve the novel's general theme. As might be expected, Andrews provides the worst example. By profession he is a composer, or at least plans to be, and Dos Passos uses his stilted meditations on music to illustrate and symbolize his spiritual development. One of the first tasks he is given in the army is to wash windows, and as he performs this mechanical chore he discovers his first theme, 'Arbeit und Rhythmus':

> Andrews started at the upper right-hand corner and smeared with soap each pane of the window in turn. Then he climbed down, moved his ladder, and started on the next window. At times he would start in the middle of the window for variety. As he worked a rhythm began pushing its way through the hard core of his mind, leavening it, making it fluid. It expressed the vasty dullness, the men waiting in rows on drill fields, standing at attention, the monotony of feet tramping in unison, of the dust rising from the battalions going back and forth over the dusty drill fields. He felt the rhythm filling his whole body, from his sore hands to his legs, tired from marching back and forth, from making themselves the same length as millions of other legs. His mind began unconsciously, from habit, working on it, orchestrating it. He could imagine a vast orchestra swaying with it. His heart was beating faster.

Later, other themes supersede this one. First, when he is wounded, Andrews toys with voluptuous images of the Queen of Sheba derived directly from a reading of Flaubert's *La Tentation de Saint Antoine*, and dreams of composing a romantic work on the subject of liberty. Later when he has finally gone A.W.O.L. he actually begins work on a piece which by this time has come to be called the 'Soul and Body of John Brown'. The last image of the novel is that of the sheets of paper containing this work blowing around his empty, desolate room after he has been dragged back to prison by the military policemen.

Dos Passos uses other techniques to objectify Andrews's conscious states but they are without exception equally clumsy. His efforts to escape into a world of purely aesthetic value have already been mentioned; he is also the first of Dos Passos's many characters who judge the present in relation to an idealized, romantic past:

> Andrews could almost see men with plumed hats and short cloaks and elaborate brocaded tunics swaggering with a hand at the sword hilt, about the quiet square in front of the gate of the Chateau. And he thought of the great, sudden wind of freedom that had blown out

of Italy, before which dogmas and slaveries had crumbled to dust. In contrast, the world today seemed pitifully arid. Men seemed to have shrunk in stature before the vastness of the mechanical contrivances they had invented. Michael Angelo, da Vinci, Aretino, Cellini; would the strong figures of men ever so dominate the world again? Today everything was congestion, the scurrying of crowds; men had become ant-like. Perhaps it was inevitable that the crowds should sink deeper and deeper into slavery. Whichever won, tyranny from above, or spontaneous organization from below, there could be no individuals.

Andrews, in fact, only begins to convince when Dos Passos shows him in the act of being humiliated and frustrated in his losing fight against regimentation, and even then his emotions tend to be over elaborated in long interior monologues.

Chrisfield, on the other hand, is a man without any accessible interior life, although under the influence of Andrews even he begins to dream of his youth in Indiana. His more typical reaction to the army and the war, however, is a purely physiological one, and Dos Passos controls the ironies implicit in his behaviouristic responses far more subtly than he does with the more articulate Andrews. Two incidents in particular combine to show the degrading and dehumanizing effects of war. The first, reminiscent of Henry Fleming's encounter in the forest 'chapel', serves ultimately to empty Chrisfield of his conditioned hatred for the enemy. He encounters a dead body in the woods:

> He kicked the German. He could feel the ribs against his toes through the leather of his boot. He kicked again and again with all his might. The German rolled over heavily. He had no face. Chrisfield felt the hatred suddenly ebb out of him. Where the face had been was a spongy mass of purple and yellow and red, half of which stuck to the russet leaves when the body rolled over. Large flies with bright shiny green bodies circled about it. In a brown clay-grimed hand was a revolver.

After this, all his rage is redirected at the man who comes arbitrarily to symbolize the amorphous inhumanity of the army as a whole, Sergeant Anderson. Eventually in the midst of battle he joyfully seizes the opportunity to blow the man to pieces with a hand grenade before sinking back into a torpor of confused and guilty conformity. Chrisfield, like Andrews, is a recurring type in Dos Passos's fiction, later to be generally associated with the violence of revolutionary politics.

Many of the elements in *Three Soldiers*, while not cohering within the particular work, have an economy and an imaginative vigour suggestive of his mature fiction. What is still lacking is the differential focus achieved in the later novels by a more subtle manipulation of the novelist's, and thus the reader's, aperture of attention. *Three Soldiers* induces monotony because Dos Passos has not yet learned to create perspective within fictional space.

IV

Between the publication of *Three Soldiers* and his next novel, *Streets of Night* (1923), Dos Passos published his book on Spain, *Rosinante to the Road Again* (1922). It is interesting now chiefly for his meditations on the art of fiction which come out of his essays on Pio Baroja and Blasco Ibanez. In their work, and in Balzac's, he discovered a fictional technique which is more like 'natural history' than 'dramatic creation', and he obviously began to realize that his pictures of American life would have to develop another dimension in order to be related to the gradual evolution and decay of such American ideals as agrarianism, puritanism and the business ethic.

Streets of Night goes some way towards enlarging Dos Passos's historical perspective by bringing to bear on a group of Bostonian intellectuals the pressure of their common New England past. Again he uses the Italian Renaissance as a point of contrast with the sterility of a decaying puritanism, but he also chooses to mediate this sense of cultural disintegration at secondhand once more, this time through the sensibilities of T. S. Eliot and Hawthorne, and the principal characters in the novel have only the most tenuous connection with either their immediate or their more general environment. Fanshaw Macdougan's Prufrockian brooding over his failure to break free from the invisible constraints of the Genteel Tradition is so vague and literary that one suspects it has its origins in Dos Passos's undergraduate notebooks rather than in his postwar experiences:

> And I'll go back and go to and fro to lectures with a notebook under my arm, and now and then in the evening, when I haven't any engagement, walk into Boston through terrible throbbing streets and think for a moment I have Nan and Wenny with me, and that we are

young, leansouled people out of the Renaissance, ready to divide life like a cake with our strong hands.

Streets of Night does not make much of a contribution to Dos Passos's development and hardly prepared the way for *Manhattan Transfer*, a novel which seems to belong to a different era altogether.

By far the most extensive and intelligent discussion of *Manhattan Transfer's* aesthetic design is Blanche Gelfant's in *The American City Novel*. Her analysis of the novel, in terms of its abstract impressionist techniques and the narrative and thematic use of urban symbols, goes a long way towards answering the complaints of critics like Edmund Wilson and Delmore Schwartz who apply to Dos Passos's fiction what are, in effect, Naturalistic canons of judgment, and condemn him for failing to express the 'whole truth' about American life. Her analysis, on the other hand, is based on the more valid assumption that Dos Passos is primarily concerned to lay bare the *essential* features of his society: the drift towards monopoly capitalism and all that is entailed by it in human terms. The fictional technique, therefore, has little in common with, say, Dreiser's; it is as much, if not more, concerned with exclusion than with inclusion.

Even so, this realization is not in itself sufficient to account for the radically different form of a synoptic novel like *Manhattan Transfer*. After all, Dos Passos had used most of the same devices before in his attempts to present immediacy of texture and a complex structure. What makes *Manhattan Transfer* so different is that it is the product of a new mode of apprehension, a different way of looking at the world. Its exclusiveness is based more on philosophical and psychological principles than on political ones. Marshall McLuhan hints at this difference when he claims that '*Manhattan Transfer* and the *U.S.A.* trilogy are not novels in the usual sense of a selection of characters who influence and define one another by interaction. The novel in that sense was a by product of biological science and as such persists today only among book-club practitioners.'[8] McLuhan traces the origins of this new vision back through Joyce, Whitman and Scott to the discovery of the artistic possibilities of discontinuous landscape in the eighteenth century. Without going quite so far it is easy to see that whereas *Leaves of Grass*, on Whitman's own admission, owes many of

[8] Herbert Marshall McLuhan, 'John Dos Passos: Technique vs. Sensibility', in *Fifty Years of the American Novel: A Christian Appraisal* edited by Harold C. Gardiner, S.J. (New York, 1968), p. 162.

its techniques to the art of still photography, *Manhattan Transfer* could not have been written without the example of the movies, and more particularly of *The Birth of a Nation* (1915) and *Intolerance* (1916).

In a campaign to publicize his own achievements, D. W. Griffith bought a full page advertisement in the *New York Dramatic Mirror* and listed his contributions to the art of the cinema: 'close-up figures, distant views as represented first in *Ramona*, the "switch-back" (i.e. cross-cutting to parallel or past action), sustained suspense, the "fade-out", and restraint in expression.' Almost every page of *Manhattan Transfer* reads like part of the script for one of Griffith's films. For example, the novel's first chapter, 'Ferryslip', is composed of five short sections grouped thematically around the subject of birth and arrival. In the epigraph, after a brief glimpse of gulls wheeling over the floating detritus of a modern industrial city, the angle of vision shifts to the arrival in dock of a ferry boat and the hourly re-enactment of the birth trauma as 'Gate fold upwards, feet step out across the crack, men and women press through the manuresmelling wooden tunnel of the ferryhouse.' Immediately Dos Passos cuts to a picture of a nurse holding a basket at arm's length containing a newborn baby who lies in the cottonwool squirming 'feebly like a knot of earthworms'. In the next section, Dos Passos introduces his first named character (though the baby in the basket was, in fact, Ellen), Bud Korpenning, in a synechdotal shift involving a movement away from imagistic montage to close-ups, fast cutting and tracking shots:

> The Young man's glance moved up from Bud's road-swelled shoes to the red wrist that stuck out from the frayed sleeves of his coat, past the skinny turkey's throat and slid up cockily into the intent eyes under the broken-visored cap.
> 'That depends where you want to get to.'
> 'How do I get to Broadway? . . . I want to get to the centre of things.'
> 'Walk east a block and turn down Broadway and you'll find the centre of things if you walk far enough.'
> 'Thank you sir. I'll do that.'
> The violinist was going through the crowd with his hat held out, the wind ruffling the wisps of gray hair on his shabby bald head. Bud found the face tilted up at him, the crushed eyes like two black pins looking into his. 'Nothin,' he said gruffly and turned away to look at the expanse of river bright as knifeblades. The plank walls of the slip closed in, cracked as the ferry lurched against them; there was

rattling of chains, and Bud was pushed forward among the crowd through the ferryhouse. . . .

EAT on a lunchwagon halfway down the block. He slid stiffly onto a revolving stool and looked for a long while at the pricelist. 'Fried eggs and a cup o coffee.'

This section is followed by the first dramatic scene of the novel, though this too is compressed and thematically dense. In it, Ed Thatcher visits his wife after the birth of Ellen, and later gets involved in a sentimental discussion of his ambitions for his daughter with a German printer, who calmly cheats him out of the price of a beer. Finally we eavesdrop on the self-imposed initiation rites of a Jewish immigrant who shaves off his beard after seeing an advertisement for Gillette safety razors. The section, and the chapter, ends with him being reborn as a true American—'a face with a dollarbland smile'.

It is easy to see why the substitution of a camera for the mediating, reflective narrator appealed so strongly to Sartre, and led him to overrate Dos Passos: he called him the greatest writer of our time. The creation of 'characterless characters' in an 'authorless novel' fortified Sartre's belief in the deceptive nature of self-consciousness, and helped to pave the way, not only for his own fiction, but also for that of novelists such as Natalie Sarraute and Robbe-Grillet.

If we pursue the implications of the techniques used in *Manhattan Transfer*, it should be possible to resolve the paradoxical phrase used to describe Dos Passos's novels at the beginning of this essay where I wrote of his 'impassioned objectivity'. Sartre talks of an indeterminacy of detail and a lack of fictional freedom in Dos Passos's world. The impersonal recording lens presents images which are, in the strict sense of the word, meaningless: 'acts, emotions and ideas suddenly settle within a character, make themselves at home and then disappear without his having much to say in the matter. You cannot say he submits to them. He experiences them. There seems to be no law governing their appearance.'[9] This is not to say, however, that the novels are without significance; that they are not open to interpretation, or that because Dos Passos uses techniques of maximum objectivity he does not write out of passionately held convictions. The condition of the world he describes itself expresses his most general and pervasive belief, that in modern society men do not have lives, they have what Sartre calls 'destinies'. The most striking and represen-

[9] *Literary and Philosophical Essays*, p. 91.

tative image in *Manhattan Transfer* occurs at the moment when Ellen makes her 'decision' to marry George Baldwin:

Ellen stayed a long time looking in the mirror, dabbing a little superflous powder off her face, trying to make up her mind. She kept winding up a hypothetical dollself and setting it in various positions. Tiny gestures ensued, acted out on various model stages. Suddenly she turned away from the mirror with a shrug of her toowhite shoulders and hurried into the diningroom. . . .

Through dinner she felt a gradual ice coldness stealing through her like novocaine. She had made up her mind. It seemed as if she had set the photograph of herself in her own place, forever frozen into a single gesture. An invisible silk band of bitterness was tightening round her throat, strangling. Beyond the plates, the ivory pink lamp, the broken pieces of bread, his face above the blank shirtfront jerked and nodded; the flush grew on his cheeks; his nose caught the light now on one side, now on the other, his taut lips moved eloquently over his yellow teeth. Ellen felt herself sitting with her ankles crossed, rigid as a porcelain figure under her clothes, everything about her seemed to be growing hard and enameled, the air bluestreaked with cigarettesmoke, was turning to glass. His wooden face of a marionette waggled senselessly in front of her. She shuddered and hunched up her shoulders.

It is a superb example of the annihilation of consciousness and the loss of identity, as she becomes an object, submerged in the materiality of her environment.

Dos Passos evidently felt the need still to oppose this pessimism with some kind of affirmation, and in a rather feeble gesture of romantic anarchy he allows Jimmy Herf to escape his own particular destiny: 'If I'd had a decent education and started soon enough I might have been a great scientist. If I'd been a little more highly sexed I might have been an artist or gone in for religion. . . . But here I am by Jesus Christ almost thirty years old and very anxious to live.' We last see him escaping back to life up the ferryslip which has now become 'a black mouth with a throat of light'. But this is the exception, fictionally unconvincing, that proves the rule; Human life cannot prevail against the machine.

V

The operation of this law is relentless in Dos Passos's next novel, *U.S.A.* The titles of the first two books in the trilogy locate the pivotal

o

coordinates in space and time of his fictional world. The Forty Second parallel slices the North American continent in two with Chicago as its hub, while 1919, the year of the Versailles Peace Conference, marks for Dos Passos the historical moment when it became certain that America had become, not a new Greece, but merely a latterday Rome; when the struggle for a humane republic finally lost out to the force that dominates the third novel of the trilogy, *The Big Money*.

The problem of extending and sustaining a fiction through large areas of space and time was not a new one. The Picaresque, Epic and Psychological novelists of the eighteenth and nineteenth centuries had shown how it could be accomplished, and indeed, one of the major impulses behind the novel as a distinct genre has been the need continually to redefine character as an identity of consciousness through extension in space and time. Dos Passos, however, despite his ability to create more vividly than most novelists the sense of life as movement and flux, clearly regards geography and duration as illusory, and contrives in *U.S.A.* to sacrifice the portrait of 'life in time' to 'life by value'. E. M. Forster, whose terms these are, claims that 'the allegiance to time is imperative; no novel could be written without it.'[10] But even granting this, one can see that the extraordinary skill employed by Dos Passos in moving characters through large areas and epochs is used not primarily in order to guarantee their 'reality', but to suggest the rootlessness and restlessness that characterize man's existence in modern civilization.

Similarly, the twenty-six short biographies inserted into the novel are seen by most critics as an attempt to buttress the general historical accuracy of the whole. They have, in fact, a much more complex function in terms of the novel's overall structure and vision. Each one is a carefully composed portrait designed to illuminate one or other of the two faces of American civilization. On one side are the Greeks (Dos Passos goes to some lengths to include appropriate allusions in each sketch)—artists, humanitarians, inventors, philosophers; and on the other, the Romans—politicians, imperialists, industrialists. These figures have an obvious correspondence with the fictional characters in the novel, but whereas Dos Passos makes no attempt to go behind the creatures of his imagination and interpret their actions directly, the subjects of his biographies have only a representative existence at best, and it is this that often leads critics to complain of their 'incomplete-

10 E. M. Forster, *Aspects of the Novel* (London, 1927), p. 29.

ness'. In Sartrean terms, the fictional characters portray the *en-soi*, the biographies the *pour-soi*. In terms of literary modes, the fiction is presented dramatically, the fact as lyric. In this way Dos Passos manages to convey both substance and significance without having to resort to the reflective techniques of narrative. The biography of J. Pierpont Morgan is typical of the way Dos Passos creates an objective correlative for his hatred of finance and financiers. The whole section is composed around a few reiterated images and refrains designed to make the great Wall Street moneymaster appear stupid, crude, vulgar and ugly— his magpie eyes and his bull neck, his love of display and his special gesture of the arm meaning 'What do I get out of it?' Here is a short passage from the middle of the piece which, if one attends to the connotations of the images, effectively serves to reduce its subject to a brutal and grasping social climber:

> Every Christmas his librarian read him Dickens' *A Christmas Carol* from the original manuscript.
> He was very fond of canarybirds and pekinese dogs and liked to take pretty actresses yachting. Each *Corsair* was a finer vessel than the last.
> When he dined with King Edward he sat at His Majesty's right; he ate with the Kaiser tête-à-tête; he liked talking to cardinals or the pope, and never missed a conference of Episcopal bishops;
> Rome was his favourite city.

The whole biography ends with a repetition of the central motif:

> (Wars and panics on the stock exchange,
> machinegunfire and arson,
> bankruptcies, warloans,
> starvation, lice, cholera and typhus:
> good growing weather for the House of Morgan.)

In contrast, this is how the editor of *Vanity Fair* described Morgan when nominating him to the magazine's Hall of Fame in 1921:

> Because, like his father, he is the banker of the widest vision and soundest ability in America; because he is a lover, collector and connoisseur of art; because he is a sportsman of the best type, and has kept the *America's* Cup in America; but chiefly because he is ever ready to help a friend, a worthy civic movement, or a deserving work of charity.

The use of the Newsreels and Camera Eye sections has also been widely misunderstood by Dos Passos's critics. They stand in a similar relation to each other as do the fact and fiction in the rest of the novel. On the one hand the badly named Camera Eye represents a disembodied sensibility interpreting experience in a pure stream of consciousness:

> revolution round the spinning Eiffel Tower
> that burns up our last year's diagrams the
> dates fly off the calendar we'll make everything
> new today is the Year I Today is the sunny morning
> of the first day of spring We gulp our coffee
> splash water on us jump into our clothes run downstairs
> step out wideawake into the first morning of the first
> day of the first year

The Newsreels, on the other hand, pile up a montage of unmediated and meaningless dramatic incident, collected from contemporary newspapers, and interspersed by snatches of popular songs:

TO THE GLORY OF FRANCE ETERNAL
Oh a German officer crossed the Rhine
Parleyvoo

Germans Beaten at Riga   Grateful Parisians Cheer Marshals of France

Oh a German officer crossed the Rhine
He liked the women and loved the wine
Hankypanky parleyvoo

PITEOUS PLAINT OF WIFE TELLS OF RIVAL'S WILES
Wilson's arrival in Washington Starts trouble. Paris strikers hear harangues at picnic. Cafe wrecked and bombs thrown in Fiume streets. Parisians pay more for meat. Il serait Dangereux d'Augmenter les Vivres. Bethmann Holweg's Blood Boils. Mysterious Forces Halt Antibolshevist March.

Those who believe that the bizarre events in the Newsreels are there to give credence to the fictional parts of the novel are as misguided as those who complain that they are not in themselves 'interesting'. On the contrary; what they induce in the reader—and are surely meant to induce—is nausea, defined by Sartre as the subject's inability to digest its experience by reflecting on it. Their random, indeterminate, neutral presentation reflects a world which is in itself impenetrable, unalterable, and devoid of essential meaning.

The supreme technical virtuosity of *U.S.A.* is much more then than a flamboyant exercise in novelistic craft by a lesser Joyce. As with all genuine works of art the expressive devices are made rigorously to subserve a particular end; in this case the presentation of a truth that is massive yet easy to overlook, simple in itself but complex in its ramifications. Any judgment of the novel must come to terms with that truth. To see Dos Passos as an author of social protest, inspired by democratic or even revolutionary zeal, is to see him altogether too narrowly. What his image of America in the twenties compels us to see and believe, is a truth become so evident that even *Life* magazine propounds it now. Twentieth-century man has created physical and spiritual environments for himself which will not allow him to go on living as a human being. Dos Passos's world has no interesting or memorable characters in it, it's true. Dick Savage, Eveline Hutchins, Charley Anderson and the rest are all in the process of becoming automata. But so are we all, Dos Passos maintains. This is the social tragedy of our times.

Note

Life and Writing

West was born in New York in 1903. His surname was Weinstein, his first name variously Nathan and Nathaniel; his names were the first of the masks behind which he juggled his identities. He went to De Witt Clinton high school, where his academic record was—in the conventional euphemism—undistinguished. Admitted to Tufts University on the strength of an entirely fictional version of his grades at De Witt Clinton, he was soon asked to leave. He then managed to enrol at Brown University, largely because the authorities there confused him with an academically sound dental student called Nathan Weinstein (West conveniently dropped the *-iel* from his name to assist them). 'West' was assumed along with the Brooks Brothers clothes, the smart dance steps and the 'collegiate' manner that he cultivated in the anti-semitic climate of the early nineteen twenties. In 1924, after graduation, West went to Paris, where he was mainly remarkable in expatriate circles for a swirling cloak and vast hat. *The Dream Life of Balso Snell* was written during this period, though not published until 1931. This was followed by *Miss Lonelyhearts* (1933) and *A Cool Million* (1934). With William Carlos Williams, West worked on the literary magazine, *Contact*, and was for a while manager of a hotel in New York during the Depression. In 1935 he took a job in Hollywood at the Republic studios, and scripted movies like *The President's Mystery*, *Five came Back*, *I Stole A Million* and *Men Against The Sky*. His last novel, *The Day of the Locust*, was published in 1939. His sister married S. J. Perelman, with whom West became close friends, and whose wit, with its passages of home-baked surrealism, is in many ways close in tone to West's. His own marriage came in 1940, to Eileen McKenney, a glittering divorcée who was the subject of the Broadway hit, *My Sister Eileen*, written by her sister Ruth. On 22 December 1940, West, a notoriously reckless driver, went through a stop-sign, and both he and his wife were killed when their station waggon smashed into a sedan. His novels have been collected, with an introduction by Alan Ross, in *The Complete Works of Nathanael West* (New York/London, 1957) (quotations from this essay are from this edition); they have also been reprinted in various paperback editions, including Bantam (USA) and Penguin (UK).

Criticism.   There are several critical works on West: James F. Light, *Nathanael West: An Interpretative Study* (Evanston, Ill., 1961); Stanley Edgar Hyman, 'Nathanael West' (*University of Minnesota Pamphlets on American Writers 21*, Minneapolis, 1962); Victor Comerchero, *Nathanael West: The Ironic Prophet* (Syracuse, N.Y., 1964), and Randall Reid, *The Fiction of Nathanael West: No Redeemer, No Promised Land* (Chicago, 1967). Leslie Fiedler offers an extravagant view of him in *Waiting for the End* (London, 1965); a more balanced view is Norman Podhoretz, 'A Particular Kind of Joking', in *Doings and Undoings: The Fifties and After in American Writing* (1965).

X

A Surfeit of Commodities: The Novels of Nathanael West

JONATHAN RABAN

IF Nathanael West did not exist, then Leslie Fiedler would probably have had to invent him. For West, after a couple of decades of critical *purdah*, has become a necessary figment of American literary mythology. Indeed, flicking over the pages of the *PMLA* bibliographies of the last ten years, one might reasonably assume that West's bones had long ago been picked clean by the assistant professors and their assiduous graduate students. The arrival, in the mid fifties, of what is now confidently termed 'the comic apocalyptic novel', occasioned an evangelical wave of ancestor baptism. In the search to legitimize recent writers like Joseph Heller, Terry Southern, Thomas Pynchon, Thomas Berger and the young novelist Edward Stewart (whose *Heads* strikes me as a very clever pastiche of the Westian style), West has been posthumously credited with a wonderfully virile and promiscuous talent for parenthood. Like most mythical figures, his powers have been variously, and exaggeratedly labelled: First American Surrealist, Sick Comedian, Dreamdumper, Nightmarist, Social Critic (of all things), Laughing Mortician. And for the mythmakers, West had an almost embarrassing abundance of convenient attributes: he was a Jew who renounced his religion; he was briefly expatriated during the twenties; he went the right distance out to the political left in the thirties; he worked in, and wrote about, Hollywood; he died young in a violent accident at the end of the decade. His four short, wildly uneven novels are a beachcomber's paradise; a junkshop of part-worn, part-used symbols and literary references. He is the indispensable minor modern novelist: once neglected, but now fully restored; use him anywhere, handy for your book or thesis. Especially suitable for Despair, Comedy and Violence.

Leslie Fiedler, who, along with Alan Ross in Britain, was among the first to open a West stall in the literary bazaar, puts the basic ingredients of the myth beautifully in *Waiting for the End*:

> He is the inventor for America of a peculiarly modern kind of book, whose claims are perfectly ambiguous. Reading his fiction, we do not know whether we are being presented with a nightmare endowed with the lineaments of reality, or with reality blurred to the uncertainty of nightmare. In either case, he must be read as a comic novelist, and his anti-heroes understood as comic characters, still as much *shlemiels* as any imagined by Fuchs, though they are presented as sacrificial victims, the only Christs possible in our skeptical world. In West, however, humor is expressed almost entirely in terms of the grotesque, which is to say, on the borderline between jest and horror; for violence is to him technique as well as subject matter, tone as well as theme.   (p. 49)

Reading Fiedler, like reading most recent critics of West who tend slavishly to echo him, we hardly know whether we are being presented with a novelist and his actual work, or with a plausible diagram of a certain kind of writer, and a certain kind of literary technique, which arguably *ought* to exist somewhere in the labyrinth of recent American fiction. In the literary histories and the books on the modern novel, West most frequently exists as a cipher for a style which is far more readily identifiable with, say, Thomas Pynchon's *V* than with his own *Miss Lonelyhearts*. And in the earnest exegetical articles, symbolist explication of West's novels has gone into a wonderland of its own, full of failed Christs, illusions masquerading as realities, phallic guns and hatchets, ritual deaths and *shlemiels* galore. But all that is a long way away from the spikey, spoiled surface of the novels, themselves, with their short sentences facetiously pursuing their own metaphors into absurdity; their desperate patter of gags working their way through the prose like a nervous tic; characters like cartoons in livid crayon; everywhere an atmosphere of the kind of surrealism which might have been rigged up by an enterprising handyman in his back garden. Nowhere can the jitterbugging craze have worked itself into the texture of literature so successfully as in the frantic phrasing of West's style.

It's a profoundly maimed style; as unambiguous as a shriek. West's work is pathetically incomplete: re-reading his novels one watches again and again as the shrill personality of the author extrudes from behind the papery mask of his assumed style. With most novelists of a comparable public stature, the work is larger, more rounded, than the biography which produced it; with West, one needs biography in order to understand the peculiar hiatuses, the grammatical breaks, the awkwardnesses and the often uncontrolled hysteria of a fictional *œuvre* that has been fractured, even ruined, by its own history.

West seemed destined to miss every available boat. He was six years younger than Hemingway, eight years younger than Fitzgerald; and by the time he graduated from college and joined the colony of expatriates in Paris, his near-contemporaries were already established writers. He was an awkward, gangling figure with an acned face, who aspired to Brooks Brothers suits and the latest dance steps. He had neither the glamour of Hemingway's war service and apprenticeship as a newspaperman, nor the polish of Fitzgerald's Ivy Leaguery. Brown University in the early twenties sounds like a dull, coltishly provincial establishment, where the sons of the small-professional and commercial middle class acted out a hammed pastiche of the Harvard-and-Princeton style. Worst, West was a Jew; he was born Nathan Wallenstein Weinstein, and grew up in a period when to be Jewish was to be stigmatized as a Robert Cohn, or one of Pound's Usurers, or Eliot's 'The jew squats on the windowsill, the owner, / Spawned in some estaminet of Antwerp . . .' No Weinstein could join any of the fraternity clubs at Brown, or participate easily in the confident protestantism of the literary tone of the twenties. And West had an agonising sense of social propriety. He seems to have spent his time at Brown developing an edgy, imitative style that would hide his Jewishness under his Coca-Cola nickname of 'Pep'. John Sanford, who knew West in New York, wrote of him:

> More than anyone I ever knew Pep writhed under the accidental curse of his religion. . . . He changed his name, he changed his clothes, he changed his manners (we all did), in short he did everything possible to create the impression in his own mind—remember that, in his own mind—that he was just like Al Vanderbilt. It never quite came off.[1]

Part of the Al Vanderbilt act consisted of West playing the country squire, surrounded by gun-dogs and toting a twelve-bore with which he was a spectacularly careless and inaccurate shot. He was an urban Jew who tried to storm WASP America with endless frantic mimicry;

[1] Quoted in James F. Light, *Nathanael West: An Interpretative Study*, p. 132.

it's hard to miss the obsessive, yearning inadequacy which characterized his life style—a desperation channelled into the relentless
acquisition of social masks. Dance floor lizard, home-town Raskolnikov, Paris bohemian (on a parental allowance), hotel clerk, hunter,
movie writer . . . Whatever West did seemed to take on the characteristics of a theatrical role; a part to be learned and played out with
slightly over-large gestures. Deeply embedded in his novels is the
notion of life as a kind of vulgar, snobbish vaudeville show. Certainly
West himself was adept at the painful clowning in which the touring
performer gets up in rouge and worn white slicker suit, to go through
a travesty of the high-life style.

He was, prototypically, a marginal man, perched uneasily on the
edge of his society. His acute sense of social conformity led him into
an infatuation with the values of the twenties which was so overdone
that it turned insidiously into conscious parody. At the same time
he inflected his own contortions with shrill, self-destructive irony;
he was simultaneously inside and out, passionately involved in his
own activity, yet able to mock it with a ribald series of Bronx cheers.
In West's early work, the social style that one recognizes from the
anecdotes of his classmates at Brown is readily turned into a literary
trick—indeed becomes, at first, his sole piece of literary equipment.

In an unpublished, semi-autobiographical story called 'L'Affaire
Beano', he treated the experience of expatriation in a tone of such
bland condescension that the writing itself becomes merely a crude
mode of exorcism:

> 'In order to be an artist one has to live like one.' We know now that
> this is nonsense, but in Paris in '25 and '26 we didn't know it.
> 'Artists are crazy' is another statement from the same credo. Of
> course all these ideas were foisted on us by the non-artists, but we
> didn't realize it then. We came to the business of being an artist with
> the definitions of the non-artists and took libels for the truth. In
> order to be recognized as artists, we were everything our enemies
> said we were.
>
> By the time I got to Paris, the business of being an artist had grown
> quite difficult. . . . When I got to Montparnasse, all the obvious
> roles had either been dropped or were being played by experts. But
> I made a lucky hit. Instead of trying for strangeness, I formalized
> and exaggerated the costume of a bond salesman. I wore carefully
> pressed Brooks Brothers clothing, sober but rich ties, and carried
> gloves and a tightly rolled umbrella. My manners were elaborate and

I professed great horror at the slightest breach of the conventional. It was a success. I was asked to all the parties.[2]

The confident air is too exaggerated; the inclusive use of 'we' too strident. West adopts a strategy of unearned absurdity: by reducing everything to short, slangy sentences, phrased in glib generalities, he achieves a thin horse-laugh at the expense of the narrator, of Paris, of the whole generation embodied in that sweeping 'we'. The passage exhibits a barely-veiled hysteria; it is *about* authorial distance; one feels West frantically disengaging himself from his subject, reaching for a language that is cool, urbane, above all, knowing. But West doesn't know when to stop, and the effect is blatantly unconvincing.

When West stepped off the boat from France, he had the manuscript of *The Dream Life of Balso Snell* in his valise. Talking to A. J. Liebling, he said that he had written his first novel as 'a protest against writing books'. Both the remark and the book itself are of a piece with West's nervously brash social style. *The Dream Life of Balso Snell* filters the figureheads of modernism—Dostievsky, Huysmans, Dada, Joyce—through the vulgarity of undergraduate revue. It is an impertinent satire, remarkably devoid of cunning, and maintains a consistent, irritating air of cocking a snook at the teachers, as West flails inaccurately around his pond of fashionable names. The core material of the novel was apparently in existence by 1924, when West lent an *ur-Balso* manuscript to Quentin Reynolds, to use as a crib for a Spring Day speech. The surprise is that West could continue living with his skittish ephemerid until 1931, when the book was finally published.

Its optimistic target was to demolish western culture with a snigger; its effect is to set in motion the lineaments of a style of contrived bogusness—a style which, in *Miss Lonelyhearts* and *The Day of the Locust*, was to be sharpened into a literary weapon of considerable force and subtlety. For the intestines of the wooden horse, where *Balso Snell* takes place, contain the remains of a stew of partially digested rhetorics. The characters—John Raskolnikov Gilson, Miss McGeeney, Maloney the Areopagite—are ciphers enclosed by the platitudes of their own languages. Together they compose a kind of Bartholomew Fair of social and cultural clichés.

It is quite clear that West had little intention of satirizing his modern humours in any detail. The parodies of *Balso Snell* are parodies of

2 Quoted by Richard B. Gehman, introduction to *The Day of The Locust* (New York, 1953), pp. xiii–xiv.

parodies; they work on schoolboy notions of 'literary English', 'avant garde writing', 'religious rhetoric' and so on. When West turns on specific authors, he assimilates them into a childish convention; as in the garbled pastiche of Molly Bloom's soliloquy at the book's end:

> Hard-bitten. Casual. Smart. Been there before. I've had police-men. No trace of a feminine whimper. Decidedly revisiting well-known, well-ploughed ground. No new trees, wells, or even fences.
> Desperate for life. Live! Experience! Live one's own. Your body is an instrument, an organ or a drum. Harmony. Order. Breasts. The apple of my eye, the pear of my abdomen. What is life without love? I burn! I ache! Hurrah!
> Moooompitcher yaaaah. Oh I never hoped to know the passion, the sensuality hidden within you—yes, yes. Drag me down into the mire, drag. Yes! And with your hair the lust from my eyes brush. Yes . . . Yes . . . Ooh! Ah!

Its badness is at least partially deliberate. For West's writing, by its very lack of satiric specificity, forces us to attend, not to the thing parodied (in this case *Ulysses*), but to the chaotic detritus of a conscious-ness brutally assaulted by this mess of styles, names, lists of objects. The random breaks, the structurelessness, the noisy nonsense, the constant posing of *Balso Snell* go to make up the actual subject of the book. And West is very good at recreating the stimuli of physical nausea as he lets his language cascade into a trough of absurdities. Again and again we are deluged by a style of gratuitous enumeration, as sentences reduplicate themselves in a runaway rhetoric, as repetitive as the flow of iden-tical articles off an assembly line:

> 'And Death?—bah! What, then, is there still detaining you in this vale of tears?' Can it be that the only thing that bothers me in a state-ment of this sort is the wording? Or is it because there is something arty about Suicide? Suicide: Werther, the Cosmic Urge, the Soul, the Quest, and Otto Greenbaum, Phil Beta Kappa, Age seventeen—Life is unworthy of him; and Haldington Knape, Oxford, author, man-about-town, big game hunter—Life is too tiresome; and Terry Kornflower, poet, no hat, shirt open to the navel—Life is too crude; and Janey Davenport, pregnant, unmarried, jumps from a studio window in Paris—Life is too difficult . . .

Here is a style of writing which sets out to prove its own sogginess, its own inadequacy under the pressure of the objects which it is forced to catalogue platitudinously. The failed surface of *Balso Snell* represents West's attempt to exhibit language and a sensibility which have been raped to a point of retching exhaustion.

As a satire, *Balso Snell* is a pretentious flop. But as the inauguration of a style, it is an auspicious technical essay, marred by grandiose overreaching and by the intrusive uncertainty of the author. For West himself shows up anxiously every few pages, nudging the reader in the ribs, all too ready to explain just what he's trying to do. The book is full of passages with the ring of deadly earnestness about them:

> An intelligent man finds it easy to laugh at himself, but his laughter is not sincere if it is not thorough. If I could be Hamlet, or even a clown with a breaking heart 'neath his jester's motley, the role would be tolerable. But I always find it necessary to burlesque the mystery of feeling at its source; I must laugh at myself, and if the laugh is 'bitter', I must laugh at the laugh. The ritual of feeling demands burlesque and, whether the burlesque is successful or not, a laugh. . . .

This poses real problems. On the one hand, West cursorily tries to incorporate the passage itself with the other exhausted rhetorics of the book, by quoting 'bitter' and slipping in the phrase about the broken hearted clown (then overdoing it with the archaism ''neath'); on the other, he allows it to stand as a *propria persona* statement. For a book as bland in its general approach as *Balso Snell*, such lapses act as remarkable confessions of insecurity. They work like distress signals, shouts for help from the centre of a muddle he clearly doesn't fully understand. He becomes the victim of his own lucidity; his language runs away with him, as if the mask had commandeered the face behind.

For West's novels, though they aspire to burlesque and laughter, rarely manage to climb out of that state of anxious self-scrutiny. His second book, *Miss Lonelyhearts* (1933), is frequently credited with being West's most assured and controlled piece of fiction; if that is true, it is only because he had learned to incorporate his uncertainty into the design and texture of his writing. Originally he was going to subtitle *Miss Lonelyhearts: A novel in the form of a comic strip*—and the tautness of that initial idea has stayed with the book, in its use of short illustrative chapters, stylized language and primary-coloured locations. The comic strip gives the novel its extraordinarily rapid tempo; working on West like a harness, so that his tendencies towards diversive extravaganza are kept firmly in check. But the apparent single-mindedness of *Miss Lonelyhearts* is deceptive: an uneasy tension throbs away in the novel, just under its carefully polished surface. (It is indicative of West's painstaking care with the book that he rewrote it more than six times: and, when working on it full-time, produced only 700–1,000 words a week.)

Like *Balso Snell, Miss Lonelyhearts* presents us with a menagerie of rhetorics; between them they make up a splintered portrait of a society that has become consumed by its own clichés. At the same time it is a novel which explores the possibility that the conventions of the Novel —its machinery of 'plot' and 'character' and psychological tensions and development—have been made unworkable by the urban industrial world of pulp media and cheapjack commodities. West does not merely create 'two-dimensional' characters; he attempts to obliterate the notion of character altogether. For the people in *Miss Lonelyhearts* —Desperate, Broken-hearted, Sick-of-it-all, Mr. and Mrs. Doyle, Shrike, Betty and the rest—act simply as labels on which to stick a jaded, received language of sickening platitudes. The book basically belongs to them; it is their confusing and contradictory *noise* which assaults both the reader and Miss Lonelyhearts.

What then of Miss Lonelyhearts himself? The first phrase of the novel is 'The Miss Lonelyhearts of the New York *Post-Dispatch* . . .' and West never fully allows him to disambiguate himself from that definite, but inanimate, article. He is a function; a vibrating diaphragm set in the centre of the communications business, as stereotyped in his available roles as the voices which beset him. He is described once in the book, and the description is made in such generic terms that it almost becomes a parodic satire on the convention of bodying-out the central 'character' in all his particularities:

> Although his cheap clothes had too much style, he still looked like the son of a Baptist minister. A beard would become him, would accent his Old-Testament look. But even without a beard no one could fail to recognize the New England puritan. His forehead was high and narrow. His nose was long and fleshless. His bony chin was shaped and cleft like a hoof.

Compare this with the other descriptions in the book: of Shrike, 'Under the shining white globe of his brow, his features huddled together in a dead, gray triangle'; of Mr. Doyle, 'He looked like one of those composite photographs used by screen magazines in guessing contests'; of Mrs. Doyle, 'Legs like Indian clubs, breasts like balloons and a brow like a pigeon.' In all cases, the similes are there, not to illuminate, but to deaden the character. West robs each of them of any recognizably human attributes, and turns them into things. The language they speak is the mass-produced grammar and vocabulary of the newspaper, the magazine, the movie. Not only are they likened to objects, but on occasions become confused with objects. Thus in the chapter, 'Miss Lonelyhearts and the Party Dress', Miss Lonely-hearts begins by encountering Betty (a splendid talking doll out of a woman's weekly) person-to-person, then slides rapidly, through a dialogue of resounding banality, into an object-to-object relationship:

> He begged the party dress to marry him, saying all the things it expected to hear, all the things that went with strawberry sodas and farms in Connecticut. He was just what the party dress expected him to be: simple and sweet, whimsical and poetic, a trifle collegiate yet very masculine.

This technique of synecdoche turns Shrike into a talking newspaper-man's eyeshade, with his glibly cynical spiels; Doyle becomes merely an extension of his enormous cripple's shoe; and Miss Lonelyhearts himself grows into a walking evangelist's soapbox. By reducing his characters to these formulae West deadens our expectations of human sympathy or change: deeply rooted in the novel is the suggestion that the only way in which we can be surprised or moved is by the introduction of things so shocking or grotesque that they transcend all normal social categories. And this is the function of the letters—

> *I sit and look at myself all day and cry. I have a big hole in the middle of my face that scares people even myself so I cant blame the boys for not wanting to take me out. My mother loves me, but she crys terrible when she looks at me.*

The only alternative to cliché is illiteracy; the only alternative to the conditioned social responses of the Shrikes and the Mrs. Doyles is gross deformity. But we should, I think, be honest enough to admit that the letters rise to such a level of crude extremity that they are merely funny. The predicaments to which they refer are so unimagin-ably awful that one takes refuge in the comic-proletarian humour of bad spelling and impossible grammar. If we are shocked by, say, the first or second letter in the book, they soon become a convention as predictable as Betty's homely flutings. The girl with the hole in the middle of her face turns, along with all the other characters in the book, into just another cliché. What is truly shocking is our own incapacity to respond to, or to make sense of, the human confusion which the novel appears to enact.

I say 'appears to' because *Miss Lonelyhearts* works like a baited trap; it assaults the reader with extremities, then leaves him wondering, embarrassedly, about his own emotional inadequacy in the face of this battering. But West effectively prevents us from responding by deliberately deadening his characters and by turning even the most bizarre rhetorics in the book into cliché. What is real in the novel is the procession of images which focus, not on any fictional predicament inhabited by the characters, but on the dilemma of West the writer, the unwilling creator of this perverse menagerie.

For the central tone of the narrative is one of jokey circumspection; it pries, investigates, works in beautifully sharp visual flashes, constantly counterpointing the violent hysteria of the novel's social world. In the second chapter, for instance, Miss Lonelyhearts crosses a park on his way to the speakeasy:

> He entered the park at the North Gate and swallowed mouthfuls of the heavy shade that curtained its arch. He walked into the shadow of a lamp-post that lay on the path like a spear. It pierced him like a spear.

One is brought up sharp by that last sentence; it looks like a facetious indulgence, a piece of verbal by-play for which there shouldn't be room in a passage supposedly centring on Miss Lonelyhearts' agony over the desperation of his correspondents' lives. But in *Miss Lonelyhearts* there always is room; the narrative continually steps back and films in sardonic slow motion. In the middle of a violent row with Betty—

> He began to shout at her, accompanying his shouts with gestures that were too appropriate, like those of an old-fashioned actor.

The narrative is positively garrulous in its readiness to stop by the way and chat, throwing in eloquent, but static, similes. Its effect is to make the social situation both trivial and unreal; it offers an alternative world of objects and exact descriptions—a world of concretes: bottles ranged above a bar, the colour of tobacco smoke, a flapping newspaper, flagstones, clothes, domestic implements. Throughout the novel, West constantly shifts from his object-like people to objects themselves, which he treats with relish. His imagery is invariably more alive than the characters who occasion it, as if the ordering process of writing were of far greater importance than the people and events out of which novels are usually, if unfortunately, made.

The reader of *Miss Lonelyhearts* becomes its proto-author; his central problem is to shape the hectic and confused voices of the book into the stylized patterns offered him by West. The subject of the novel becomes the desperate play of sensibility as it attempts to reconcile the noisy, heterogeneous fragments of a mass-media world. The images become more contorted, to the point of growing surreal; the noises get louder; the paper characters dance frenziedly on the spot. But our attention remains fixed on the jugglery of West, the most psychologically convincing character in the novel, as he tries to keep all those multiple, crude voices and objects in balance. The trouble is that West seems to be in love with his own failure. The grotesquerie of the letters, of Miss Lonelyhearts' eventual death at the hands of Doyle, of the snatched sex and casual speakeasy brutality in the book, is carried out with a kind of sadistic delight. West's tone, as he transforms his people into mechanical devices or exhibits their pathetically stereotyped rhetorics, is never less than gay. He, not Miss Lonelyhearts, is the failed hero of the novel; he subsides under its pressures like an old-style tragedian, waving his arms and bellowing with obvious enjoyment.

As a novelist, West establishes himself by destroying his own creations with the easily-won indifference of a god. He grossly indulged himself in *A Cool Million* (1934), accurately subtitled, 'The Dismantling of Lemuel Pitkin'; an extended act of writer's vengeance on the notions of 'character' and 'society'. By reducing his hero to an innocent who is even flatter and more simple-minded than Alger's Ragged Dick, and by turning American fascism into a society more lurid than that of most horror comics, West gives himself the opportunity to write in a vein of extraordinary nastiness:

> He also made an unsuccessful attempt to find Mr. Whipple. At the Salvation Army post they told him that they had observed Mr. Whipple lying quietly in the gutter after the meeting of the 'Leather Shirts', but that when they looked the next day to see if he were still there they found only a large blood stain. Lem looked himself but failed even to find this stain, there being many cats in the neighbourhood.

P

One would surely have to be very insensitive indeed to find this humorous; it goes considerably further than the letters in *Miss Lonelyhearts* in its direct exploitation of a literary trick, enabled only by the complete unreality of the fictional characters and situations involved. There is a totalitarian streak in West's writing; a tendency to turn his novels into Charentons, where he can victimize his witless characters at his pleasure. For a novelist, it seems an odd revenge.

And West appears to have realized this in the five years that followed before the publication of *The Day of the Locust* (1939). In Tod Hackett, the Tiresias-like artist through whose eyes we see the waste land of Hollywood, West partially embodied his own predicament as a writer. When he first encounters Homer Simpson, the retired hotel clerk from Iowa, on the landing of the San Bernadino Arms, he behaves remarkably like West's authorial persona:

> Tod examined him eagerly. He didn't mean to be rude but at first glance this man seemed an exact model for the kind of person who comes to California to die, perfect in every detail down to fever eyes and unruly hands.

Through Tod, West is able to inflect his own aesthetic sadism with a degree of irony. But West and Tod jockey for position in the novel, and it's often difficult to determine who is in control where. So, after the marvellous description of Hollywood as a landscape of pure artifice and simulation, the last paragraph of chapter one reads:

> It is hard to laugh at the need for beauty and romance, no matter how tasteless, even horrible, the results of that need are. But it is easy to sigh. Few things are sadder than the truly monstrous.

Its tone is both apologetic and sententious. Does it belong to Tod or West? It reads like most professions of sentiment in West's fiction, as if it ought to go into quotation marks, yet its positioning in the chapter suggests that it is an authentic narrative voice which we must accept if we are to continue to collaborate with the novel. In combination with the passage describing Tod's specimen-hunting approach to Homer Simpson, it is a strong indicator of West's unease. In *The Day of the Locust*, he covers himself both ways by creating a promiscuous irony with which to ambiguate almost everything in the book.

The structure of *The Day of the Locust* is that of an exactly timed series of improvisations. It is built round its set-pieces: two celluloid battles, a Hollywood party, a cheap rooming house inhabited by the dreamers, a funeral, a cockfight and a gala première. Each of these major scenes are 'long shots'; they display the characters at a distance and treat them through a filter of imagery that rubs out their individual details and emphasizes their generic characteristics. They are balanced by interlinking flashback-biographies and close-ups which continually test the individual characters against the large thematic patterns proposed by Tod as he assembles the material for his painting, 'The Burning of Los Angeles', and tacitly underwritten by West. This dialectical structure works smoothly and eloquently; for the first time, West is able to use the Novel as mode of exploration rather than flat statement.

More powerfully than ever before, the destruction of character grows organically out of the texture of the fiction. The magnificently realized location of Hollywood—the luric illusions of the studio lot and the Cape Cod colonial house in paper and plaster, the antiseptic smelling corridors of the San Berdadino Arms, the sickly, pervasive heat in which Harry Greener peddles his cans of home-made polish, the mawkish kitsch of the Californian way of love and death—provides a backdrop of epic dimensions, against which the characters scuttle pitifully, reduced to twitching puppets by the overpowering articulacy of their environment. And West manages his structural devices with a new cunning. In the fourth chapter, for instance, he alternates between brief, cruel portraits of the guests at Claude Estee's party and their tinny dialogues; then, just when the rhythm of the section demands a new portrait of a partygoer, West introduces the black mass at the bottom of the darkened swimming pool:

> A row of submerged floodlights illuminated the green water. The thing was a dead horse, or, rather, a life-size, realistic reproduction of one. Its legs stuck up stiff and straight and it had an enormous, distended belly. Its hammerhead lay twisted to one side and from its mouth, which was set in an agonized grin, hung a heavy, black tongue.

It is perfectly timed, and the party never recovers from the insidious suggestion of that passage: the twisted penis and the hanging tongue carry, like sustained bass notes, into the next chapter, where the party migrates to a brothel to watch blue movies.

In *The Day of the Locust*, the shifts of tone are rapid and unexpected; West darts in and out of his characters like a skilled saboteur. Describing Homer Simpson's move into his cottage, he spends four paragraphs of neutral narrative, in which the reader is allowed temporarily to inhabit Homer as a character, before shifting, through an intermediary paragraph, into a passage of brilliantly managed detachment:

> He got out of bed in sections, like a poorly made automaton, and carried his hands into the bathroom. He turned on the cold water. When the basin was full, he plunged his hands in up to the wrists. They lay quietly on the bottom like a pair of strange aquatic animals. When they were thoroughly chilled and began to crawl about, he lifted them out and hid them in a towel.

This is far more fully developed, and less flashy, than the comparable images of *Miss Lonelyhearts*. Almost every character in the novel— Abe Kusich, the dwarf who is initially mistaken for a pile of soiled laundry; the cowboy, Earle Shoop, who has 'a two-dimensional face that a talented child might have drawn with a ruler and compass'; Harry Greener who behaves like an overwound mechanical toy when he had his first heart attack—is transmuted into the kind of object that can be found on the garbage dumps of an industrial society. But West does not simply leave it at that; he gathers the threads of his images together to project them into a large and complete metaphor of estrangement. In Hollywood, the dreams are faked in the studios; the houses are faked on the hillsides; emotions are faked (consciously and with style) in Harry Greener's music hall routines; religion, and even death, are faked by the funeral industry (where Harry's shaved and rouged corpse is made to look 'like the interlocutor in a minstrel show'); and people are faked in a relentless process of image-making. The novel itself works like a production line; it takes the scattered ingredients of a recognizably real Hollywood and turns them into the hard, bright patterns of cheap industrial design.

For West never allows us to lose sight of the artifice of his own novel; his carefully managed structure is often deliberately obtrusive. One watches the novelist keep Harry Greener alive until the time is ripe for the funeral; then West, without warning, snuffs him out. And Tod's insistent interior monologues, as he collects characters and bits and pieces for his painting, are a way of reminding us that it is the process of the novel that is at stake; the characters and their situations are merely the bundles of hair and leaves and mud out of which the glittering structure may be composed. The final effect is of a lunatic baroque edifice which stuns the onlooker with its sheer brazenness, its air of suffocating overpopulation. *The Day of the Locust* obsessively accumulates its details; characters are switched into objects and added to the pile; objects themselves take on a bizarrely vivid life of their own; the landscape of Los Angeles is broken down into a heap of brightly painted junk. The apocalyptic finale, when the rioting mob lynch Homer Simpson, is both a description and an encapsulation of the process of the novel: the heat, stench, frustration and noise of a packed crowd is expanded to breaking point. Then one is left only with a quietened shuffle of people round an ambulance, while the artist goes into an hysterical imitation of the sound of its klaxon.

West never got beyond that point. His unease is taken to the edge of hysteria and left there. On the one hand there is the shrill confidence of his imagery, the harshly didactic rhythm of his sentences. He strains all the time for a literary voice that will carry the ring of the stern authoritarian, and rules his novels like a dictator. On the other, there is a strain of excruciatingly evident insecurity. His irony teeters between the gross (as in *A Cool Million*) and the nervously diffuse. His style of masquerade slips frequently into lapses of embarrassing earnestness. He is, pre-eminently, the novelist as victim.

West's fictional world is essentially one of objects, of commodities. When people enter it they become transfixed and assimilated into the dime-store jumble of parti-coloured rubbish. On this account, West is often called a surrealist (a title which he himself vehemently rejected). And, clearly, there are deliberate echoes of Huysmans's *A Rebours* in all of West's novels; the glutted consciousness, fed to the point of nausea with sensations, images, people, things, which forms the centre of each narrative often seems exactly like a coarsened and vulgarized version of Des Esseintes. It is almost as if Huysmans's hero had lived into the post-war boom of industrial manufacturing, and found his dreams on sale at every Woolworths'. But this is why West's work is a far cry from European surrealism; his wildly juxtaposed objects always belong to an explicitly commercial context. The passage most frequently quoted as evidence for his 'surrealism' is that section from *Miss Lonelyhearts* in which Betty and Shrike compete for the fevered columnist's soul. Lying ill in bed—

> He found himself in the window of a pawnshop full of fur coats, diamond rings, watches, shotguns, fishing tackle, mandolins. All these things were the paraphernalia of suffering. A tortured high light twisted on the blade of a gift knife, a battered horn grunted with pain . . .

A trumpet, marked to sell for $2.49, gave the call to battle and Miss Lonelyhearts plunged into the fray. First he formed a phallus of old watches and rubber boots, then a heart of umbrellas and trout flies, then a diamond of musical instruments and derby hats, after these a circle, triangle, square, swastika. But nothing proved definitive and he began to make a gigantic cross. When the cross became too large for the pawnshop, he moved it to the shore of the ocean. There every wave added to his stock faster than he could lengthen its arms. His labours were enormous. He staggered from the last wave line to his work, loaded down with marine refuse— bottles, shells, chunks of cork, fish heads, pieces of net.

It is too easy merely to see that here are the lineaments of a painting by Ernst or Dali. We shouldn't miss the fact that the vision starts in a pawnshop; that the objects over which Miss Lonelyhearts exercises his sickened imagination are either pieces of rubbish or things in hock. West turns his hero into a crazed consumer, haphazardly patterning the goods on display; his revulsion is focussed on a peculiarly American style of mass commercial wastage. If it is surrealism, it is the home-town surrealism of the neighbourhood supermarket. One can echo this with passages from any of West's books; for instance, when Homer Simpson goes shopping in *The Day of the Locust*:

The SunGold Market into which he turned was a large, brilliantly lit place. All the fixtures were chromium and the floors and walls were lined with white tile. Coloured spotlights played on the show-cases and counters, heightening the natural hues of the different foods. The oranges were bathed in red, the lemons in yellow, the fish in pale green, the steaks in rose and the eggs in ivory . . .

Behind West's chilling, cartoonlike treatment of people and objects (and people-as-objects) there always lies the chink of money and the grinding of the industrial machine. He is a surfeited realist. The surface strangeness and 'violence' of his novels never rises far above the simple level of being sickened by the excess of an overstocked refrigerator or a sweaty crowd on a Christmas-shopping spree.

It seems helpful to remember Fitzgerald's thorny transition from the twenties to the thirties. In *The Great Gatsby* he was able to allow Daisy to weep over the beauty of Gatsby's opulent shirts; to catalogue with open-eyed wonder the magnificence of that machine for gutting oranges and the brilliant yellow of Gatsby's car. But in *Tender Is The Night*, his tone hardens. Nicole, the child of American success, is discovered in a psychiatric clinic which is explicitly described by Fitzgerald as a kind of spunging-house for a society that is going sour on its own affluence. Nicole, the consumer heroine—for whose sake

> trains began their run at Chicago and traversed the round belly of the continent to California; chicle factories fumed and link belts grew link by link in factories; men mixed toothpaste in vats and drew mouthwash out of copper hogsheads; girls canned tomatoes quickly in August or worked rudely at the Five-and-Tens on Christmas Eve; half-breed Indians toiled on Brazilian coffee plantations and dreamers were muscled out of patent rights on new tractors— these were some of the people who gave a tithe to Nicole and, as the whole system swayed and thundered onward, it lent a feverish bloom to such processes of hers as wholesale buying, like the flush of a fireman's face holding his post before a spreading blaze. She illustrated very simple principles, containing in herself her own doom, but illustrated them so accurately that there was grace in the procedure, and presently Rosemary would try to imitate it.

—shakes hysterically in the bathroom, immersed in some obscure schizophrenic fit. Surrounded by the *embarras de richesse* which he acquires with Nicole (and which prominently includes another pneumatic rubber horse), Dick subsides into broken alcoholism. The wealth of possibilities which seemed once to extend, like the green light over Daisy's dock, has narrowed down to the rank aftertaste of used commodities. Fitzgerald accommodates these opposites in his fiction with a wonderful doubleness of vision; West works obsessively around only the seamy underside of that flowed dream.

For West had a more parochial, mean and hysterical talent than the best of his contemporaries. Like Nicole, he vividly expressed the ruin that came in the wake of the spree; but unlike her, and unlike Fitzgerald too, he never participated in the style which the spree temporarily enabled. Perhaps his novels have been overvalued because American literary history has needed a scapegoat—a novelist so violated that he stands as a symbol for the violent estrangement with which the thirties looked back on the hopes and excesses of the previous decade. He created a voice of shrill, high-pitched nausea; and his mutilated novels are as much symptoms as they are diagnoses of the disease.

Note

Studies of the nineteen twenties which pass beyond a simple literature-plus-background approach and tackle the cultural field as a whole are yet to be written. Meanwhile, Daniel Snowman, *USA: The Twenties to Vietnam* (London, 1969) is a useful opening out; Christopher Lasch, *The New Radicalism in America, 1889–1963* (New York, 1965) and Henry F. May, *The End of American Innocence* (New York, 1965) take a wide range of writing as documentation (Randolph Bourne and *The New Republic*, Sherwood Anderson and Robert La Follette, Mabel Dodge Luhan and Lincoln Steffens). Some of the significant changes in psychological attitudes are explored in Philip Rieff, *The Triumph of the Therapeutic* (New York, 1966); in American art in the last sections of Barbara Novak, *American Painting of the Nineteenth Century* (New York, 1969) and Barbara Rose, *American Art Since 1900* (New York, 1967); in American music in Gilbert Chase, *America's Music* (New York, 1955) and Gunther Schuller, *Early Jazz* (New York, 1968). W. B. Rideout, *The Radical Novel in the United States, 1900–1954* (Cambridge, Mass., 1956) examines politics and fiction together, containing information on neglected figures (M. H. Hedges, Samuel Ornitz); also see Daniel Aaron, *Writers on the Left* (New York, 1961). On black Americans and their writers, see the beginnings of an account in Robert A. Bone, *The Negro Novel in America* (New York, 1958), the opening sections of Harold Cruse, *The Crisis of the Negro Intellectual* (New York, 1967) and Herbert Hill, ed., *Anger and Beyond* (New York, 1966).

For the general literary climate of the nineteen twenties, see Edmund Wilson, *The Shores of Light* (New York, 1952) and *The American Earthquake* (1958). Further reports are in Mabel Dodge Luhan, *Movers and Shakers* (4 vols., New York, 1933–7); Man Ray, *Self-Portrait* (1963); Gertrude Stein, *The Autobiography of Alice B. Toklas* (New York, 1933); Samuel Putnam, *Paris Was Our Mistress: Memoirs of a Lost and Found Generation* (New York, 1947); Alfred Kreymbourg, *Troubador: An Autobiography* (New York, 1925); Robert McAlmon, *Being Geniuses Together* (London, 1938); Sherwood Anderson, *Autobiography* (New York, 1942); William Carlos Williams, *Autobiography* (New York, 1951; London, 1968) and his novel *A Voyage to Pagany* (New York, 1928). *Gertrude Stein: Writings and Lectures, 1911–1945*, ed. Patricia Meyrowitz (1967), contains the essay 'Composition as Explanation' and other valuable documents. Carlos Baker, *Ernest Hemingway* (New York and London, 1969); John Unterecker, *Voyager: A Life of Hart Crane* (New York, 1970); Gershon Legman, *Love and Death* (New York, 1963); Mark Schorer, *The World We Imagine* (London, 1969); Charles Norman, *Ezra Pound* (New York, 1960; London, 1969) all contain valuable detail about New York, Paris and London in this period. Nelson M. Blake, *Novelist's America: Fiction as History* (New York, 1969), suggests ways of reading novels of the period as documents of a culture.

XI

The Hostile Environment and the Survival Artist: A Note on the Twenties

ERIC MOTTRAM

I

IF WE take Philip Rieff's 'problem of explaining cultural change [as] a psychohistorical process'[1] as a line of approach for one more assay into the critically much-frequented and analysed twenties, one way of getting into the field is by aligning attitudes towards money, war and synoptic schemes or overall theories of process as these emerge in the writings of the decade. The intellectuals of the twenties returned to many of the characteristic obsessions that had dominated radical America since the Civil War: the problems of the fiscal economy and the attempt to redeem money from the hands of and scandals of the wealthy banking class; the issues of war and peace, international adventures and reform or revolutionary violence; and the effort to produce large-scale and possibly stabilizing schemes of explanation and justification for men's situation and their desires, whether the schemes came from Herbert Spencer or Darwin, Marx or Freud or Spengler. The writers of the nineteen twenties also found themselves within a certain existing framework of thought, a debris from the previous two decades which included: a 'genteel tradition' or 'puritanism' which questioned nothing except the assumptions of the newly emergent American intelligentsia and the associated diabolism known as 'The Reds'; various strands of thought which had come into the reform tradition from about 1900 and which Christopher Lasch disentangles as 'a movement away from the dogma of natural rights toward a relativistic, environmentalist, and pragmatic view of the world', along with a tendency 'to forsake the role of criticism and to identify with what they [the new radicals] imagined to be the laws of historical necessity and the working out of

[1] Philip Rieff, *The Triumph of the Therapeutic* (London, 1966), p. 2.

the popular will'[2] (cf. the novels of Jack London); and a tendency to see youthful idealism as quickly compromised or disillusioned. The last mood is best exemplified in Randolph Bourne's *Youth and Life* (1913), and his comment that 'the tragedy of life is that the world is run by these damaged ideals', the ideals of youth travestied in middle middle age, is in fact the theme motivating Eugene O'Neill's play *The Fountain* in 1926 and Clifford Odets' *Awake and Sing!* ten years later.

In O'Neill's play there is also clear evidence of the vitalism which infected the intellectual mood of the decade. The 'psychographer' Gamaliel Bradford wrote in his *Journal* for 1926, registering his rare resistance to Spengler:

> The whole book [*Decline of the West*] is rather like so many meta-physical systems, an assertion of the man's individual egotistical conception of the universe rather than an objective system that has objective bearings for the rest of us.

But since Freud's *The Interpretation of Dreams* had been translated into English in 1913 and his *The Psychology of the Unconscious* in 1921, it was possible by 1922 (the year of *Ulysses, The Waste Land* and *Babbitt*) for Spengler's vitalist analysis of the process of civilizations to compete with these psycho-philosophical grids of explanation for the determinist trophy—that grail sought as the explanation for all conflict in all histories. The tendency towards such controlling accounts runs deep in the literary postures of the twenties. Where in American painting a certain eclecticism healthily cuts into the willingness to imitate schematic formulae from Europe (George Bellows' *Dempsey and Firpo* and Arthur Dove's mixed media *Portrait of Ralph Dusenberry* both date from 1924), literature functioned more towards the stabilizing of the accepted area of conflict than towards the changing of social structure by invention and legislation. The twenties can therefore be read as an arrested version of the sixties. The differences are the earlier period's self-consciously vigorous sense of a chance for new beginnings within the recently volcanic barbarism, and a fresh faith in rites, codes, parties and get-together grids of all kinds. The notorious self-consciousness of being part of a permissive Jazz Age is only too similar to the feeling of the sixties; but it is a good place to insert a probe to ascertain the nature of the times. In spite of the urge towards vitalism, jazz, apart from

[2] Christopher Lasch, *The New Radicalism in America, 1899–1963: The Intellectual as a Social Type* (New York, 1965; London, 1966), pp. xiii–xv.

skeletal forms of ragtime, hardly penetrated white consciousness. His critics and his own self-enamoured image apart, the 'Jazz Age' Fitzgerald had really little idea of the art of Louis Armstrong, Bessie Smith and James P. Johnson, nor of the meaning of Duke Ellington at the Cotton Club in 1927. Beside the superb growth of jazz, the first major black American poetry is feeble. Even so, among the most significant events of the decade in the arts was that scheme of black arts known as the Harlem Renaissance. Writing in the early twenties, Franklin Frazier offered this programme for black survival:

> If the masses of negroes can save their self-respect and remain free of hate, so much the better, but . . . I believe it would be better for the Negro's soul to be seared with hate than dwarfed by self-abasement.

This exactly exposes the dualism of the Renaissance. Claude McKay's poem 'The White House' begins:

> Your door is shut against my tightened face

and concludes:

> I must keep my heart inviolate
> Against the poison of your hate.

As M. B. Tolson's *Harlem Gallery* later celebrated, the poets met at 'The Dark Tower' on 136th street (not far from where LeRoi Jones was operating his Black Arts Repertory theatre in 1965). They did not care much for being called Negro poets, let alone black poets: McKay edited the *Liberator* with Max Eastman. But the future inhered in Langston Hughes's *The Weary Blues* (1926)—in 'They'll see how beautiful I am / And be ashamed— / I, too, am America', and in 'Dream within a dream, / Our dream deferred.' Negro poetry was the most significant proletarian poetry of the interwar years, more intelligent and less politically hidebound than the *New Masses* dogmatists, if less politically defined towards action in its complexities.

But a clue to the more common split between art and life, the more invidious pattern of ideology and Americanism, is deftly suggested in Kenneth Fearing's 'Cultural Notes' (1929), whose precise articulations and long-breathed line helped to liberate poetry in the nineteen sixties:

> Professor Burke's symphony, 'Colorado Vistas',
> In four movements,

I Mountains, II Canyons, III Dusk, IV Dawn,
Was played recently at the Philharmonic.
Snapshots of the localities described in music were passed around
    and the audience checked for accuracy.
All O.K.
After the performance Maurice Epstein, 29, tuberculosis, stoker on
    the S.S. Tarboy, rose to his feet and shouted,
'He's crazy, them artists are all crazy,
I can prove it by Max Nordau. They poison the minds of young
    girls.'
Otto Svoboda, 500 Avenue A, butcher, Pole, husband, philosopher,
    argued in rebuttal,
'Shut your trap, you.
The question is, does the symphony fit in with Karl Marx?' . . .

Meanwhile back at the Browning Writing League (Mr. Pound had
already assimilated his Browning), the literary Mrs. Ralston-Beckett
declaims Sir Henry Parke-Bennett's verses to Beauty:

'O Beauty,' she said,
Take your fingers off my throat, take your elbow out of my eye,
Take your sorrow off my sorrow,
Take your hat, your gloves, take your feet down off the table,
Take your beauty off my beauty, and go. . . .'

Such acuteness obviates whole books of literary criticism, but at least
it can be noted that an actual fission between 'hairy ape' decadence and
political thuggery is rare in the literature of the twenties. The average
good political city novel, like Samuel Ornitz's *Haunch Paunch and Jowl*
(1923), concerned itself more with the tenacity of ingrown power.
Ornitz's Mayer Hirsch—corrupt lawyer, corrupt politician and corrupt judge in rapidly uprising career—is the rotten centre of a system
towards which M. H. Hedges' *Dan Minturn* (1927) just as surely gravi-
tates. It is a curiously typical novel of the Minneapolis–St. Paul rebel
who sells out. Dan's education is typically mixed between Marx,
H. G. Wells and Upton Sinclair, but so is his yielding to the fetishism
of property and total alienation from self. Neither of these novels in-
terprets the possible processes of change; they explore and expose the
nature of the power structure without benefit of metapolitics.

The process of generational change and stabilizing is the obsessive
structure of Gertrude Stein's *The Making of Americans* (written in

1906–8 and published in 1925). The style necessarily involved is the core subject of her 1926 lecture, 'Composition as Explanation':

> Each generation has something different at which they are all looking. . . . Nothing changes from generation to generation except the thing seen and that makes a composition . . . the only thing that is different is what is seen when it seems to be being seen, in other words, composition and time-sense. No one is ahead of his time, it is only that the particular variety of creating his time is the one that his contemporaries who are also creating their own time refuse to accept.

This kind of clarity is rare in the decade's general tone, which is compounded of a certain brash postwar sense of confused but lively spree which suffers change and stability as external afflictions. Escape from stale principle was assumed to confer genius on an artist. When George Antheil's *Ballet Mécanique* appeared in 1924, it was thought to glorify machines because it used percussion and mechanical sound sources for its structural effects. To Antheil, his work was not simply fashionable, but 'escape from the iron grip of the tonal principle' and a Spenglerian advance into musical vitalism, 'the barbaric and mystic splendour of modern civilization—mathematics of the universe in which the abstraction of "the human soul" lives.' To most of his audience, the work was deliciously wicked, suggesting primitive and mechanical erotics. The *New York Times* reporter happily treated it as visual–aural sensation producing cheers and hisses from the smart set, bohemians and intellectuals.

Like Gertrude Stein, Antheil observed certain cubist principles of the day: 'I used time as Picasso might have used the blank spaces of his canvas.' But this piece was not in fact new; it continued the music demonstrating Russolo's Milan manifesto of 1913. Antheil, however, lived over 'Shakespeare and Company' and moved in the Pound–Satie set to whom the new was largely restricted to an immediate American–Parisian axis, remote from Hirsch and Minturn. At the time when Pound reached Canto XII of what he called his 'uncanny forecast, something like Stendhal's', he invited Antheil to help him transcribe his Villon opera, a medievalist work which argued, he said, 'far greater rhythmic variety than modern laws of music admit'. During a riot at his *Ballet Mécanique*, Antheil reports in his autobiography, he 'felt for the automatic under his arm and continued playing'; and at a performance in 1926, Sylvia Beach reported that Pound was seen 'hanging head downward from the top gallery', roaring. Ten days later the Villon was performed. William Carlos Williams commented that Pound 'doesn't know one note from another', but in fact it sounds like the lines of Satie's *Oedipe* transposed into fourteenth-century French musical styles. As Pound said, his aim was 'the motz el sons just the way the old troubadours did', and without fixed notation. As in his Violin Sonata, the aim is clear and simple monodic rhetoric, the equivalent of the continuity which connects the spatial forms of the *Cantos* when Pound reads them. When his violinist, Olga Rudge, tried to convert Mussolini to 'modern music and machines' (a letter of 1927), Pound was pleased when the Duce accepted Antheil's piano as a percussion instrument, saying 'So it is.' This is where the Pisan experience began, in the midst of the confusions of style in the twenties. Pound was sickened when Antheil went to Hollywood, the American centre of mechanized art between the wars, and the centre of American incipient fascism, as Fitzgerald and Nathanael West were to show in the thirties.

Pound's *Villon* opera expressed a reaction to romantic Teutonic American music of the earlier twentieth century; it takes its place with the French-trained Americanism of Copland and Thomson of the period. What Pound admired in Antheil were 'the short hard bits of rhythm hammered down, worn down so that they were indestructible and unbendable . . . monads'—as if the imagism of Hulme's brevities had been musically shaped under Cocteau's demand in *Rappel à l'ordre* (quoted in *Guide to Kulchur*) that music be 'like tables and chairs'. Pound adds: 'That goes with Mantegna's frescoes'—a main imagic example in the *Cantos*. He saw the twenties as 'the sorting out, the rappel à l'ordre, and . . . the new synthesis . . . the totalitarian'. But his master Frobenius shrewdly commented on *Villon*: 'Not satiric, naïve. Wrong to use royal instruments for proletarian music.' Pound required his ideal performance to take place in the open air, sung by Ethel Merman and Ezio Pinza, and presumably he believed such an act would at least not detract from fulfilment of the need to nourish 'an actual productive order' to replace 'the great swindling confidences in usury, commodity speculation, money changing and inflation'; or in the words of Robert Duncan, 'both words and moneys are currencies that must be grounded in substance of real worth if they be virtuous. Abstraction from meaning meant manipulation of public trust.' In all his work, Pound shows forth the twenties impulse to responsibility; the *Cantos* are, at that stage of their course, far more than any of the large naturalist novels, the great polemical monodic rhetoric of exploration for change—

'a river of speech', as Duncan says, which shows the information and emotion required for cultural change, and whose only ally is the combination of *Ulysses* and *Finnegans Wake*. The work began before the turn of the century.

So Henry Murray exaggerates in his description of the war and 'the moral revolution of the nineteen twenties . . . [which] shattered the prohibitions of puritanism and Victorianism, and opened a wide vent for the eruption of the repressed instincts and emotions.' In 1926, Murray was teaching at Harvard, where he later became professor of clinical psychology, and must have felt the impact of the minimal unveiling that took place:

> sex chiefly, but also hatred of the dominant powers, plutocracy, mediocrity, and finally Mechos, the cold-blooded dragon of impersonal matter-of-factness and technics, of business, advertising, and upward mobility, of hollow showmen and spurious prestige; the machine-god that seemed to be getting grosser and more implacable every day and shaping more and more robots in its own image to propagate still more impotent machines.[3]

These conditions were not the straightforward cause of a sense of isolation in the responsible artist, since, as Christopher Lasch makes clear, the alienation was established well before the war. Murray—born in 1893—is a typically twenties intellectual, however, preferring 'the immense possibility of a saving myth' to 'a regressive, self-dissolving course, inward and backward, yielding to the lure of disintegration'. His Spenglerian fatalism appears in the suggestion that increasing violence precedes 'the trauma of rebirth', a typical twenties cliché to be found in writers as otherwise divergent as Yeats and Mann. Such analogies from biology are part of the common reversion to vitalist images of organicism which the despairing intellectuals of the century have insisted upon as value. Barbarism is supposed to be in hand because it is inevitable within some cruel metaphysical grid.

The *Ballet Mécanique* can therefore be regarded as an example of the hostile twenties environment reproduced as cultural barbarism, a characteristic style of the period. John Dos Passos's novel, *Manhattan Transfer* (1925), for example, treats New York externally and expressionistically as the function of its role-playing inhabitants. With the aid of the multiple narrative of Griffith, the montage of Eisenstein and

[3] Henry A. Murray, 'Conrad Aiken: Poet of Creative Dissolution', *Wake* II (Spring, 1952).

spatial discontinuities associated with Joyce, Dos Passos created the fictional equivalent of that technological expressionism which received its first major sculptural form in Duchamp-Villon's *The Great Horse* in 1914. The novel organized information about the city as a machine for living death; whereas Antheil controlled part of the impact of machine technology on postwar tenderness as music that did sound like machines but which did not have to be listened to by mechanized citizens. The Dos Passos fiction did read like that reductive collectivity which tenderness and egoism resisted—a collectivity which actually mechanized by depriving men and women of their energies within the dehumanizing *polis*. In this context, Pound's opera is a return to the medieval-naïve, a sophistication of pastoral technique which is nearer the core of Antheil—primitivism as a return to an order that becomes totalitarian when an open society is denied through simplifying mechanisms.

Primitivist alibis wreck the art and politics of the twenties. It is clear in O'Neill's play *The Hairy Ape* (1922), but it is there, too, in the expressionistic psychological space, visible and rather crudely obvious, in *Strange Interlude* (1928), with its actualizing of the 'unconscious' through visible stage action and audible soliloquy. The Scopes trial of 1925, savaged by H. L. Mencken in the *Baltimore Sun* and scoffed at in *The Sun Also Rises* (1926), can be understood as an intuitive group refusal of the invitation to regress to the primitive, to be collectivized into a barbarism without resources. But, of course, Tennessee itself contributed to that hostile environment to which Faulkner's airman returned, as incongruously as the propellers appearing in Antheil's ballet. Tennessee rebelled against the North as city intellect probing a society of selves who needed to be static and unexamined. The Southern self was beginning those reinforcements which have since climaxed in a white feudalism, whose development William Faulkner began to chart with such fierce and degenerate beauty in *The Sound and the Fury* (1929). 'The Great Monkey Trial' gave Main Street an opportunity to protest its familiar anti-intellectualism, a form of unwillingness to entertain any analysis whatsoever of its precariously held dignity within a wretchedly degrading society. Only the lawyer, Clarence Darrow, emerged with credit from the Scopes affair. H. L. Mencken wrote:

> Imbecilities you say live on? They do. But they are not as safe as they used to be. Some day, let us hope, they will be put down. Whoever at last puts them down will owe half his bays to Clarence Darrow.

Darrow's spirit is clear in a speech he made at Columbus, Ohio, in 1929:

> The fear of God is not the beginning of wisdom. The fear of God is the death of wisdom. Skepticism and doubt lead to study and investigation, and investigation is the beginning of wisdom.[4]

In fiction that wisdom is not offered in the South by Faulkner but by Erskine Caldwell: *The Bastard* (1929) is a strong documentary of life in the depressed strata of a semi-industrialized agrarian economy, a way of life so accustomed to scarcity that in itself it demonstrates the lie of an affluent American Way of Life. The facts of the twenties are often forgotten by critics in perpetual hunt for their own bourgeois values. It was a decade of instability encrusted with official statements claiming national prosperity, supposedly indicated by the fake progress of visible technology—cars, telephones, radios and refrigerators for the first time in any profusion. The middle and upper classes felt inventions playing into their lives and assumed justification. The norm of 'normalcy' was conflict, the nightmare of rich versus poor:

> the top one per cent earned about 15 per cent of all earned incomes. . . . In 1929, one third of all personal income was being earned by the top five per cent.[5]

In 1926, 207 individuals paid taxes on one million dollars or more in a single year, but poverty was national and largely ignored. Certainly any talk of values in literature and criticism which ignores such facts is valueless. The sheer incompetence of capitalism is itself a disgrace: goods produced failed to find a consumer market for the simple reason that few could afford the spending spree, and as producers overextended their activities, the number of the relatively poor increased. The Crash appears to have been planned, or at least desired. From 1919 onwards strikes and social violence were commonplace, and the rounding up of 'Reds'—aliens, dissenters, unionists—with a total denial of civil liberties, paralleled the revival of the KKK, and the first large-scale race riots.

The action of *The Bastard* is, therefore, documentary. A hoochie-coochie dancer bears the hero into her tent; when he sees a photograph

---

[4] *Clarence Darrow: Verdicts out of Court* edited by A. and L.Weinberg (Chicago 1963).

[5] Daniel Snowman, *USA: The Twenties to Vietnam* (London, 1969), p. 13. Most of the social facts instanced here can be found in this work.

of her on the back of a postcard, he automatically uses his automatic on the total stranger who shows it to him. Gene Morgan has been raised by a Negro woman in a town where 'cotton absorbed the blood of the white man'; his only chance to stabilize himself away from the 'grinding whine of the augering worms in the feeding troughs'—the machinery of a cotton-seed mill—takes the form of singing to himself, 'My name is Morgan but it ain't J. P.' His female counterpart is the married girl who gives a hoochie-coochie performance for the workers, deploying her mechanical rhythms for their machine-earned money, affording a relief from tension paid for through sex enacted without desire or consumption.[6] This is not fashionable barbarism but an accurate record of the action of a lawless economy. Beside it, *Manhattan Transfer* looks more than ever like a pattern of noisy and wilful cubist surfaces. Caldwell presents minimal technology and maximal uncontrolled human energy in combustion; the nearest in Faulkner would be the Jason Compson section of *The Sound and the Fury*, except that Caldwell does into indulge in pathetic determinisms labelled Circumstance and the Player through which to thrust rotten human lives into a philosophically condoned pattern.

Both novelists describe a frontier inability to allow law to become an internalized moral action. Ring Lardner's understanding of how morality is eroded in the hostile environment emerges in the controlled opening sentences of 'Champion':

> Midge Kelly scored his first knockout when he was seventeen. The knockee was his brother Connie, three years his junior and a cripple. The purse was a half dollar given to the younger Kelly by a lady whose electric had just missed bumping his soul from his frail little body.

Lardner understood that combat is the condition of America. The complete range is in Alibi Ike's use of language as a strategy of survival in the baseball world. He has endless compulsive alibis for avoiding attack. Shovelling potatoes into his mouth, he remarks, 'Doctor tells me I needed starch', and adds, 'Nothin' like onions for a cold.' His reply to the coach, Carey, cuts through layers of lies and ignorance: 'Sure they taught writin', but he got his hand cut off in a railroad wreck.'[7]

[6] Erskine Caldwell, *The Bastard and Poor Fool* (London, 1963), pp. 11, 14, 17, 29.

[7] *The Portable Ring Lardner* edited by Gilbert Seldes (New York, 1946), pp. 365, 314, 328.

As Josephine Herbst once wrote of Lardner, 'like Charlie Chaplin, he had won an immense popular audience before the critics got around to consider him an artist.' In Lardner's writing 'it is not so much a case of exploring the mechanism of the mind as of owning up to every-day facts and ordinary emotions. Lardner does not seek evidence that requires damnation, does not look for quick moral returns.'[8] Nor did he suffer from the 'national disease' of hero-worship, and that at a time when the disease reached the rabid stage with Lindbergh in 1927, Aimee Semple McPherson in 1926 and Henry Ford year after year (Dos Passos's *U.S.A.* is largely centred on the cult). As a war-reporter, Lardner did not, as Hemingway did, find glory in his work, nor did he 'attempt to put himself in the role of a combatant'. He restricted himself to exposing ignorance and ineptitude. But as Mencken noticed, he could not maintain his style:

> Of late a sharply acrid flavour has got into Lardner's buffoonery. His baseball players and fifth-rate pugilists, beginning in his first stories as harmless jackasses, gradually convert themselves into loath-some scoundrels. The same change shows itself in Sinclair Lewis; it is difficult, even for an American, to contemplate the American without yielding to something hard to distinguish from moral indignation.[9]

Lardner's sporting lives are commentaries on virility cults as much as Sinclair Lewis's exposures of health, progress and optimism in *Zenith*. When Babbitt declaims on 'the Real He-Man, the fellow with Zip and Bang', on men with 'hair on their chests and smiles in their eyes and adding machines in their offices', we are in the presence of the scan-dalous mosaic of aggression which consists of spurious virility, naked business aggression and belief in the weaponry of machines. The result in practice is laid open in the Lynds' *Middletown: A Study in Contempor-ary American Culture* (1929), an analysis of generational and class conflict reported with a power beyond most criticism and fiction of the period.

II

One of the very few Americans to maintain stability without smug-ness or lunging towards ideological securities—to retain what Scott

[8] Josephine Herbst, 'A Language Absolutely Literary', introduction to *Gullible's Travels, etc.* (revised edition, Chicago, 1925).
[9] H. L. Mencken, *Prejudices: Fifth Series* (New York, 1925).

Fitzgerald called 'the ability to function', was William Carlos Williams, a major fictionist of the interwar years, as well as a great poet. His radical forms—the early prose 'improvisations' and the early poems—are not barbaristic or primitivist or excitedly mechanistic, but locations of fact fully engaged into his life as a New Jersey doctor. He was as much part of an international art and literature scene as Man Ray, at one time his neighbour at Ridgefield art colony,[10] as well as in Paris (Ray arrived 14 July 1921). Williams's life as a doctor continually threatened to become wholly work, the condition of the people he served and whom he recognized as being stunted by labour and city conditions. His *Autobiography* reports something of how he resisted the contingent. In the chapter called 'Of Medicine and Poetry', he considers how medicine, rather than being simply a matter of cures for somatic conditions, turned out to be more like a baseball game, with home team and visitors alternatively winning. Surgery never attracted him in the same way as physiology, or the nervous system. He recalls a surgeon who used to rub a hunk of malignant growth, which he had just cut out, under his own armpit:

> Never knew why. It never hurt him, and he lived to a great old age. He had imagination, curiosity and a sense of humour, I suppose.[11]

What interested Williams was 'the secret of life' which was not subject to surgery, plumbing, cures or fashions in art:

> And my 'medicine' was the thing which gained me entrance to these secret gardens of the self. It lay there, another world, in the self. I was permitted by my medical badge to follow the poor, defeated body into those gulfs and grottos. And the astonishing thing is that at such times and in such places—foul as they may be with the stinking ischio-rectal abscesses of our comings and goings—just there, the thing in all its greatest beauty, may for a moment be freed to fly for a moment guiltily about the room. In illness, in the permission I as a physician have had to be present at deaths and births, at the tormented battles between daughter and diabolic mother, shattered by a gone brain—just there—for a split second—from one side or the other, it has fluttered before me for a moment, a phrase which I quickly write down on anything at hand, any piece of paper I can grab.

[10] Man Ray, *Self-Portrait* (London, 1963), p. 38.
[11] *The Autobiography of William Carlos Williams* (New York, 1951), pp. 286–7.

It is an identifiable thing, and its characteristic, its chief character is that it is sure, all of a piece and, as I have said, instant and perfect: it comes, it is there, and it vanishes. But I have seen it, clearly. I have seen it. I know it because there it is.[12]

It is that security what Williams brings to his major two prose works of the twenties, *In the American Grain* (1925) and *A Voyage to Pagany* (1928). These are acts of discovery leading to his masterpieces of the thirties and forties, the novel trilogy and *Paterson*. *In the American Grain* discovers a continuity of America since the seventeenth century, as a stabilizing myth rather than a saving myth (Williams did not require rigidity) in a dislocating time. He measures the changes in American cultural history, from the first heroes, the founders and their 'open assertion' (the ring-leader is Paul Jones) of bourgeois belief in the possibility of an action between capitalism and communism (it is the main project of the novel trilogy as well). *A Voyage to Pagany* discovers necessities Williams required from German medicine, Parisian art and European complexities and subtleties of personal relations as against 'the seclusion and primitive air' of New Jersey. As an artist he drew his strength, then, from being both provincial and cosmopolitan, but poised enough to be overwhelmed by neither the wide range of contemporary artists and intellectuals he knew, nor the contingency of his Rutherford practice. Of his writing he remarked: 'it'll be good if the authentic spirit of change is on it.'[13] And:

> The true value is that particularity which gives an object a character by itself. The associational or sentimental value is the false. Its imposition is due to lack of imagination, to an easy lateral sliding. The attention has been held too rigid on the one plane instead of following a more flexible, jagged resort. It is to loosen attention, my attention since I occupy part of the field, that I write these improvisations.

Williams accurately understood the significance of the local object as a revelatory field, and it was this, of course, which gave him a common interest with Zukofsky, Reznikoff and Oppen in the Objectivist group, and can be observed in Emerson's *Journal* entry in 1865:

> there are times when the cawing of crows, a flowering weed, a snowflake, a boy's willow whistle, or a porter's wheelbarrow is more

[12] *Ibid.*, pp. 288–9.
[13] Preface to *Kora in Hell* (New York, 1920).

suggestive to the mind that the Yosemite Gorge or the Vatican would be in another hour.

The Great American Novel (1923) witnesses Williams's ability to transfer immediate experience as husband and doctor into the more public city world of the already fetishistic automobile, with humour and serious relevance. (More than eight million passenger cars were registered in 1920, and about twenty-three million by the end of the decade.)[14] In *Kora in Hell* he had already exposed the 'popular superstition' of possession—'a house has no relation whatever to anything but itself'; it is 'more than a skin' but may threaten to become a drug. *The Great American Novel*[15] begins with a statement about art—

words are not permanent unless the graphite be scraped up and put in a tube or the ink lifted. Words progress into the ground—

and proceeds to play with what *is* necessary: nourishment for the senses, for love, for balancing on a bicycle, for planting goldenrod. He concludes:

You cannot deny that to have a novel one must have milk . . . Progress from mere form to the substance . . . Milk is the answer.

You may 'catch up a dozen good smelly names and find some reason for murder', but a car runs through the 'fog of words'; therefore the words must be broken and reformed, just as the brain reforms the external pressures of environment. A novel is a union which does not take the form of a pyramid, a tomb. The novelist says to his model, America, 'Turn your head a little to the left please.' Williams, the doctor, adds:

her whole pelvis is full of intestine but aside from the ptosis I find nothing really wrong. The uterus appears to be normal. The bleeding may come from a cyst. At least there is no good reason for removing —for a hysterectomy. There it is. Like some tropical fruit colour of the skunk cabbage flower. There it is, that mystical pear, glistening with the peritoneum. Here the cavern of all caverns. Alpha if not omega. Talk politely and obey the law. But do not remove it.
Oh my country. Shall it be hysterectomy?

Politically, Williams finally came to rely on that good old bourgeois

14 Daniel Snowman, *op. cit.*
15 William Carlos Williams, *Imaginations* (New York, 1970), pp. 158, 159, 161ff.

standby 'personal integrity', as much as, say, Arthur Miller had to. Capitalist democracy destroyed the Elsies but Dr. Williams's novels tried to solve the problem through individual integrity, resisting collective action, without the despair of Dos Passos's *U.S.A.* But in terms of literature, it was not such a lonely operation. He learned, like Sherwood Anderson, Hemingway, Fitzgerald and many others, from Gertrude Stein how to say, for instance, 'the American background is America.... The background of America is not Europe but America.' He saved himself the expatriate plights of Pound and Eliot partly because he can go one better than the pupil of William James, herself an exile:

There is a constant barrier between the reader and his consciousness of immediate contact with the world. If there is an ocean it is there.[16]

The common process of reification in Williams probably begins in chapter 19 of *Spring and All* (1923), and it is a form of contentment in a troubled time and place. But he also sardonically fears how America lives as a great adventure novel of wars and future wars, 'the orthodoxy of its stupidity'. He finds himself forced to reinterpret that confident sense of assimilative power—stabilizing change—which is classic Americanism. Even he is infected by the theory of the Spenglerian barbaric curve, so rife at this time:

The imagination, intoxicated by prohibitions, rises to drunken heights to destroy the world. Let it rage, let it kill. The imagination is supreme. To it all our works forever, from the remotest past of the farthest future, have been, are and will be dedicated. To it alone we show our wit by having raised to its honour not the least pebble. To it now we come to dedicate our secret project: the annihilation of every human creature on the face of the earth. This is something never before attempted. . . . Then at last the world will be made anew. . . . A marvellous serenity broken only by bird and wild beast calls reigns over the entire sphere. Order and peace abound.

But immediately the ironies become clear—the holocaust, inflicted for love on a whole race, is a black spring from which is to emerge 'we, the Great One among all creatures . . . contemplating our self-prohibited desires as we promenade before the inward review of our own bowels—et cetera, et cetera, et cetera . . .'

16 *Ibid,* pp. 88, 90-1.

Williams's radical insight into the erotic nature of catastrophe theories differs from most others of the period in its unwelcoming irony. War had produced a widespread taste for orgiastic oblivion and theories to support it, such as Freud's wicked pseudo-philosophizing in 'Thoughts for the Times on War' (1915) and its imitators and extenders. The First World War itself shaped many young Americans and left them with a burden of experience and inclination which prohibited living even in the fake peace they returned to in America. Cadet Julian Lowe's anger at the beginning of Faulkner's *Soldier's Pay* (1926) must have been typical:

> they had stopped the war on him. So he sat smouldering in disgusted sorrow, not even enjoying his Pullman prerogatives.

Joe Gilligan, his travelling companion, is accurately sardonic: 'Excuse me, madame, I got gassed doing k.p. and my sight ain't been the same since.' He is interrupted by the other kind of truth—Donald Mahon, the man with wings, facial scar and withered right hand. The South is about to be invaded by the young remnants of an explosive technology in the hands of insane leaders, and will, according to Faulkner, assimilate them into its own hostile environment. To Mrs. Powers, her young husband's death in France is 'a rotten trick'[17] he has played on her. We are already in the world of Hemingway—of luck as the active metaphor of determinism. 'Rotten luck' is the only non-fake emotion left, but at the end of the novel, Dick's death is still resented—nothing has been understood: 'How well you got out of this mess!' The only serious statement in the book comes from a Christian rector, a man who requires relief, though not from orthodoxy, since that has been eroded by luck, trick and general hypocrisy at least between 1914 and 1918, if not long before. His belief is shredded. He is an entirely postwar, twenties man:

> Who knows, perhaps when we die we may not be required to go anywhere nor do anything at all. That would be heaven.

But not for the last time, Faulkner takes spurious refuge in the heat and dark of a Negro church—'the crooning submerged passion of the dark race' singing 'Feed Thy Sheep' as an example of 'Oneness with Something, somewhere', themselves 'inevitable with tomorrow and

[17] William Faulkner, *Soldier's Pay* (London, 1951), pp. 31, 36, 289, 324.

sweat, with sex and death and damnation'. Faulkner never moved substantially beyond this wretched state of mind at the end of his first novel.

The war was, of course, a trick, but not in the sense intended by Mrs. Powers or Ernest Hemingway. Nor was it, as Hemingway fondly believed, part of a universal 'biological trap', his key phrase in *A Farewell to Arms* (1929). Henry James could at least comprehend the war as a shocking surprise in his famous letter of 1914:

> No one was more innocent than I of the impending horror. . . . The plunge of civilization into this abyss of blood and darkness by the wanton feat of two infamous aristocrats is a thing that so gives away the whole long age during which we have supposed the world to be, with whatever abatement, gradually bettering, that to have to take it all now for what the treacherous years were all the time making for and *meaning* is too tragic for any words.[18]

Such ignorance, self-regarding liberalism and hysterical replacement of historical fact with superficial dramatics ought to have been a clue to the nature of James's inbred obsessions with erotic power. Instead we have been fobbed off with academic chatter about his Christian values and humanist insights. But at least he is shocked, whereas Faulkner and Hemingway accommodated themselves to forms of the primitive and agrarian, the elitist and the reactionary, those processes of what Jean Piaget calls equilibration, rather than the critical exploration of detailed knowledge.

III

The twenties begin to exhibit that 'degeneration of knowledge' and 'deprivation of nourishment' which betrayed intelligent political men of the thirties and which Norman Mailer dramatizes in *Barbary Shore* in 1951. The achievement of Scott Fitzgerald was to have slowly transcended simplifying fashions and stabilities, from the end of *This Side of Paradise* in 1920 and its tentative move towards some kind of responsible action beyond wars and egotism, through to a need to rediscover 'the ability to function', beyond the suicidal 'crack-up' and jumpy allegiances to Marx, Freud and D. H. Lawrence so typical of the thirties and forties. With the help of Edmund Wilson, Fitzgerald understood

[18] *The Portable Henry James* edited by M. D. Zabel (New York, 1951), p. 676.

the need to combine the knowledge available in Marx and Freud into a viable model for responsible action (the evidence is in the *Crack-Up* collection and in the letters)—in the words of Norman O. Brown:

> the outcome of the collision between Marx and Freud is their unification
> the perception of the analogy between the two
> the analogy between social and psychic
> society and soul
> body and body politic.[19]

Fitzgerald found a way of writing from this crucial centre, the starting point for Mailer's novels and for those post Second World War writers who can use Wilhelm Reich. The beginnings were not hopeful. Edmund Wilson remembered visiting the Fitzgeralds at Ellerslie after their return from America in 1927, and in his chronicles, with a customary insinuative manner, he states how Fitzgerald had just discovered the war:

> For our entertainment, a choice of listening to records—which were still a novelty then—of *Le Sacre du Printemps* or of looking at an album of photographs of horribly mutilated soldiers. Scott had discovered the war, and this explained . . . his just having pointed out to me, hanging on the wall of his study, the trench-helmet which, not having been sent overseas, he had never worn in action.[20]

But, as Wilson must have known and, in his feline way, conceals, Fitzgerald understood more of the hostile environment than this. His first novel makes a start on defining that 'ability to function' he formulated in 1936: 'to be able to see that things are hopeless and yet be determined to make them otherwise.' Amory Blaine rejects those who shouted 'that they had found it . . . the invisible king—the elan vital—the principle of evolution . . . writing a book, starting a war, founding a school.' His Catholicism and his brash acceptance of postwar boom affluence are replaced by an ideal of being 'free from all hysteria' and holding to 'responsibility and a love of life', of helping to provide 'a sense of security'. He rejects 'the outworn system' and chooses some form of radicalism against the naturalism he had grown up in, the belief that 'men were blind atoms in a world as limited as a stroke of the pendulum.'

[19] Norman O. Brown, 'From Politics to Metapolitics', *Caterpillar* 1 (New York 1967).   [20] Edmund Wilson, *The Shores of Light* (New York, 1966).

Fitzgerald read Spengler while writing *The Great Gatsby*, and he wrote to Maxwell Perkins, 'I don't think I ever quite recovered from him.' But he then adds: 'he and Marx are the only modern philosophers that still manage to make sense of this horrible mess.'[21] Back in 1921, he was already trying to resist 'the flabby semi-intellectual softness in which I flounder with my generation.' Four years later, *The Great Gatsby* shows the level of resistance he had achieved, and it is focussed on his sense of the party as a necessary conspicuous consumption of happiness in the rich and celebrated, on his sense of the automobile as an instrument of careless power and mobility in the rich, and on his sure knowledge of the erosion of energy in the leisure classes at the centre of consumer society, of their violence in action, their beliefs in racialism and Spenglerian necessary barbarism. The movements of Nick Carraway from the Probity Trust to the fantasy area called Wall Street, and on to the partying of Great Neck, are an accurate chart of events leading to the Crash of 1929. The lawlessness of Gatsby and the Buchanans demonstrates the reach of frontier egoism into the American city, and the failure of American money to produce the new aristocracy that would justify it, the dream of Theodore Dreiser and of Henry James too. Tom Buchanan reads *The Rise of the Coloured Empires* at a time when the Harlem Renaissance begins to indicate the path towards Greenville, North Carolina in 1960, and it reinforces his membership of 'the dominant race', the Nordics who 'produced all things that go to make civilization'. Daisy whispers over her twenties cocktail, 'we've got to beat them down', and Gatsby is caught in the justificatory self-reliance of the Swastika Holding Company. Whatever God there may be available appears as an advertisement of hypnotic control and retribution in 'the valley of ashes'. In his *Notebooks* Fitzgerald wrote:

> D. H. Lawrence's great attempt to synthesize animal and emotional —things he left out. Essentially pre-Marxian. Just as I am essentially Marxist.

This passage delineates Fitzgerald's edge over Hemingway or Faulkner as a diagnostic novelist of the period. Hemingway did, of course, go 'overseas', and Carlos Baker's biography shows him, in 1919, in 'a cloth cap with a visor and a black leather jacket lined with sheep skin', living it up on veteran's tales in Petoskey, wallowing in the wartime

[21] *The Letters of F. Scott Fitzgerald* edited by Andrew Turnbull (New York and London, 1964), p. 289.

torture and killing of prisoners, and indulging in knife-throwing and duelling. At the Ladies Aid Society he spoke of his wartime life wearing a sweeping cloak, with silver clasps, and cordovan boots, and exposing his 'well-riddled khaki breeches'. Seven years later, *The Sun Also Rises* proved to be a book of victims written by just such a dandy—a dandy in the sense defined in Baudelaire by Jean-Paul Sartre. As Don Stewart, the Bill Gorton of the novel, and others recognized, some only too clearly, it was 'a very clever reportorial *tour de force*'.[22] But, of course, it was rather more than that. Against the depredation of the war and the Treaty decadence of Paris, Hemingway set a totalitarian primitivism. Beautifully written and completely reactionary, the book comprises a single complex image fused from Ecclesiastes and agrarian Spain, a way of life promulgated in action by the novelist himself and neatly demolished by Fitzgerald in a letter to Ernest in 1927. Instead of the ritual of parties at Great Neck, Hemingway offers something nearer to the determinist and totemistic primitivism of Faulkner's *Go Down, Moses*. The trivialization of killing in war is to be redeemed and re-established by the ritualization of killing and violence in the bull ring. The trenches are to be blotted out through another kind of existential confrontation with terror, the khaki riddled breeches relinquished for a suit of lights. Animals do not have self-conscious courage and they are therefore an example for men. Ceremony provides an arena for regaining the orgiastic moment of oblivion. The survival artist constructs a declarative prose through which to record and propogate the rites of spring.

But once the fiesta is experienced there is nothing to be done with your experience. Impotence is the ground condition for courting killing situations. That 'separate peace' which Hemingway found for Nick Adams in 1924 remains separate, a blasted privacy, the condition Hemingway himself recreated with wit and pathos to the end. *The Sun Also Rises* is the masterpiece of a competitive man whose father shot himself behind the right ear with an old Smith and Wesson .32 revolver out of pain, loss of sleep from diabetic disorders and angina pectoris, and financial decline. Hemingway had to believe that the condition of life was a 'biological trap'.

Beside the sacramental arena stands the sacramental bar, and beyond these the cathedral where one may drink the sacramental Host. Slaughtered animals and the slaughtered saint are to resurrect the energies of

[22] Carlos Baker, *Ernest Hemingway: A Life Story* (London, 1969), pp. 92, 193, 223.

postwar men, and women may tag along and get what joy they may. Of course, nothing of the kind occurred, and we can learn from Claude Lévi-Strauss's more pertinent analysis that sacrifice commonly concerns substitution. To whom did Hemingway offer his sacrifices in sacramental hope? To what god in need of propitiation in 1926? His rite is more expiatory than propitiatory; it is a 'rite of communion' intended to 'bring about a solution of continuity'.[23] Self-sacrificing is what he is really after, and it is Brett who is permitted to achieve it (Jake Barnes gained his involuntarily in the war). It is rare indeed in Hemingway's writing for women to be allowed into the inner sanctum of either church or dance. The men of S. Fermin dance around Brett, not with her. Prayer is not her capability, as it is for the 'technical' Catholic, Jake Barnes. Blood only appears in *The Sun Also Rises* when Romero hands her the bull's ear. In brutal terms, Gershon Legman is right most of the time:

> Openly transvalued from sex, the death that Hemingway sells is frank and bold. He makes no pretense of 'mystery' behind his murders, no genuflection to law and justice, not even to lynch-law. He is out to kill because he is a *man*, and castrated death and frightened killing—he says—are man's work.[24]

The Sun Also Rises proposes stability through ceremonialism within a barbaric male-dominated, agrarian culture whose religion takes what it chooses from Mithras and the Roman Catholic God. The next logical step taken is towards the politics of violence in *The Fifth Column*.

The stylistic inventions of Gertrude Stein had come a long way from the deployment of Cézanne's absoluteness and Picasso's cubist plasticity, and from their reinforcement of the plainness and essentiality of Sherwood Anderson. The division is clear between Hemingway's obsession with absolutes and Anderson's concentration on the local—less detailed than Williams but nearly as humane:

> A man keeps thinking of his own life . . . life itself is a loose, flowing thing. There are no plot stories in life.

Hemingway is like one of the grotesques in *Winesburg, Ohio*, a man seized by single truth, under intolerable pressure. Hemingway told Fitzgerald that *Winesburg, Ohio* was his first model, and it in turn was composed under the instance of *Three Lives* (1910). Edmund Wilson

[23] Claude Levi-Strauss, *The Savage Mind* (London, 1966), pp. 223–5.
[24] Gershon Legman, *Love and Death* (New York, 1963), p. 90.

recognized the connections in his *Dial* article of 1921 and Mark Schorer writes them up excellently in 'Some Relationships'.[25] One of the most salient points in Schorer's essay is where Anderson recalls in his *Memoirs* the patronizing letter with which Hemingway accompanied a copy of *The Torrents of Spring* (1926)—written in ten days after reading *Dark Laughter* and discussing it with Dos Passos. Anderson wrote: 'it was a kind of funeral oration delivered over my grave.' Meeting Anderson in a Paris bar later, Hemingway behaved exactly like his own Robert Cohn, offering him a beer in amelioration and quickly walking off: a sportsmanlike gesture of no hard feelings and a brief contact of spurious good will. Sport never was a decent basis for human relationships. Hemingway believed to the contrary.

He certainly understood the need for the postwar rejuvenation of language, as the famous passage on 'sacred, glorious, and sacrifice and the expression in vain' (*A Farewell to Arms*) suggests. But in fact he maintained a context for its continued devaluation. As Marilyn Gaull indicates, the twenties' approaches to language were everywhere related to the semantics of Korzybski, Richards, Sapir and Hayakawa, which attack the use of words as absolute values enforcing a gap between language and social, political and moral reality:

> The individual who operated within such a system was necessarily the victim of a debilitating intellectual determinism, reduced to interpreting his environment and experience passively according to the predisposition of an inherited language.[26]

The reinvention of language for E. E. Cummings became a necessity for the survival of the self in a time of shifting incoherence, rising mechanization of human responses and official hypocrisy. As R. P. Blackmur understood and disliked with his characteristic conservativism, Cummings tries to 'wipe out altogether the history of the word, its past associations and general character', leaving the reader, according to Blackmur, with 'only the free and *uninstructed* intuition'. The result is 'a general movement away from communable precision'. In practice Cummings relies on a core of sentimental good sense, a sort of general humane decency with an emphasis on privacy and love which constitute an anarchist response to a disastrous time. *The Enormous Room*

25 Mark Shorer, *The World We Imagine* (London, 1969).
26 Marilyn Gaull, 'Language and Identity: E. E. Cummings's *The Enormous Room*', *American Quarterly* XIX(4) (Winter, 1967).

(1922) attacks the society of orthodox language which betrays its men and women, and particularly the young. Cummings's novel pivots on the difference between official language and the language of known life, and parodies the assumed sacred and sacrificial by exposing the official sacral area of church and state. Survival collides with two forms of tyrannical nationalism—the state, whose citizens are supposed to be patriots, and thereby under strict control, *Haute surveillance* as Jean Genet calls it; and the church which gives immorality a cosmic context.

Cummings's novel is an early recognition of the twentieth-century theft of dignity and freedom in America. It concerns civil rights, quite as much as the Scopes trial, and does so by parodying *The Pilgrim's Progress*. The Heaven offered to the prisoners of La Ferté Macé by its mechanical priest is only a liberty on terms prescribed by a god. It is therefore as insulting as liberty offered on any terms from any authority. The Enormous Room becomes the image of a place where self and community are not at loggerheads and language is not the instrument of the coercive state-church system. As Dos Passos remarked on the book in the *Dial* in 1922, 'it is nearer the conventions of speech than those of books', and it is untrue to say that Cummings's people have no role but their own existence, since the Room is the example of the space of their created society—'the finest people'—speaking eleven languages and living together against enforced filth and herding at the hands of international official authority. The Room is one more example of the search for survival stabilities in the twenties. What Cummings, Hemingway and Fitzgerald produced were examples of that structure of equasiveness which Cesare Pavese so usefully noticed in Theodore Dreiser: an equation of emotions and information hopefully offered towards stability without deathly stasis.

Dreiser is central to the search for equilibration, to use Piaget's term again—that equilibrium between what Dreiser called 'chemic impulses and appetites', 'instinct toward individuality' and 'the law of balance and equation', over none of which, separately or in combination, no man and no society has 'any control whatever'. If Whitman crying 'Hurrah for positive science! Long live exact demonstrations!' had waited for an answer he might have heard something like Dreiser's indifferent deterministic equasiveness. In 1925 Dreiser managed to allow Clyde Griffiths a measure of stoic pathos as he goes to the chair, but nothing more. Even the boy's defiance is blurred. *An American Tragedy* is a long demonstration of fascination with raw materials, a refusal to accept easy and dogmatic solutions. But it is also a confession of bewilderment, honest and impressive. The crux is a problem at least as modern as Dostoievsky, and before him, in America, Hawthorne—the location of responsibility for the criminal act. Dreiser sets up a relationship that includes the doctor's morality in refusing an abortion, the lower-classes' ignorance of contraceptives, the fact that law cannot be impartial since it is organized by lawyers and the state, and the fact that any act has to be defined through internal mechanisms and 'chemisms', the forces of social pressure and the structure of 'the unconscious' (Dreiser, it will be recalled, used Brill's translations of Freud). Dreiser's moral indignation is overwhelmed by his fascination with evidences of this kind; the novel is necessarily huge. Its keys are characteristically confused, and inherent in the ideological arrogance of the West: they are self-reliance, which has become in Clyde 'a secret sense of his own superiority', and the concept of destiny, that recurrent alibi set up inside the word 'destined'.

An American Tragedy is an epic poem of logic. Its internal terror moves compulsively towards that final turning of Clyde to religion and confession, through a sexually repressed and morally confused Christian clergyman, for a solution to an insoluble equation. Even Jake Barnes had the decency to call himself only a 'technical Catholic'. Few other writers saw the equation in such fullness. Hart Crane realized something of the falsity of the religious solution when he designed his long poem The Bridge as a critique of and a reply to The Waste Land, using, as Blackmur observes, 'the private lyric to write the cultural epic'. It was Crane who warned the dogmatic Yvor Winters in 1927: 'Watch out you don't strangulate yourself with some countermethod of your own.' Using The Waste Land as his seamark, Crane defined his own action:

I take Eliot as a point of departure towards an almost reverse direction. His pessimism is amply justified in his own case. But I would apply as much erudition and technique as I can absorb towards a more positive, or if I must put it so in a sceptical age, ecstatic goal. . . . I feel that Eliot ignores certain spiritual events and possibilities as real and powerful now as, say, in the time of Blake. Certainly the man has dug the ground and buried hope as deep and direfully as it can ever be done. . . . After this perfection of death—nothing is possible in motion but a resurrection of some kind.[27]

[27] John Unterecker, Voyager: A Life of Hart Crane (London, 1970), p. 272.

Like Conrad Aiken, Crane worked for what he called his 'symphonic form', already present in 'The Marriage of Faustus and Helen' in 1922–1923—a way of synthesizing the exterior environment and the interior model offered to writers in the twenties. Where Crane challenged Eliot through the writer he used to call 'Rimbodd', both H. D. and Conrad Aiken defined character through the spatial, mechanistic metaphors of Freud, an attempt also carried out by O'Neill in his plays of 1928 and 1929. Where 'H. D.' managed—as Robert Duncan is in the process of demonstrating in his major series of articles based on her poetry—to fuse her psychoanalytics back into a more broadly-based tradition of erotic culture, notably in *Palimpsest* (1926), Aiken aimed for a synthesis which is classic in its desperation. The preface to *The House of Dust* (1920) speaks of 'a totality of emotional and sensory effects'; but the result is a unity of tone rather than a coherence of experience. Diagnosis of evil is shifted from the public to the private action, as if public and private were separable zones. Freudian psychologizing replaces true analysis as an orderly system at once public and fashionable and yet still private. Aiken was aware of the ridiculous and nihilistic dangers of psychoanalysis, and its consequences for language as a *rappel à l'ordre*. ('Changing Mind', 1925, is one piece of evidence.) But Freud still became his 'saving myth', to use Henry Murray's term again. William Demarest, the autobiographical hero of his novel *Blue Voyage* (1927), is provided with an 'unconscious' minted from the mould of the Master. Art for him is neurosis and defined as a complex from which no traveller returns. To an analyst it is the creative curse, to Demarest a humiliation made tolerable by being schematized into someone else's system: 'I take what refuge I can in a strictly psychological scrutiny of my failure.' He is fascinated more by his 'unconscious' than by his creativity, more by passivity than action. His location in external environment is sacrificed almost entirely to what Hans Selye, the analyst of stress diseases, calls the interior environment. Narrative becomes monologue within the confines of a ship's cabin, the escapist's answer to 'chaotic flux'.

Aiken's 'dark world' is a worried twenties version of that 'involuntary unconscious' which the arch-vitalist Carlyle sowed like dragon's teeth in 1838, in his essay 'Characteristics'. Aiken fails to present Demarest as 'the consciousness of modern man'—a grotesquely pompous aim—mainly because of his reliance on the predominance of the involuntary, emotional and symbolic 'unconscious'. Searching for causes for the failure of 'the ability to function' he comes up with a recurrent set of images of travel, travellers, voyages, ships, trains and movements between countries. The result is a false mobility and an illusion of living. The emphasis remains with his other image collection—the web, the net, the mesh, the fine-strung prison. In 'A Basis for Criticism' (1923), he states principles: the criterion of beauty is a pattern of 'associations . . . woven together', 'expression' rather than 'experience'; the ideal would be a complete retreat into 'a sense of unlimited impression'. 'Psychological interpretation' is primary since it explains 'the implicit mode of thought and feeling' in the artist. For the masses (and the web-prison is never—for the bourgeois—the daily life of the labouring classes) beauty lies in cheap literature which 'gives these people illusion, escape from themselves'. The people want 'revelation and the illusion of transcending itself'.

Aiken is fundamentally part of that genteel New England ethos which would place sex and change in the realm of the 'irrational', the 'sub-basement' of the erotic, the underground. Such a model of life can only too well be supported from Freud's archaic literary divisions of the human into over, under and middle. Aiken stands as an *art nouveau* Edwardian, all erotic lineality without erotic substance. Levels of meaning replace full analysis of actual social life. Demarest, for example, attacks the snobbery of class distinctions but not the social structure which manufactures them. Aiken's inward-turning characters are as grotesque as the townspeople of Winesburg or Zenith, or the menageries of Djuna Barnes. The frustrated passion, introspective perversion and compulsive behaviour of these characters in the novelists' scenes resemble some monstrous Diaghilev ballet or the later works of that Robinson Jeffers of dance, Martha Graham. And it is indeed Robinson Jeffers who is a key to the inner barbarism of the twenties; he is not the eccentric Pacific coast loner he is frequently taken to be. His aim, in speaking of his *The Women of Point Sur* (1927), is explicit:

> to uncentre the human mind from itself. There is no health for the individual whose attention is taken up with his own mind and processes; equally there is no health for the society that is always introverted on its own members.

Jeffers' narrative poems of the twenties characterize both the locale and the more widespread nature of sickness, tension and decay; their characters' self-consumption is exactly that of the urban and suburban figures in Sinclair Lewis's *Main Street* (1920) and *Babbitt* (1922)—

Americans seen as 'an exhibition of essential elements'. Babbitt's conclusive crime, for which there is no punishment other than his own exhaustion and decay, is to hand on to his son Ted the responsibility for change. Sinclair Lewis offers a futility more immorally jejune than anything in Jeffers's *Roan Stallion* or *The Tower Beyond Tragedy*. Babbitt asks his son to revolt in the vacuum created, or at least maintained, by his lifelong participation in the American Way of Life—business, real estate, boosting, underground erotics. In chapter five, section 3, Paul Riesling, the local intellectual, observes:

> Oh, I don't mean I haven't had a lot of fun out of the Game; out of putting it over the labour unions, and seeing a big cheque coming in, and the business increasing. But what's the use of it. . . . All we do is cut each other's throats and make the public pay for it!

But this tame bleat from a tar-roofing business man and ex-near-thinker, is near-socialism to Babbitt. When Riesling adds the increase in suicides—Fitzgerald and Nathanael West were to record greater increases in the thirties—the Substantial Citizens jumping into war for reasons not exactly patriotic, and the sheer boredom of living in Zenith, Babbitt can only regard it as part of 'a maze of speculation' which makes him 'elephantishly uneasy'. Riesling is no more than uncertainly bold.

In chapter 14, section 3, in his Annual Address to the Zenith Real Estate Board—'held in the Venetian Ball-room of the O'Hearn House'—Babbitt describes the Ideal Citizen, the Sane Citizen, in a rhetoric designed to jerk his fellow businessmen through the Pavlovian mazes of boosterism: he is 'in politics and religion . . . the canniest man on earth' and in the arts, the man of 'natural taste which makes him pick out the best, every time', such as reproductions of Old Masters and Verdi 'rendered by the world's highest-paid singers'. But, when on the last page of the novel, Ted rejects the university for 'twenty dollars a week in a factory right now', Babbitt realizes he has accomplished nothing 'except just get along', and he hands the rotten world he had supported to his son: 'maybe you'll carry things on further . . . Go ahead, old man! The world is yours!' They exit Hollywood fashion, with their arms around each other's shoulders. *Babbitt* is strictly a horror novel, an unconscious prophecy of a future America of drop-outs and organization men. Lewis cannot condemn the man who does not work for his organization but belongs to it, or the man who betrays his leisure to labour. Instead he gave his Main Street readers security—he 'managed at once to open their eyes and give them a feeling of superior vision.'[28] The terror in *Babbitt* is an early form of the terror in *Death of a Salesman* and Philip Roth's *When She Was Good*; just as the mixture of despair, suicide and transcendentalism in *The Grapes of Wrath* extend through into 'Howl'.

Standing with astonishing steadiness and intelligence in the midst of this disaster area is not a novelist but a cultural critic, Lewis Mumford. His nerve for what America had achieved, as a basis for building a recovery, did not permit him to believe in either Main Street or Washington, nor in the mystic of organicism, curves of barbarism and crudities of vitalism which affected Yeats, Shaw, Eliot, Lawrence and the rest. His essay on Spengler is critical. His *The Golden Day* (1926)— the title comes from Edward Taylor—is 'a study in American experience and culture', a diagnostic healing by way of reference to the years between 1800 and 1860, of which he says, 'this period nourished men, as no other has done in America before or since.' In 1924, Mumford made his *Sticks and Stones*, 'a study of American architecture and civilization', a critique of the romantic eclecticism of the 'machine-ego'. His lectures of 1929 which became *The Brown Decade: A Study of the Arts in America* sought to establish American culture 'beneath the crass surface' at a time when 'the architect, the engineer, the landscape architect, the painter, all rode together on the rising tide of industrialism.' His examples are Sullivan, Richardson, Wright, Roebling (the designer of Brooklyn Bridge), Olmstead (who planned Central Park), Ryder, Eakins, Fuller, Homer and Stieglitz. Mumford's political sense was not highly developed, but he places the positions of the Philistine for whom art and design were accessory to business, and the Bohemian for whom avant-garde art and literature were the only possible attack on Philistinism, as extremes equally absurd and dangerous.

The twenties were the flourishing time of those born roughly in 1900 and who were roughly twenty in 1920:

> The child born in 1900 would, then, be born into a new world which would not be a unity but a multiple . . . where order was an accidental relation obnoxious to nature; artificial compulsion imposed on motion, against which every free energy of the universe revolted; and which, being merely occasional, resolved itself back again into anarchy at last. . . .

[28] Leon Howard, *Literature and the American Tradition*, (New York, 1960), p. 268.

The new American child . . . must be a sort of God compared with any former creation of nature . . . The new American must be either the child of the new force or a chance sport of nature.

In 1970, Henry Adams's words of 1906 in *The Education of Henry Adams* might appear to be only too prophetic. Writing in 1961 of her life in the twenties, Josephine Herbst felt compelled to call her key year, 1927, 'a year of disgrace'. Her reasons are first-hand and authentic:

The law was on the side of what the literary left in its new-found exuberance called the Philistine and made a rallying point for the young for whom freedom to write was synonymous with freedom to love. . . . It was with something like pride that the editors of *transition* had announced in Number 7 that Numbers 3, 4, 5, and 6 had been confiscated on grounds of obscenity or other pretexts. . . . Brancusi's sculpture was taxed by the port of New York on the ground that it 'wasn't sculpture but metal'. A few weeks later they passed in the Hope Diamond free on the ground that it was a work of art.[29]

The avant-garde did nourish itself with an energy far beyond Natalie Barney's Paris salon:

The era that gave the Model-T Ford to the farmers opened the world to its literary young on a scale never before ventured and not equalled since.

But it was a mobility of fragments. If the twenties had any unity at all, it was probably, as Josephine Herbst says, this potential energy:

all flux and change with artistic movements evolving into political crises, and . . . ideas of social service, justice and religious reaction had their special spokesmen. You might be invited to look forward to the social millenium or to the mechanical millenium; you might beat a retreat to Jeffersonian agrarianism.

At the New York première of *Ballet mécanique* on 10 April 1927, William Carlos Williams came in from Rutherford and Pound's parents from Idaho; but it was also the day on which, after seven years in prison, the death sentence was passed on Sacco and Vanzetti, not bohemian players at anarchy but real anarchists. It was America's Dreyfus Case and played as such, whatever the truth of the sentence might today seem to be.

[29] Josephine Herbst, 'A Year of Disgrace', *The Noble Savage* 3 (1961).

The most perceptive men and women of the twenties did begin to see how the first half of this century was to be—to comprehend the limits of recovery from the capitalist war of 1914–18, and the need to discover 'the ability to function' through nourishment which would not rigidify but contribute towards the stability of process and change, without unnecessary violence. These men and women, particularly the writers among them, function as pathologists of the decadence created and maintained by politicians, economists, theoretical historians, churchmen and the activists of the military-business nexus. The twenties is what we, in the second half of the century, see in that rear-view mirror Marshall McLuhan hands to us as a device: determinism, feminism, permissiveness, military governance and aristocratic bargaining with the lives of the masses. The difference is simply that the early decades did not possess our sense of permanent disaster, nor the sense of America's being a closed terminal condition which the rest of the world must obey.

Index

Index